Even the Rat
Was White

Second Edition

Even the Rat Was White

A Historical View of Psychology

Classic Edition

Robert V. Guthrie

**With new Foreword
by William H. Grier**

Boston   New York   San Francisco
Mexico City   Montreal   Toronto   London   Madrid   Munich   Paris
Hong Kong   Singapore   Tokyo   Cape Town   Sydney

Series Editor: Carolyn Merrill
Editorial Assistant: Carolyn Mulloy
Marketing Manager: Wendy Gordon
Production Editor: Paul Mihailidis
Manufacturing Buyer: JoAnne Sweeney
Cover Administrator: Joel Gendron

For related support materials, visit our online catalog at *www.ablongman.com.*

ISBN 0-205-39264-4

36 2022

Printed in the United States of America

To the memory of my Mother, Father, and Brother:
Lerlene C. Guthrie, Paul L. Guthrie, and Paul L. Guthrie, Jr.

Contents

► Foreword

Nothing in life is so rare and surely nothing more precious than an original idea. One scholar turns the light of inquiry on what was a blank void, and a new world springs into being. The course of scholarly work changes course and the world has changed forever. One new idea.

Dr. Guthrie shed light on the embarrassment that was early psychology and it's extraordinary dedication to racism and, with his work, changed that discipline forever.

Early psychological study was bound hand and foot with anthropological studies of "racial mixing" and with a maddening search for definitions of mulattoes and the implications of race mixtures for behavior. Psychologists/anthropologists spent careers studying the kinkiness of African-American's hair and trying to define the hair as coming from a quarter, eighth, or sixteenth mixture with European. Careers were devoted to determine whether kinky hair would "felt."

Men spent lifetimes measuring the differences in skin color. Complex mechanical devices were created to measure the slightly lighter or darker skin tone. Skulls, skeletons, nerves, noses, ears, lips were measured. Phrenology was serious science and the endless measurements were designed to distinguish non-white human beings from white and to establish scientifically that non-whites were limited intellectually.

The power of the conviction of the universal superiority of the white race was so great that Darwin's work had no significant effect on it aside from the notion of "the survival of the fittest" in which idea some psychologists found support for the racism of the day. The simplistic ideas of eugenics were quickly turned to support the most shameful public policies afloat. An array of methods were suggested to suppress the reproduction of "undesirables." Psychologists became the gatekeepers determining who was "unfit" and passing them on into a system of segregation, birth control, and restrictive marriage laws. The most widely used method for suppressing the "unfit" was sterilization, adopted officially as the method of "purging the society of the unwanted."

Sterilization of the "unfit" was widespread and enthusiastically performed throughout the United States. The sterilization of persons determined appropriate for this treatment was law in a majority of states and was, in fact, social policy in the United States, which lasted from the nineteenth century until long after the demise of the Nazi regime.

At the turn of the century experiments became more common and ultimately psychological tests became the more favored instrument of psychological research and practice. Psychologists developed sensory measurement devices, impressive statistical tables, curves, ranges, and distributions all of which, as expected, proved the mental superiority of white Europeans and European Americans. They persisted with statistical studies of increasing complexity which were designed to prove the mulatto hypothesis, that the mental ability of African-Americans was proportionate to the amount of "white blood" they possessed.

There seems in retrospect an astonishing abandonment of the scientific method, which was coming to guide other fields of serious inquiry. Psychological tests were devised and interpreted to demonstrate that not only were black's intellectually inferior to Europeans but that they were particularly well suited to perform manual labor, as if this pseudoscience had as its purpose providing a scientific basis for slavery and peonage.

When public attitudes turned against the increased immigration of Southern Europeans of Mediterranean origins, the psychologists devised tests which would filter out these "undesirables" and label them inferior to Northern Europeans.

Psychologists, evolving more and more arcane psychological tests, emerged with the IQ tests, which were promoted as the most scientific of its permutations and which gained wide public acceptance. But the IQ test, along with its predecessors, remained simply a vehicle for the meanest elements of public policy makers, and, with few objections, offered itself as the instrument of racist exclusionists.

Dr. Guthrie elegantly spells out the racist uses of psychological tests, how they became madly entangled in the efforts of World War II, and became anachronistic at the time of their most widespread use. He describes the steady increase in the numbers of black psychologists and how they brought their scholarship to bear on the perversion of what was contemporary psychology.

To give full dimension to the impact of widespread racist attitudes, Dr. Guthrie spells out the systematic manner in which black scholars were denied the opportunity to study psychology, denied the opportunity to publish their work, and vigorously denied academic appointments from which they might propose a more rational psychology. These previously anonymous scholars have been carefully unearthed, identified, and given their appropriate place in the pantheon of psychological pioneers.

While the scene of psychology is a more benign one as this is written, when *Even the Rat Was White* was first published, smoke still rose from the decades-long battles in which it had positioned itself far from the side of the angels.

Even the Rat Was White exposes this unfortunate past, sets it firmly behind us, and makes it possible for psychology to organize itself as a true scientific discipline. Psychology and all of us owe congratulations to Dr. Guthrie for his original insight and for the dramatic beam of light he has brought into darkness.

William H. Grier

Preface to the
Second Edition

One fall afternoon in the 1950s, while an undergraduate student at Florida A&M College, I happened to stroll past the downtown U.S. Post Office in Tallahassee and was startled to see a Ku Klux Klansman in full regalia standing inside. Judging from the printed literature that I later saw, he was recruiting KKK memberships. (I also learned that the Klan's "Grand Wizard" lived in Tallahassee.) That same afternoon at a football game, while playing clarinet in our college marching band, I along with all the other band members wore recently discarded University of Florida band uniforms. To this day, I wonder if anyone at the then all-white University of Florida felt the impact of how unequal the two state-supported schools were when they gave us their cast-off uniforms. Oddly, in retrospect, we happily wore the uniforms even though they displayed the wrong school colors; in our defense, we had no other uniforms to wear. These inequities occurred regularly but all was not unequal at A&M; the college was a cornucopia for knowledge and experiences and was a petri dish for concepts concerning the psychology of human behavior. For example, I remember learning about similarities between humans rather than differences—quite a dramatic departure from what was stressed in our textbooks. Fortunately, we fought against the traditional concept of differences. This line of reasoning would have wreaked havoc on the equal rights struggles of the era, not to mention the racist bedfellows we would have acquired if we had accepted the possibilities of genetic differences among races.

Later, when I attended a large southern university, I was dismayed when no mention was made during class discussions or lectures of any contributions by Black or other minority scholars. It was especially bewildering how the contributions of Mamie and Kenneth Clark were ignored or at best mentioned as a sidebar discussion in social psychology classes. I had not read Ralph Ellison's *Invisible Man* at this time, unfortunately, for it would have helped me to gain a perspective on why certain materials were unmentioned, slighted, or dismissed in my classes.[1] But, of course, the mandates of the Brown decision were far from being accepted throughout America's Southland. Billboards and other posters announced "Impeach Justice Earl Warren," and states-rights agendas were popular devices for the segregationists.

In spite of it all, Black students matriculated, the academic production pipeline began to trickle, and a second generation of Black doctoral-level psychologists became available to "pick up the cudgel" to relieve the earlier small cadre of psychologists discussed in Chapter 7. This earlier group fought uphill battles against the popular notions of the inferiority of Black people and these second-tiered Black psychologists supplied a surge of talented energy. Psychologists such as Robert Williams, Joseph White, Adelbert Jenkins, Edward Barnes, Henry Pitts, Charles Thomas, Robert Green, Carolyn Payton, Edmund Gordon, Leslie Hicks, Dalmas Taylor, Joseph Awkard, Kitura Whitehead, Reginald Jones, Pearl Dansby, Asa Hilliard, Henry Tomes, and others who were located in the Black colleges and universities became advocates for the civil rights struggles. They also provided a sense of equilibrium for students, both majority and minority, who viewed themselves as standing on intellectual fault lines separating traditional concepts and emerging minority-inspired theories.

Black psychologists were not alone in this scenario: Mexican Americans, Asian Americans, and Native Americans were undergoing similar challenges; they organized constituency groups to voice their concerns. Led principally by Alfredo Castaneda, Manuel Ramirez, Martha Bernal, Stanley Sue, Carolyn Attenave, and Robert Ryan, minority coalitions were formed, and their voices joined Black psychologists to become unifying factors for sensitizing the American Psychological Association to minority concerns. A number of leading white psychologists played indispensable roles by supporting and endorsing minority platforms. George Albee, M. Brewster Smith, Thomas McKeackie, Theodore Blau, Benjamin Kleinmuntz, Thomas Pettigrew, and George Miller worked with minority caucuses to ease the way in the formation of ethnic minority concerns within APA governance structures. Also during this time, a number of the nation's universities escalated their efforts to increase their numbers of minority professors and students: Pittsburgh, Maryland, Michigan State, and Southern Illinois became early leaders in supporting the need for training and producing Black psychologists. On the other hand, the vast majority of the nation's psychology departments possessed no minority faculty nor was there an increase of minority students.

It continues to be business as usual, for it is indeed uncommon to find minority professors in many academic havens. This is either due to an unwritten "cloning criteria" of existing faculty or a general lassitude in spite of rosters, curricula vitae, academic skills banks, and advertisements proclaiming equal opportunity clauses. The resulting bottom line is that most departments of psychology, without the existence of minority professors, maintain a singular biased attitude concerning traditional values in psychology. This tunnel vision encourages myopic views of past, present, and future ideas. Consequently, the problem of subjectivity constricts the importance of alternative ideas and even historical accounting of the profession. In 1991, Korn and others polled a distinguished group of psychology historians to obtain a ranking of the most important psychologists of all time and noted the necessity for establishing criteria for such determinations.[2] One participant in this study pointed out that a "popularity contest" would ensue. She further clarified this by adding that the results would inevitably favor those who are "white, male, from large institutions, and those who have had large networks of students and colleagues to sing their praises." An analogous situation occurs when one is asked to name significant events in the history of psychology. Traditionalists will quickly summon known biographies, which underscores the adage that there is "no proper history, only biography." Wundt's establishment of his psychological laboratory in 1879, or James's work with his metronome, horopter, and other bits of hardware in a tiny room at Harvard, or the series of debates between Watson and McDougall become the historical "gold standard." Just how important or significant were these particular events and to whom? Also embedded in this query is: What is the rationale for excluding one set of biography and events and immortalizing others? Schultz and Schultz (1996) aptly refer to this situation as "the politics of identity," which includes the omission of women in the determination of eminence and general historical accounting.[3] There is no doubt that selectivity reflects the values and preferences of the recorders and often becomes a weapon as in the Orwellian sense: "Who controls the past, controls the future: who controls the present controls the past." Then, is it possible for historical objectivity to become a realistic goal? While I agree with Novick (1988) that objectivity is an elusive task and is much like trying to nail jelly to the wall, a historical reporting of psychology involving the gleaning of knowledge

from archival documents is an essential goal.[4] Materials from *The Journal of Negro Education*, *The Crisis: A Record of the Darker Races*, *The Competitor*, *National Era*, *Voice of the Negro*, *Alexander*, *Messenger: The World's Greatest Negro Monthly*, *Presence Africaine*, *Journal of Negro History*, and *Douglass Monthly* must figure into the archival equation in order to insure perspectives and data to increase objectivity.

The first edition of *Even the Rat Was White* was published with these goals in mind, for instance, using nontraditional sources of documentation for the purposes of presenting, documenting, and analyzing vignettes meaningful to the study of psychology from a nontraditional perspective. The present edition continues within the spirit of these aims. Throughout Part One, Psychology and Racial Differences, new and expanded historical materials that formed scientific precursors to racial stereotypes and negative views toward Black Americans are presented. Discussions that provide early concepts of how Africans first viewed Europeans are contrasted with how Europeans first reported Africans. Expanded discussions concerning the introduction of psychometry in racial difference have been added to the chapter Psychometric Scientism. Part Two, Psychology and Psychologists, is updated with specifics of what and how psychology was taught in the pre–1960 Black colleges with emphases on philosophical directions in teaching individual differences. Discussions concerning the philosophical forces that brought about the formation of the first group of Black psychologists in 1938 to the formation of the Association of Black Psychologists in 1969 are presented. The chapter that documents the trials and tribulations of Francis Sumner, the first Black American to receive the Ph.D. degree in psychology, contains additional materials and expands on his publications. Part Three, Conclusion, advances discussions on the implication of new historical information for the field of psychology as it relates to Black America.

As a closing note, it seems necessary to me to capitalize the word *Black*, contrary to some prevailing style manuals, when the word refers to a specific people. I have also written "Black" whenever it has seemed to me an exact synonym for "African American." Maybe because of my longevity, or the law of parsimony, or stubbornness, I find the syntactical application of the word *Black* easier to use. I hope I have not upset some of my readers with these preferences.

Finally, I would like to acknowledge the following individuals who reviewed the manuscript for Allyn and Bacon: William Grier, M.D., San Diego; Caroline Murray, University of California, Riverside; Joseph L. White, University of California, Irvine; and Todd Zakrajsek, Southern Oregon State College.

R.V.G.

NOTES

1. R. Ellison, *Invisible Man* (New York: Random House, 1952).
2. J. Korn et al., "Historians' and Chairpersons' Judgment of Eminence Among Psychologists," *American Psychologist* (July 1991): 371–374.
3. D. Schultz and S. Schultz, *A History of Modern Psychology* (Fort Worth: Harcourt Brace, 1996).
4. P. Novick, *That Noble Dream: The "Objectivity Question" and the American Historical Profession* (Cambridge: Cambridge University Press, 1988).

Preface to the First Edition

This book is an attempt to present, document, and analyze vignettes in the study of man as viewed from one historical perspective. The book is divided into three parts: Part One, Psychology and Racial Differences; Part Two, Psychology and Psychologists; and Part Three, Conclusion. Part One seeks to establish some social antecedents of psychology by outlining the relationship between psychology and anthropology. Growing from this discussion are historical analyses of early psychological testing and eugenic philosophies. Chapter 1, Brass Instruments and Dark Skins, presents methodologies used to collect and measure human physical characteristics. There are discussions of the investigations of skin color, hair texture, and other characteristics. Various schemata of black-white racial combinations are evaluated and discussed. In Chapter 2, Psychology and Race, the union between psychology and anthropology is explored with emphases on early research patterns and speculations between black-white differences. Events which reinforced the nativistic themes of individual differences are explored. Chapter 3, Psychometric Scientism, is a historical analysis of the background of mental testing, with emphasis on the concept of the "mulatto hypotheses" of the 1920s. Documentary evidence illustrates the obsession of early white American psychologists with the testing of black people. Lewis Terman, of Stanford-Binet test fame, is discussed in regard to his philosophies. The ill-fated attempt by black and brown scholars during the 1930s to prevent mass IQ testing, their arguments, and their precautions against the use of psychological testing are related. Chapter 4, Psychology and

Eugenics, is devoted to a discussion of the relationship between the race-betterment movement in America and the role psychologists played in supporting this concept.

Part Two discusses the development of psychology as an independent field of study and its impact on formal education in black colleges and universities. A history of those black Americans who earned doctorates in psychology and educational psychology is found in this section. Chapter 5, Psychology and Education in Black Colleges and Universities, traces the involvement of psychology in the growth and development of higher education for blacks. Early staffing and research patterns are outlined and the importance of psychology in teacher training programs is stressed. Chapter 6, Early Black Psychologists, deals with black Americans awarded the doctorate in psychology and educational psychology from 1920 to 1950 and lists dissertation titles and granting institutions. Biographical sketches outline the interests and accomplishments of most of these scholars. Chapter 7 is devoted to the first black American to be awarded the doctorate degree in psychology, Francis Cecil Sumner. A man of profound talent, Sumner's vitae warrants his recognition as the Father of Black American Psychologists.

The final section, Part Three, Conclusion, is a backward look into the material presented and a brief glance into contemporary occurrences.

In many ways, writing this book was an exciting adventure. Because much of the material was not readily available, there was a good deal of painstaking research in which I had the satisfaction of uncovering information that had appeared lost through the passage of time. There were moments of despair and frustration; yet, what seemed to be dead-end roads often led to new vistas. Tracing the black Ph.D. recipients in psychology did not offer the difficulties encountered in discovering the names of the educational psychologists. The educators were harder to locate because in most cases their degrees had been awarded by schools of education without speciality specifications. I tried to include as much information as possible in the biographical sketches in order to fill this void in our history.

Germination for this book came in 1969 with the opening sentence of an American Psychological Association journal article, "The Negro Psychologist": "Little is known about the origins, education and training of Negro psychologists."[1] This declaration of void stimulated my appetite for more information and, as a result, I formally began researching the origins and training of early black psychologists in 1972. That research resulted in Part Two of this book.

Years ago, during my own undergraduate and early graduate training in psychology, it became obvious, at least to me, that the profession of psychology had maintained an unhealthy alliance with several racist themes. The similarities in attitude, approach, and interest between psychology and anthropology appeared to be highly interrelated. In order to document these alliances, I began a formal study of this area in 1973. The resulting data led to Part One of this book.

I owe a particular debt to the research facilities of the University of Pittsburgh, Howard University's Moorland-Spingarn Research Center, and the Archives of Clark University. In addition, the libraries of the National Institute of Education, Smithsonian Institution, University of Maryland, Morehouse College, George Washington University, Tillotson College, Stanford University, University of Washington, and the Library of Congress were valuable sources of information.

Special acknowledgments are extended to Max Meenes, James Bayton, Oran Eagleson, S. O. Roberts, Martin Jenkins, Frederick Watts, Mae Claytor, James Morton, Miriam Kyle, Carlton Goodlett, Montraville Claiborne, Ruth Howard, Alberta Turner, Katharine Beverly, J. Henry Alston, Charles Thompson, Mamie Clark, Julia Bond, Lorraine Morton, Lily Brunschwig, Howard Wright, Julia Canady, Roger Williams, and Kenneth Clark—all of whom provided valuable information.

During various phases of my research and writing, discussions with Pittsburgh colleagues Edward Barnes, George Fahey, Michael Gladis, Norman Dixon, and Raymond Hummel were especially stimulating. Appreciation is extended to a Washington colleague, Eunice Turk, who read the entire manuscript with helpful suggestions. Tribute is given to Joyce Harris who did a most thorough job of typing the manuscript. Finally, unestimable credit is given to my wife, Elodia, whose encouragement from the beginning insured that this book had to be written.

R.V.G.

NOTE

1. L. Wispe, P. Ash, J. Awkard, L. Hicks, M. Hoffman, and J. Porter, "The Negro Psychologist in America," *American Psychologist* 24:2 (1969), pp. 142–150.

▶ Part I

Psychology and Racial Differences

Chapter 1
"The Noble Savage" and Science

Chapter 2
Brass Instruments and Dark Skins

Chapter 3
Psychometric Scientism

Chapter 4
Psychology and Race

▶ 1

"The Noble Savage" and Science

*Negros of goodlie stature, shape and personage,
and yonge of yeres beinge the choise and
principall of all the negros w'ch wer gotten.*
—MASTER JOHN HAWKINS, ESQ., Captain, slave ship
Jesus *commenting on his cargo in 1564–1565.*

Long before the dawn of literary history, great African states of civilization emerged and flourished. For example, the Yorubas were masters of bronze casting at a time when no craftsman in Europe knew how to cast a life-size bronze.[1] Sub-Saharan Africans manufactured and used iron while Europeans were still in the Stone Age.[2] The Shona constructed massive stone edifices during the Great Zimbabwe-Kame culture before the arrival of the Portuguese. The Tomb of Huy in the reign of Tutankhamum reveals the glory of the Nubians in the largest kingdom along the Nile.

The Kingdom of Songhai produced enviable learning centers—at Sankore, Gao, Walata, Timbuktu, and Jenne—which flourished at about the same time Spanish explorers were busy plundering the Americas and Portuguese and English voyagers were searching the shores of West Africa for ivory and gold. Yet, Europeans knew little about the peoples of Africa, and their ignorance contributed to and nourished negative reactions toward Africa and its inhabitants long before the first European set foot on the African continent. As far back as the seventeenth and eighteenth centuries, black was regarded as repulsive and decidedly inferior as witnessed in England's poetic and artistic expressions.[3] The French de-

The Homage of the Nubian Princes: Tomb of Huy.
Source: N. G. Davies and A. H. Gardiner, *The Tomb of Huy: Viceroy of Nubia in the Reign of Tut'ankhum* [No. 40]. The Egypt Exploration Society, 1926.

scribed the interior of Africa as being inhabited by monsters. The Spanish spoke of "moreno" savages with temples of gold, and the English reported "blacke soules" with mounds of glistening ivory. When the Britons encountered Africans, they perpetuated their perceptions of the inhabitants of Africa in clear and often poetic detail:

> And entering in (a river), we see
> a number of blacke soules,

Whose likeliness seem'd to be,
Their Captaine comes to me
as naked as my naile,
Not having witte or honestie
to cover once his taile.[4]

According to W. D. Jordan (1968), description of the African's skin color as *black* was "an exaggerated term in itself for it suggests that the Negro's complexion had powerful impact upon their perception."[5] Negative attitudes toward Africans were carried by interlopers and sailors and the impact of contact with the Africans reinforced the negative black imagery by Europeans. Furthermore, it is important to note that the term *black* was used to describe all the inhabitants of Africa regardless of their varying degrees of skin color. Since Europeans believed humans originally were white, the blackness of Africans was seen as a degeneration of mankind. This explains the impact of the English language in placing extreme negative connotations on the concept of blackness contributing to the immediate fears and disdain English-speaking people had for Africans. And, because the Africans' skin color struck Europeans as unusual, a number of explanations, religious and philosophical, were advanced to explain this difference. For example, some believed Africans had a special skin layer that turned black after birth; women who had painted their bodies with black paint exerted a prenatal influence on the color of their offspring; and the popular concept that blackness was due to exposure to the sun.[6] As a further outgrowth of the negative notion of blackness, the Caucasian standard of beauty was quickly foisted upon the African, who was variously described as ugly, disfigured, or cursed from this frame of reference.

Beyond missionary notes and slaver captain logs, little is left to record the impression of white-skinned Europeans from the eyes of the African. However, Omosegbon (1995) explained that the African possessed little if any bias toward the Europeans who came initially to the shores of Africa. "Africans," according to Omosegbon, "curiously accepted them chiefly as foreigners who had either lost their way and therefore needed assistance . . . or as genuine partners arriving at the African shores."[7] Evidence of this hospitality can be seen in the following specimen of eighteenth-century West African poetry:

The winds were roaring, and the White Man fled,
The rains of night descended on his head;
The poor White Man sat down beneath our tree,
Weary and faint, and from home was he:
For him no mother fills with milk the bowl,
No wife prepares the bread to cheer his soul;
—Pity the poor White Man who sought our tree
No wife, no mother, and no home has he.[8]

But, it was not long before the African, himself, would be stripped of his own wife, mother, and home—enslaved, with no pity.

Notes from an African who was sold into slavery describe his experience of the "middle passage" and make reference to the widespread fear among captured Africans that they were to be cannibalized by the white men: "I asked them if we were not to be eaten by those white men with horrible looks, red faces, and long hair."[9] (It is interesting to note that the Yoruba word for a European means "a peeled man.")

RELIGIOUS VIEWS

Since Europeans firmly believe that "original" man was white, attempts to explain the presence of Blacks in foreign lands often came from interpretations of selected religious writings. These interpretations were widely used to support the inferiority of Blacks. One view held that the African's dark skin and his consequent enslavement by other men had been a proclamation from God. As one story from the Old Testament was interpreted, Ham had looked at his father's drunken and naked body while his other brothers, Shem and Japheth, had covered their father, Noah, without looking at him (Genesis 9:20–25). When Noah sobered up and awoke, he blessed and rewarded Shem and Japheth for their tolerance; for Ham's ridicule, he made Canaan, Ham's son, a servant to Ham's brothers. With Canaan now designated a "servant of servants," his descendants were doomed to a role of subjugation by supreme authority. The verses said nothing of skin color, but various interpretations held that because the descendants were to be enslaved, it was logical they had to be black. The Hamitic myth had relegated Blacks to the lowest order of humanity. Still another view, interpreted from the Old Testament, held that Africans were descendants of Cain, another cursed biblical figure. The Canaanites were described as a debased people, and by the time of Solomon, most were reduced to human servitude.[10] This becomes disputable since all mankind except Noah and his family were wiped out by the flood.

The oral tradition of the Jews, as presented in the Babylonian Talmud (200–600 A.D.), held that Ham was cursed for another reason. As this story goes, God forbade anyone to have sexual relations while on the *Ark*, and Ham disobeyed the proclamation. Thus, Ham was condemned to blackness and his descendants to perpetual servitude. In each of these religious explanations, Ham was accused of wrongdoings, and blackness was the direct punishment, along with the curse of slavery.[11]

In clear and lucid language, the *Book of Mormon* equates dark skin with "loathsomeness and filth" (2 Nephi 5:21) and dark-skinned individuals were the result of a curse placed by God against a rebellious leader named Laman.[12] The *Book of Mormon* is quite clear in its descriptions of skin color differences in the juxtaposition between "good and evil."

PHILOSOPHICAL AND SCIENTIFIC VIEWS

Beyond the religious speculations for dark complexion, ancient white philosophers held that the African's blackness and woolly hair were caused by exposure to the hot sun, while the inhabitants of northern areas were white as a result of the colder climate and those in warm, temperate areas were intermediate in color.[13] Later philosophical views also proposed similar relationships between the climate and skin color. Blumenbach, the founder of physical anthropology, held that blackness was caused by a tendency in the tropics for carbon to become embedded in the skin. Schweinfurth, in *Heart of Africa,* wrote that "dark skin is based on the ferruginous nature of the laterite soil."[14] Waitz felt that "hot and damp countries favour the darkening of the skin and that within the same race the skin tends to be much darker in low marshy districts than on the neighbouring uplands."[15] Both of these theories advanced the concept that the darkness of skin color increased in proportion to the nearness of the equator and that the geographical latitude of one's home could be inferred from that person's skin color. However, as explorers began to encounter people of dark skin in many corners of the globe, the equatorial hypothesis was shattered.

THE NOBLE SAVAGE VIEW

As a outgrowth of explorers' observations and the deductions by some European philosophers, a concept emerged (circa 1730) arguing that although nature is created innocent, all things degenerate when touched by civilization. The idea becomes a double-edged sword in that, while the concept suggests inherent evils of so-called civilization, it labels dark-skinned people as savage thus lending themselves to Eurocentric investigations, measurements, and studies. The myth of the Noble Savage emerged and moderated somewhat the disapproving European attitudes toward dark-skinned people in general but did not prevent most Europeans from maintaining a view of the African as barbaric and liable for enslavement.

SMITHSONIAN INSTITUTION

With the negativism of religious and philosophical ideas toward dark-skinned peoples, science provided a mechanism to assess physical differences between humans. This avenue enabled scientists to contribute emotional, intellectual, and sensory data gleaned from their instrumentations. At the turn of the twentieth century, the Smithsonian Institution (Washington, D.C.), intrigued by human variations, vigorously proceeded to increase data collection of various human physical characteristics. Having recently acquired an anthropological collection from the Army Medical Museum, the Smithsonian showed a growing concern with the educational possibilities of the study of civilization. To this end, a Division of Physical Anthropology was established at the Smithsonian with Ales Hrdlicka as assistant curator-in-charge. In short order, Hrdlicka undertook the task of publishing instructions for standardizing measurement and observation of human characteristics. His "Directions for Collecting Information and Specimens for Physical Anthropology" joined the library of the impressive *Smithsonian Institution Bulletin*. Previous sections of the *Bulletin* had given directions for collecting birds, insects, rocks, and minerals; Hrdlicka's contribution humanized the listing. His instructions included collection techniques in physical anthropology, involving crania, brains, and skeletons, and general observation. He called for the necessity of using appropriate aids and instruments to measure "the special senses; the pressure or traction force; to make, on healthy individuals valuable observations on pulse, respiration, and temperature; to test for swiftness or endurance in running; to observe the capacity for carrying burdens, enduring hunger and thirst, and capacity for excess in food."[16] Since skin color differences had occupied the attention of Europeans, it was natural that physical anthropologists would focus on measurement of this characteristic.

SKIN COLOR MEASUREMENT

To standardize measurement of skin color differences, Hrdlicka created techniques and presented them in precise instruction to his students:

> In this particular (skin color), it is first of all necessary to choose for comparison the same parts of the skin, and among those who wear the clothes, preferably those parts that are usually covered. The upper part of the arm or the back is especially suitable for this purpose. In this case the color should invariably be compared with and recorded by some well known standard, and the observation should be extended to both sexes and numerous individuals. It was largely a lack of precision in reporting the

color of the skin that made a red man of our brown Indian, and other similar examples.[17]

Hrdlicka's preference for skin color standards designed by Broca (1879) was evidenced by his reference to them in several of his publications. Essentially, Broca's technique was a matter of comparison. A set of pattern colors resembling the color selection cards seen in many of today's paint stores was used to match the skin hue of the subjects. A numbering system accompanied the color standards, allowing subjective observation to be converted into statistical objectivity.[18] While Broca's standards were designed to measure only skins of color (those normally outside the Caucasian groupings), his technique was praised for its accuracy. "Broca's set of pattern colors records the colour of any tribe he is observing with the accuracy of a mercer matching a piece of silk,"[19] was one statement typical of the praise.

Following the spirit of these color standards, various other attempts were made at skin color assessment utilizing paints, oils, lithography, and other tools. All met with general failure. The more interesting methods utilized devices called the tintometer (1918); the color top (Davenport, 1912); color blocks (von Luschan, 1918); color standards (Fritsch, 1916); and the photometer (Shaxby and Bonnell, 1918; Dice, 1930).

Tintometer

John Gray's tintometer (Figure 1.1) was designed for measuring the amount of pigmentation in hair and eyes, as well as in the skin:

> It consists of a single tube of rectangular section (1 inch by 1¼ inch) and 4 inches in length. At one end of the tube is an eye-piece with a lens, and in the other end are 2 rectangular apertures, side-by-side. Surrounding one of the apertures is a sheath or pocket into which one of the standard-coloured glasses is dropped. The bottom of the rectangular tube is extended about 2 inches beyond the end of the one, where it is turned up nearly at right angles. On one side of this upwardly projecting piece is pasted a strip of white paper to form the white surface opposite the coloured glass; and on the other side is a rectangular opening which is placed over the hair, eye, or skin whose pigment is to be measured.[20]

The tintometer failed to show much promise in spite of its technically interesting properties. One of the chief reasons for its lack of popu-

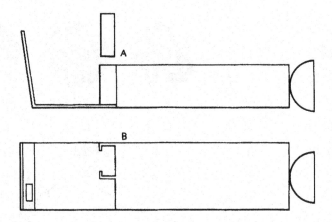

FIGURE 1.1   The Tintometer or Pigmentation Meter: (A) side view, (B) top view

Source: J. Gray, "A New Instrument for Determining the Colour of the Hair, Eyes, and Skin," *Man* 8, no. 27 (1908): 54. Reprinted by permission of the Royal Anthropological Institute of Great Britain and Ireland.

larity was the increasing interest shown in a top originally manufactured to show school-age children the properties of color mixture.

Color Top

The color top, made at the turn of the century by the Milton Bradley Company in Springfield, Massachusetts, was a little device designed for expressing color quantitatively (Figure 1.2). The toy, later called "The Pupil's Color Top, No. 8109," had disks of standard black, red, yellow, and white colors arranged so that varying proportions of each were exposed as sectors of a circle. (The four color variables were labeled: Nigrum (N), Red (R), White (W), and Yellow (Y). When the top was spun, the colors blended. By varying the proportions of the sectors (with small dissecting forceps), the color of the blend was altered. When this hue matched the color of an individual's skin, percentages were recorded. Careful instructions called for comparisons to be made with that part of the skin that was not exposed to sunlight; the deltoid region of the upper arm was often used. Specifics of this operation followed much the same procedure previously outlined by Hrdlicka:

> Skin color is to be taken on an unexposed and an exposed por-
> tion of the skin. The underside of the upper arm, which is not

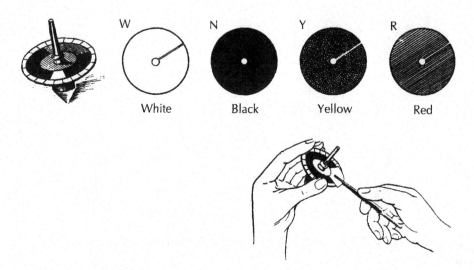

FIGURE 1.2 The Color Top and Method of Adjusting the Color Disks

Source: Louis R. Sullivan, *Essentials of Anthropometry: A Handbook for Explorers and Museum Collectors,* revised by H. L. Shapiro (New York: The American Museum of Natural History, 1928), 21. Courtesy of The American Museum of Natural History.

usually exposed is a good place to record skin color unexposed to light and wind. If this part has been exposed, the chest will serve. The cheek is usually studied for the effects of light and wind in pigment. Both are important . . . If a color top is employed, hold the spinning top as near the skin surface as possible, adjusting the disks until an approximate match results. Then record by letters and percentages the portions of each disk exposed.[21]

Even with these precise instructions, technical complaints began to be sounded in two respects: the problem of producing the desirable color and individual variances in interpreting the match between the color of the top and the color of the skin. As early as 1921, Todd and Van Gorder warned that "If the Bradley color top is to be used in the estimation it is essential to make necessary correction for the occurrence of a considerable amount of black in the red disc."[22] Later, Todd and others reiterated "there is one problem which must be faced before we can proceed . . . namely the amount of black (N) in the red disc."[23] In 1930, Bowman declared the situation hopeless: "We cannot therefore hope for uniformity in the red disc of the color top." Herskovits (1926) recognized similar problems in his use of the top.[24] Nevertheless, before the top's popularity

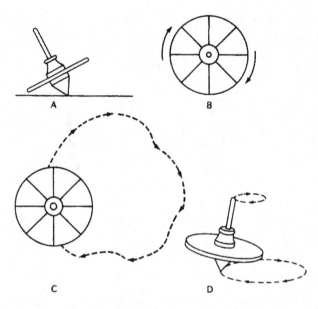

FIGURE 1.3 The Several Possible Movements of a Spinning Color Top: B always occurs, C is usually present, A and D generally occur.

Source: H. A. Bowman, "The Color-Top Method of Estimating Skin Pigmentation," *American Journal of Physical Anthropology* 14, no. 1 (1930). Reprinted by permission of the publisher, Wistar Press.

began to diminish, researchers had thoroughly overworked its usefulness. From movements of the spinning top (Figure 1.3) to the effects of lighting (Figure 1.4) to the possibilities of uniformity in speed and movement (Figure 1.5), the top was researched into oblivion.

Color Blocks

Felix von Luschan's porcelain scale of skin color standards was internationally acclaimed by virtue of his stature and esteem in the field of anthropology.[25] (His classic treatise, *Voelker Rassen Sprachen,* was a popular textbook for many early anthropologists.) The technique for using this scale was simple: The color blocks were held next to the skin until the match was made. Each block was numbered similarly to Broca's plates and the results were recorded in much the same manner. Bowman's (1930) criticism was typical; he found that the test raised resentment in the subject against an European or white standard.[26]

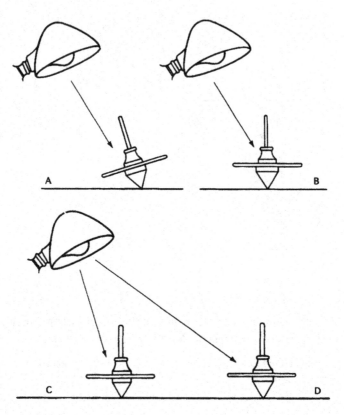

FIGURE 1.4 Effect of Incidence of Light on the Color Top: Tops A and C register a lighter shade than tops B and D because the latter are more obliquely illuminated.

Source: H. A. Bowman, "The Color-Top Method of Estimating Skin Pigmentation," *American Journal of Physical Anthropology* 14, no. 1 (1930). Reprinted by permission of the publisher, Wistar Press.

Color Standards

Gustav Fritsch (1916) attempted to quantify skin color variations on racial grounds using seven subdivisions, each of which contained variations of seven shades.[27] He duplicated these shades with oil colors painted on strips of special paper. In order to highlight these colors to improve the color recognition, the strips were surrounded by a dark field. A total of forty-nine strips were formed into a small case that was easily carried. Fritsch's oil colors received scant acceptance even though they were used for many research endeavors.

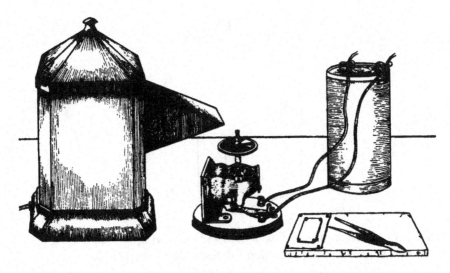

FIGURE 1.5 Color Top Mounted on Ajax Motor with Dry-Cell Connection, a Forerunner to the Modern Color Wheel Apparatus

Source: H. A. Bowman, "The Color-Top Method of Estimating Skin Pigmentation," *American Journal of Physical Anthropology* 14, no. 1 (1930). Reprinted by permission of the publisher, Wistar Press.

Photometer

J. H. Shaxby and H. E. Bonnell (1928) proposed an interesting method for quantifying the luminance of various skin colors. Utilizing a photometer (Figure 1.6), the researchers took a light source, such as a candle, and set it a foot away from the photometer. The arm of a subject was then moved until the color of the subject's skin matched the brightness reflected by the candle onto the screen inside the photometer. Then after measuring the distance of the subject's arm to the photometer, the luminance of the skin was calculated with the equation:

$$I_1 / D_1^2 = I_2 / D_2^2.$$

In spite of the mathematical aspect of this technique, research into the photometer's ability to measure skin color differences met with consistent failure. The reflecting degrees of various skin colors were minuscule, thus proving no significant differences between races of people.

Finally, in the waning days of skin color measurement, these instructions were written by Hrdlicka (1939):

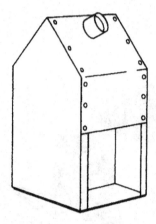

FIGURE 1.6 The photometer was used for measuring the luminating power of a stimulus. The photometer dates back to the 1800s.

On the pectoral parts of the chest may also be made certain tests developed by the writer which in many instances of doubtful mixtures between Whites and Indians or other Yellow-browns, and between Whites and other colored races, will help us to arrive at a conclusion. They are tests for the blood reaction of the skin. In a full-blood individual of the Yellow-brown or other dark races, if the chest is exposed and the observer makes three or four vertical lines over the pectoral parts by drawing his finger nail over the skin with a certain amount of pressure, there will be little or no visible reaction; but if there is any mixture with Whites the lines will show as fairly broad red marks, and the flush will be of some duration . . . both features being the more marked the more white blood is present in the individual under examination, provided he is in the ordinary state of health.[28]

Beyond the many attempts to measure skin color variations, other human physical attributes were subjected to measurement: Hair color and texture and the thickness of lips became particularly important. Focus on these features also played a part in later psychological measurements.

HAIR TEXTURE MEASUREMENTS

Scientific discussions relative to hair texture differences date to the nineteenth century. Pruner Bey maintained that hair constituted the best means of race identification: "A single hair representing the average form characteristic of the race might serve to define it." J. C. Prichard (1855) claimed that the hair of the Black man was decidedly different from that of any of the other races of man. He felt that the hair of the Black man was wool, not hair. He later expounded the difference between sheep's wool and "Negro" hair as the degree of "crispation."[29] For a long time it was felt that "tufted" hair grew in separate bunches that, while scattered evenly over the scalp, were isolated tufts with intervening bald spaces. Rudolf Virchow (1895) added to the debate by stating that "between these peppercorns there occur apparently bald spaces which gives the impression that all the hair forming each grain grows from a single spot."[30]

Bey classified hair into three categories:[31]

1. Short, crisp, or fleecy, usually called "woolly," almost invariably jet black; characteristic of all black races
2. Long, lank, or cylindrical, horse-mane type, mostly black; characteristic of all Native American and Mongoloid peoples
3. Intermediate, wavy, curly, or smooth, every shade; characteristic of Caucasian people

Paul Broca (1879) classified hair into three similar categories, which he then further subdivided according to length and color:[32]

1. Straight-haired

    Dolicho (long): Eskimo
    Brachy (short): (red) Prairie Indians; (olivaster) Mexican, Peruvian; (yellow) Guarani, Samoyede, Mongol, Malay

2. Wavy- or curly-haired

    Dolicho: (blond) Cimmerian, Scandinavian, Anglo-Saxon; (brown) Mediterranean (Basque, Corsican, Berber), Semite; (black) Australian, Indo-Abyssinian; (red) Fulah, Red Barabra (Nubian)
    Brachy: (blonde) Finn; (chestnut) Kelt, Slav; (brown) Iranian, Galcha

3. Woolly-haired

    Dolicho: (yellowish) Bushman; (black) Oceanic, Papuan, African, Kafir
    Brachy: Negrito

Much later, Sullivan (1928) considered straight hair "natural" hair, and attempted to calibrate other types using special measurement techniques. He first described three degrees of "waviness" (Figure 1.7):

> Following straight hair, three degrees of waviness are recognized. While they are described in terms of depth only as low, medium, or deep waves, the degree is really determined by the depth in relation to the width of the wave. The width of a wave is the distance from the apex of one wave to the apex of the next wave. The depth is the distance from a line tangent to these two points to the greatest depth between the two waves. When the depth is from $1/12$ to $1/10$ of the width, the hair is described as low waved. When the depth fluctuates above or below $1/6$ of the width, it is described as a medium or moderate wave. When the depth fluctuates above and below $1/2$ of the width, it is described as deeply waved.[33]

Sullivan also described three forms of hair (curly, frizzy, and woolly) and went into further detail concerning measurement (Figure 1.8):

> Real curly hair is rare . . . Before a hair can be called curly it should form at least three-fourths or more of a circle . . . It is not to be mistaken for the matted-woolly hair of Negroes. It is easily distinguished from this by the diameter of the curl or spiral which fluctuates around 2 centimeters near the head and dwindles gradually as the spiral continues. Frizzy hair is hair with a very short deep wave, but it does not form a curl or a spiral. It is distinguished by the small dimensions of the wave. A low wave is frequently about 5 centimeters wide and about .5 centimeter deep; a medium wave is about 3.5 or 4 centimeters wide and 6 or 7 millimeters deep; a deep wave is about 2.5 centimeters wide and about 12 millimeters deep, but frizzy hair has a wave only about 5 millimeters wide, and about the same depth or slightly less. Wooly hair is the familiar Negro hair consisting of more or less closely coiled spirals linked together forming a matted mass . . . One frequently sees very closely coiled hair grouped together in tufts which are more or less isolated from each other. The scalp is clearly visible between the tufts.[34]

Other speculations in hair texture research included Berstein and Robertson's (1927) conclusion that "negroid hair . . . weighs less than

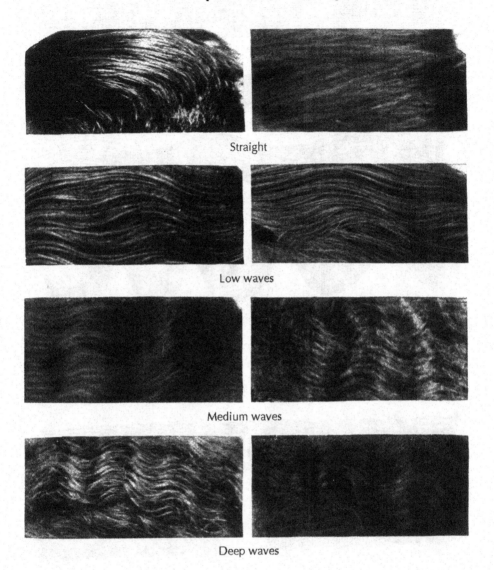

Straight

Low waves

Medium waves

Deep waves

FIGURE 1.7 Degrees of Hair Waviness

Source: Louis R. Sullivan, *Essentials of Anthropometry,* 47. Courtesy of The American Museum of Natural History.

that of the average Caucasoid . . . the hair of negroids contains numerous air bubbles of large sizes not evident in the hair of Mongoloids and Caucasoids."[35] Because of differences in hair classification proposed by these and other researchers, Sullivan warned his readers to use the standards that he outlined and study them until they were firmly fixed in

FIGURE 1.8 A Standard to Aid in Describing the Form of the Hair: (A) straight, (B) low wave, (C) medium wave, (D) deep wave, (E) and (F) curly, (G) frizzy, (H) woolly, (J) coiled or spiral tufts.

Source: Louis Sullivan, *Essentials of Anthropometry*, 47. Courtesy of The American Museum of Natural History.

mind: "Keep them constantly with you in the field since one easily loses the perspective in the new racial environment."[36]

Hexa, Penta, Tria

Browne's (1895) speculation that the hair of the white man would not felt while the "wool" of the black man would led to some complicated terminologies. Essentially, Browne suggested that two distinct species of man existed. When racial crossings occurred, the question of hybridization was complicated:

> Browne found that the hair from the heads of "hybrids" formed by the crossing of any two "species" of man consisted of filaments characteristic of each of the parent species. That is, the hair of a mulatto born of a "pure" white are both eccentrically elliptical and oval. By close observation he could determine the "degree of hybridity" of any given individual, and he prepared an elaborate set of tables which gave the nomenclature of human hybridity, of hybrids both "simple" (the offspring of two species only) and "compound" (the offspring of the crossing of all three species). Using the term "mulattin" to denote all crosses of the black and white species (or mixtures of oval and eccentrically elliptical types of hair) he found that the simple crossing of black and white could produce seven degrees of hybridity: "Helpta Mulattin" (14 parts white to 2 parts black), or {14:2}, "Hexa Mulattin" {12:4}, "Penta Mulattin" {10:6}, "Tetra Mulattin" {8:8}, "Tria Mulattin" {6:10}, "Di Mulattin" {4:12}, and "Mono Mulattin" {2:14}. Applying the same prefixes to the terms "costin" and "Mestisen," he gave the degrees of "simple hybridity" between the black and Indian and white and Indian, respectively. Compound hybrids led to such linguistics feats as "Hypta-hypo-mono-mulattin" and "Penta-hyper-mono-mulattin."[37]

MEASURING HAIR COLOR

Far more emphasis was placed on the measurement of hair texture than of hair color. Nevertheless, techniques were developed for measuring the degree of variances in hair color, and one of them used the color wheel for that purpose. Bellamy (1930) proposed a method of matching cuttings of hair to existing color charts from which percentages of color mixtures were calculated (for example: 85 percent black, 12 percent red, and 3 percent yellow).[38] Bellamy went so far as to suggest that the prevalence of blondness or brunetness should be indicated on regional maps for the purpose of further research.

MEASURING THICKNESS OF LIPS

Davenport's *Guide to Physical Anthropometry and Anthroposcopy* (1927) delineates no fewer than 35 "observations" of the human body. Among these "observations" is a discussion concerning the measurement and classification of lip sizes.

> When lightly closed, height measured at the maximum to one side of median; width to angles; then lips may be classified by height divided by width ratio as:

Thin	below 0.20 millimeters
Medium	0.20–0.29 mm
Thick	0.30–0.44 mm
Very Thick	0.45 mm and over[39]

Another technique for estimating sizes of lips was offered by Sullivan in a similar guidebook, *Essentials of Anthropometry.* This procedure called for the matching of the subject's lips to a set of illustrated drawings (Figure 1.9).

ANTHROPOMETRY AND BLACKS

Attempts to categorize hair texture, skin color differences, and lip sizes suggest the importance that many researchers placed on anthropometric measurements. These findings were often used to support assumptions of racial differences by comparing races with European standards. In spite of the widespread emphasis placed on comparing races to European standards, Franz Boas and his students encouraged research on African and African American cultures in order to learn specifics of each culture and to synthesize the uniqueness of Black culture. Boas's leading student and later distinguished scholar, Melville Herskovits, believed that Black culture and white culture, "were the same pattern only a different shade."[40] In order to prove this theory, he conducted extensive studies of physical measurements of Blacks in New York City and students at Howard University with the idea of illustrating the "sameness" in human beings.

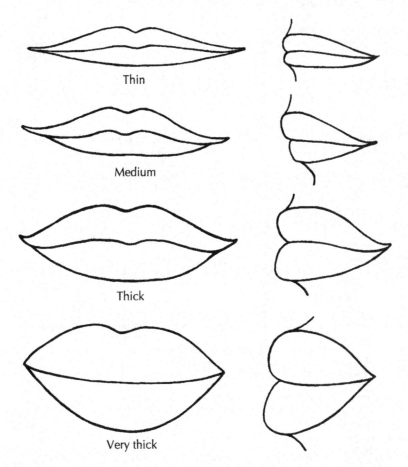

FIGURE 1.9 Standard to Aid in Describing the Thickness of the Lips

Source: Louis Sullivan, *Essentials of Anthropometry,* 58. Courtesy of The American Museum of Natural History.

With the assistance and recommendations of Howard professors Alain Locke and Ernest Just, Herskovits began to conduct anthropometric studies and to teach at Howard in the spring of 1925.[41] Using a long, detailed form (Table 1.1) to insure uniformity in his collection of data, Herskovits made an extensive study of the physical measurements of Black students at Howard University. (Ten other anthropometric studies of Blacks, made in the United States from 1925 to 1930, are listed in Table 1.2.) Herskovits summed up his findings and the state of affairs in the opening chapter of his book, *The Anthropometry of the American Negro* (1930):

TABLE 1.1 Form Used for Collecting Anthropometric and Genealogical Information (Howard University and New York City)

Anthropometric Information

Form H 1   **No.**

Length of Head:	Width of Head:	Index
Height of Nose:	Width of Nose:	
	al-al	
	sp-tip	
	cr-tip	

Thickness of Lips: center   right   Width of Mouth:
Height of Face: n-a   n-gn   Bizygomatic Width:
Height of Ear: Width of Ear:
Metacarpale laterale to M. mediale   Phal. III to Dak. III
Skin-color: Inner Upper Arm   N   R   Y   W
                  Outer Upper Arm   N   R   Y   W
Minimum Width of Forehead: Angle of Eyes:
Distance between Inner Corners of Eyes: Outer:
          Interpupillary Distance:

Height of Head:
Acromial Width: Width of Hip:
Weight: Height: Height sitting:

Genealogical Information

Note: This information is strictly confidential. No reference will be made to it in any way other than by number.

By *Negro* is meant *all* Negro, that is, African or descent from African, with *no* mixture of White or Indian blood.

By *Mixed* is meant mixed Negro and White, that is, neither all White nor all Negro.

By *White* is meant *all* White, without any mixture of Negro blood.

If you have Indian blood, indicate this in the proper place by the initial (I).

Are you Mixed?	Negro?	White?
What is your father's name?		
When was he born?	Where?	
Is he Mixed?	Negro?	White?
What is your mother's name?		
When was she born?	Where?	
Is she Mixed?	Negro?	White?
What was your father's father's name?		
Where was he born?		
Was he Mixed?	Negro?	White?
What was your father's mother's name?		
Where was she born?		
Was she Mixed?	Negro?	White?
What was your mother's father's name?		
Where was he born?		
Was he Mixed?	Negro?	White?

Name _____ Date of Birth _____ Class _____ Date _____

Address _____ Place of Birth _____

TABLE 1.2 Anthropometric Studies Conducted in the United States, 1925–1930

Location	Subjects	Researcher
New York City	Native Born Blacks	Herskovits
New York City	Native Born Blacks	King
New York City	West Indian Born	Herskovits
New York City	West Indian Born	King
New York City	Native Born, Upper Class Blacks	Hurston
West Virginia	Native Born Blacks	King
Howard University	Black Students	Herskovits
Fisk University	Black Students	Blackwood
Tennessee A & I College	Black Students	Blackwood
St. Louis	Blacks	Von Luschan
Tuskegee Institute	Black Females	Blackwood

Source: M. J. Herskovits, *The Anthropometry of the American Negro* (New York: Columbia University Press, 1930), 12. Reprinted by permission of the publisher.

The American Negro has long been recognized as constituting one of the major social and economic problems of the United States. Although there have been numerous studies resulting from this recognition, most of these deal with the more imperative phases of the problem of the association of Negroes and Whites. Nor is this strange, for the presence of a considerable body of individuals among a large population from whom they differ in physical type, and particularly in such an easily recognized trait as skin color, must inevitably bring on a body of taboos, repressions, conflicts, and social and economic complications of more or less grave import.[42]

DEFINING RACIAL DIFFERENCES

Differences between the physical measurements of Blacks and whites led to a number of discussions of racial classification. Such questions as By what criteria is an individual classified as white? Or Black? Or whatever? became increasingly difficult to answer. It was obvious that visual observations were confusing; large numbers of Blacks with mixed ancestry complicated the matter of identification. While Herskovits felt that the number of Blacks who claimed Indian ancestry, for example, was inaccurate because "Indian ancestry has distinct prestige value among American Negroes," it was obvious to even the most casual observer that significant numbers of persons with mixed ancestry existed.

White researchers became leery of visual techniques for the identification of races and called for warnings of being misled by the effects of skin bleaching, hair dyeing, hair straightening or by the use of wigs, hair pieces, and so forth. To help avoid the potential errors inherent in casual observation, Sullivan (1928) called for the solicitation of hearsay information. He encouraged the recording of such evidence as "looks part white" or "neighbor says he is part Negro" for anthropological data gathering. The United States Census Bureau, while recording only Black-white mixtures (Table 1.3), called for the classification of "Negro" if even one relative could be traced to African descent. Not allowed the wide variances permitted whites, which disregarded ethnic subdivisions, Blacks were placed in a single category, regardless of their language or point of origin.

In 1910, the sixty-first Congress accepted from the Immigration Commission a unique book, *The Dictionary of Races or Peoples,* prepared by Daniel and Elnora Folkmar.[43] The Folkmars, following Blumenbach's broad racial classification of black, white, red, yellow, and brown, implemented a "Comparative Classification of Immigrant Races or Peoples" for their research (Table 1.4). While the *Dictionary* treated more than 600 subjects in its classification system, Black people were placed in a single, narrow category. The *Dictionary* stated that the Negro belonged to "that grand division of mankind distinguished by its black color and, generally speaking, by its woolly hair."[44] This classification included "aliens whose appearance indicates an admixture of Negro blood, whether coming from Cuba or other islands of the West Indies, North or South America, Europe, or Africa."[45]

TABLE 1.3 Population Figures for Black and Mulatto U.S. Citizens, 1850–1920

Year	Total Negro	Black	Mulatto	% Black	% Mulatto
1920	10,463,131	8,802,577	1,660,554	84.1	15.9
1910	9,827,763	7,777,077	2,050,686	79.1	20.9
1890	7,488,676	6,337,980	1,132,060	84.8	15.2
1870	4,880,009	4,295,960	584,049	88.0	12.0
1860	4,441,830	3,853,467	588,363	86.8	13.2
1850	3,683,808	3,233,057	405,751	88.8	11.2

Source: M. J. Herskovits, *The Anthropometry of the American Negro* (New York: Columbia University Press, 1930), 19. Reprinted by permission of the publisher.

TABLE 1.4 Comparative Classification of Immigrant Races or People

Race	Stock	Group	People	Ripley's races with other corresponding terms
Caucasian	Aryan	Teutonic	Scandanavian: Danish Norwegian Swedish German (N. part) Dutch English (part) Flemish	I. TEUTONIC H. Europæus (Lapouge) Nordic (Deniker) Dolicho-leptorhine (Kohlmann) Germanic (English writers) Reihengräber (German writers) Kymric (French writers)
		Lettic	Lithuanian	
		Celtic	Scotch (part) Irish (part) Welsh	Part Alpine
		Slavonic	Russian Polish Czech: Bohemian Moravian Servian Croatian Montenegrin Slovak Slovenian Ruthenian Dalmatian Herzegovinian Bosnian	II. ALPINE (OR CELTIC) H. Alpinus (Lapouge) Occidental (Deniker) Disentis (German writers) Celto-Slavic (French writers) Lappanoid (Pruner-Bey) Samatian (von Höider) Arvernian (Beddoe)
		Illyric	Albanian	
		Armenic	Armenian	
		Italic	French Italian (part) Roumanian Spanish Spanish-American Mexican, etc. Portuguese	Part Alpine Part Mediterranean III. MEDITERRANEAN H. Meridionalis (Lapouge) Atlanic-Mediterranean and Ibero-Insular (Deniker) Iberian (English writers) Ligurian (Italian writers)
		Hellenic	Greek	Part Mediterranean
		Iranic	Hindu Gypsy	Part Teutonic
	Semitic	Arabic	Arabian Hebrew	Part Mediterranean
		Chaldaic	Syrian	
	Caucasic		Caucasus peoples	Doubtful
	Euskaric		Basque	
Mongolian	Sibiric	Finnic	Finnish Lappish Magyar Bulgarian (part)	
		Tataric	Turkish, Cossack, etc.	
		Japanese	Japanese, Korean	
		Mongolic	Kalmuk	
	Sinitic	Chinese	Chinese East Indian (part i.e., Indo-Chinese)	
Malay			Pacific Islander (part) East Indian (part)	
Ethiopian			Negro	
American	(Indian)			American Indian

Note: Based on Brinton (cf. Keane)

Source: D. Folkmar and E. Folkmar, *Dictionary of Races or Peoples,* Document No. 662 (Washington, D.C.: Immigration Commission, 1911).

CLASSIFICATION OF BLACK-WHITE MIXTURES

In order to classify those Blacks of mixed racial background, specific terminology was created by academicians. *Mulatto* described the off-spring of the union of a pure white person with a pure Black person. The term appears to have been derived from the Latin word, *mula*, meaning mule. This offers an interesting parallel, for the mule is a hybrid ani-mal—resulting from the union of a horse and a jackass—which is des-tined not only to be a creature of burden, but also genetically unable to reproduce its own kind. For many years, in fact, it was argued that Blacks and whites were unable to interbreed successfully and produce fertile offspring: While children could be produced from a Black-white combi-nation of parents, it was believed that two mulatto offspring could not reproduce.

Other fractionated divisions in racial makeup were designated *quad-roon*, the child of a mulatto and a white, three-fourths white and one-fourth Black, and *octoroon*, the child of a white and a quadroon, seven-eights white and one-eighth Black.[46] While there was no com-monly agreed upon term for the child of a pure Black and a mulatto (three-fourths Black and one-fourth white), Ferguson (1916) suggested the ridiculous term *Sambo*.[47]

In some instances, psychologists used far less complicated systems of identification. Ferguson (1916) classified Black children into four groups—"pure," "three-fourths," "mulatto," and "quadroon"—based on skin color, hair texture, and general facial and cranial data. Strong (1913) labeled Blacks as "dark," "medium," or "light." Crane (1923) devised the following scale: (1) so light as to be possibly mistaken for a white person at first glance; (2) very light, but instantly recognizable as a "colored" person; (3) medium dark; (4) very dark; and (5) pitch black, African in appearance.

CULTURAL ANTHROPOLOGISTS

Initially, voices of dissent directed toward anthropometric philosophies were limited because the nature of anthropology called for the investiga-tion of darker people. The "discovery" mode of anthropologists was much like the establishment and maintenance of the world's zoos, for example identifying, collecting, and classifying exotic animals. The ob-session for discovery of darker races compelled anthropologists to iden-tify, measure, and contrast peoples regarded as primitive. To those who did not investigate darker peoples in other parts of the globe, the focus and concept of "degenerate families" in the United States became vogue. (See Chapter 4.) In both cases, the concept of comparative research was paramount. A symbiotic relationship grew between sociology and anthropology with each discipline focusing on culture and society.[48] Anthropologists became concerned with the environmental effects of human variations and conditions, and with psychology's embroilment in their nature versus nurture dispute, the concern was magnified. In the vanguard of the environmentalist perspectives were prominent women scholars such as Ruth Benedict, Hortense Powdermaker, Rachel Davis, and Margaret Mead. Their egalitarian perspectives, along with Boas, Lloyd Warner, and Herskovitz, began to stimulate Blacks who were aware of the deleterious results of most anthropometric studies. Judging from the viewpoints of these people, an eminent African American anthropologist, St. Clair Drake, declared that Blacks began to feel that "anthropology must be on their side."[49]

EARLY BLACK ANTHROPOLOGISTS

"Anthropologists of color have a long and rich history of shaping the shifting discourse on race, culture, and diversity as well as challenging the oppressive forces which shape racial constructs," Lee Baker stated in his discussion of Black anthropologist Louis E. King.[50] (King was one of a small number of Black graduate students who worked with leading white researchers; his later contributions played an important role in U.S. public school desegregation.) Despite the lack of course work in anthropology taught in Black colleges and universities, however, a few Black students began to trickle into the graduate training pipeline. White anthropologists used their Black apprentices to assist them in negotiating with Black communities for research ventures and to provide necessary academic skills. Notably, graduate students such as Zora Neale Hurston and Katherine Dunham assisted with and contributed to several anthropological studies.[51] Drake, in his "Reflections on Anthropology and the Black Experience," identified Caroline Bond Day as possibly the first African American with a doctoral degree in anthropology. He also identified eminent University of Chicago professor Allison Davis as a doctoral student during the late 1930s.[52] Drake and Davis led a small number of Black anthropologists into the cultural-social anthropologist camps that subsequently contributed immensely in combatting racist themes of prior studies.

"NO SCIENTIFIC BASIS FOR DISCRIMINATION"

The heavy emphasis placed upon the categorization of races and the subsequent psychological testing of various groups of people often led to conclusions of racial superiority and inferiority. The brewing anti-Semitism in Europe led to a realization, among some scholars in the United States, that erroneous conclusions had been made of its "scientific" data. In 1928, at its annual meeting, the American Anthropological Association adopted a resolution, which declared in part: "Anthropology provides no scientific basis for discrimination against any people on the ground of racial inferiority, religious affiliation, or linguistic heritage."[53] This proclamation came about not because scientists were convinced of Blacks' racial equality, but because of the European situation. Psychologists issued a similar disclaimer in an attempt to erase the interpretations made from psychological testing data. (See Chapter 3 for further discussion.)

NOTES

Chapter Epigraph: Richard Hakluyt, *Principal Navigations, Voyages, Traffiques, and Discoveries of the English Nation* (Glasgow, 1903–1905).

1. S. Vogel, *Yoruba: Nine Centuries of African Art and Thought,* ed. H. Drewal, J. Pemberton III, R. Abiodun (Abrams, New York), 10.

2. P. Curtin et al., *African History: From Earliest Times to Independence* (London: Longman Group, 1995).

3. W. B. Cohen, *The French Encounter with Africans* (Bloomington: Indiana University Press, 1980), 2.

4. R. Hakluyt, "The First Voyage of Robert Baker to Guinie," in *Principall Navigations, Voiges and Discoveries of the English Nation* (London, 1589), 132.

5. W. D. Jordan, *White Over Black* (Chapel Hill, N.C.: University of North Carolina Press, 1968), 5.

6. Cohen, *The French Encounter,* 9.

7. O. Omosegbon, "The Unequal Exchange: European Contacts with Africans in Precolonial Times," unpublished manuscript, Southern Illinois University, 1995.

8. J. Montgomery, *Poetical Works* (London, 1841).

9. O. Equiano, *The Interesting Narrative of the Life of Olaudah Equiano or Gustavus Vasa, The African* (New York, 1791), 1:49–62.

10. Cohen, *The French Encounter,* 11.

11. Much of this indictment was based on the Canaanite religious rites, which deeply shocked the Hebrews. It is interesting to note that the Canaanites invented three different alphabets, one of which (the Phoenician) became the ancestor of practically all alphabets of the Western world.

12. *Book of Mormon*, 2 Nephi 5:21, 30:5–6. Mormons of Black African descent were denied the male priesthood of the church until 1978. Native Americans have always been eligible for positions in the church's hierarchy with the promise that they will become white and delightsome. This "goal" applies to all people the Mormons call "Lamanites"—Mexicans, Latin Americans, Hawaiians, and Polynesians who convert.

13. F. Welsing, as quoted by Genevieve E. Kaete in "Soul: The Sixth Sense," *New Directions* 1, no. 3 (Spring 1974): 12–17. An interesting reversal of the "black-skin-deficit" philosophy can be viewed in interpretations by Black psychiatrist Frances Welsing. She advances the notion that Adam and Eve were the first albino children of Black parents in the Garden of Eden (Africa) and that they were ashamed of their skin's whiteness. Welsing further explains that Africa's first albinos then wandered "into Europe into a climate where there was less sun and their pigmentation could function in the environment."

14. J. Schweinfurth, *Heart of Africa* (Berlin: Junker and Dunnhaupt, 1938).

15. T. Waitz, *Introduction to Anthropology* (London: Longmans, 1863).

16. A. Hrdlicka, "Directions for Collecting Information and Specimens for Physical Anthropology," (Part R, No. 39) (Washington, D.C., United States National Museum, 1904), 25.

17. Ibid.

18. P. Broca, "Instructions generales pour les recherches anthropologiques a faire sur le vivant," 2nd ed., Paris, 1879.

19. J. Deniker, *The Races of Man: An Outline of Anthropology and Ethnography* (Freeport, N.Y.: Books for Library Press, 1900), 47.

20. J. Gray, "A New Instrument for Determining the Colour of the Hair, Eyes, and Skin," *Man* 8, no. 27 (1908): 54–58.

21. L. R. Sullivan, *Essentials of Anthropometry: A Handbook for Explorers and Museum Collectors*, rev. ed., H. L. Shapiro (New York: American Museum of Natural History, 1928), 43.

22. T. Todd and L. Van Gorder, "The Quantitative Determination of Black Pigmentation in the Skin of the American Negro," *American Journal of Physical Anthropology* 4, no. 3 (1921): 239–260.

23. T. Todd, B. Blackwood, and H. Beecher, "Skin Pigmentation," *American Journal of Physical Anthropology* 11, no. 2 (January–March 1928): 187–205.

24. M. Herskovits, "Age Changes in Pigmentation of American Negroes," *American Journal of Physical Anthropology* 9, no. 3 (1926): 323.

25. F. von Luschan, *Voelker Rassen Sprachen* (Berlin: Welt Verlag, 1922).

26. H. A. Bowman, "The Color-Top Method of Estimating Skin Pigmentation," *American Journal of Physical Anthropology* 14, no. 1 (January– March 1930): 59.

27. G. Fritsch, "Bermerkungen zu der Haufarbentafel," *Mitt Anthrop Ges Wien* 16:H, Berlin (1916): 183–185.

28. A. Hrdlicka, *Anthropometry* (Philadelphia: Wistar Institute of Anatomy and Biology, 1939).

29. P. Bey, as quoted by J. C. Prichard in *Natural History of Man,* E. Norris, ed. (London: Wilson and Ogilvy, 1855).

30. R. Virchow, *Zeitschrift fur Ethnologie* (Berlin: Heft 11, 1895), 152.

31. Bey, *Natural History,* 79.

32. P. Broca, *Atlas d'anatomie Descriptive du Corps Humain* (Paris: G. Masson, 1879), 37. Other recognized schema were interestingly prepared by Muller (1900), Deniker (1900), and Haeckel (1866). Deniker's scheme was based on a fusion of two, three, or more "races," which set forth "thirty types" based on the different textures of the skin.

33. Sullivan, *Essentials of Anthropometry,* 44–48.

34. Ibid., 48–49.

35. M. Berstein and S. Robertson, "Racial and Sexual Differences in Hair Weight," *Journal of Physical Anthropology* 10, no. 3 (July 1927): 379–385.

36. Sullivan, *Essentials of Anthropometry,* 50.

37. W. Stanton, *The Leopard's Spots, Scientific Attitudes Toward Race in America 1815–1859* (Chicago: University of Chicago Press, 1960), 152.

38. R. Bellamy, "Measuring Hair Color," *American Journal of Physical Anthropology* 14, no. 1 (January–March 1930): 75–77.

39. B. Davenport, *Guide to Physical Anthropometry and Anthroposcopy* (Cold Spring Harbor, N.Y.: Eugenics Research Association, 1927), 42.

40. W. Jackson, "Melville Herskovits and the Search for Afro-American Culture," in G. W. Stocking, Jr., ed. *Malinowski, Rivers, Benedict and Others* (Madison: University of Wisconsin Press, 1986), 102.

41. Ibid.

42. M. Herskovits, *The Anthropometry of the American Negro* (New York: Columbia University Press, 1930).

43. D. Folkmar and E. Folkmar, *Dictionary of Races or Peoples,* Document No. 662 (Washington, D.C.: Immigration Commission, 1911), 150.

44. Ibid., 100.

45. Ibid., 101.

46. During antebellum days in New Orleans, female octoroon parties were fairly common events for the entertainment of white men.

47. G. Ferguson, Jr., *The Psychology of the Negro: An Experimental Study* (New York: The Science Press, 1916).

48. Anthropology and sociology share common departmental arrangements in many institutions.

49. St. C. Drake, "Reflections on Anthropology and the Black Experience," *Anthropology & Education Quarterly* IX, no. 2, pp. 85–109.

50. L. D. Baker, "Moving the History of Anthropology from the Memorial to the Contextual: The Case of Louis E. King," unpublished manuscript, 1994.

51. Drake, "Reflections on Anthropology," 95.

52. Ibid. Also for an informative discussion on W. Montague Cobb (1904–1990): L. M. Rankin-Hill and M. L. Blakey, "Physical Anthropologist, Anatomist, and Activist," *American Anthropologist* 96, no. 1 (March 1994) 74–96.

53. "The New York Meeting of the American Anthropological Association," *Science* (New Series), 89 (1939): 29–30.

► 2

Brass Instruments
and Dark Skins

Something of an academic coup occurred late in the nineteenth century
with the emergence of the new science of psychology. The established
sciences of biology and physics looked to the new discipline with great
expectation and excitement. Both the new adherents and older scientists
watched with the hope that psychology would be a deliverance from the
scientific doldrums and fads of the eighteenth and nineteenth centuries.
By declaring itself the study of the mind, psychology claimed ownership
of all that dealt with animal and human behavior. Wilhelm Wundt's
(1879) influence on the field of scientific psychology was tremendous.
From his laboratory in Leipzig, Germany, his students and followers
formed the roster of founding fathers and leaders in American and
European psychology. They travelled from afar and later scattered to all
parts of the globe arousing new interests and methodologies for ex-
ploring human behavior with the "brass instruments" of physiology.
Laboratories were established in major universities with the intent of
investigating differences among human beings. It was little wonder that
these techniques would be used in comparing physiological reactions of
so-called primitive people. The new discipline cut a wide swath through
the ivy walls of academia at a time when the Western Weltanschauung
was infected by racism and social Darwinism, and psychology eventually
became an important contributor to the era.[1]

The concept of race and its later development to racism originated
during the precolonial phase of English history. As European nations
vigorously competed with one another for wealth and power, the justification for the subjugation and enslavement of other peoples was seen as

a mandate to improve a superior group. It was this unequal human formula that sanctioned the annihilation and enslavement of dark-skinned peoples in the name of progress and civilization. Not only did the English language support the negativism attached to skin color differences, but also it allowed for the philosophical thought promoting the subsequent political, economic, social, and scientific reactions to dark-skinned peoples. Finally, religion supplied the "saving of souls" as a rational for dominating a group of people.

ETHNICAL PSYCHOLOGY

Psychology and anthropology were bedfellows during an emerging golden age of racism during the nineteenth century; both searched for, and consequently magnified, the existence of differences in racial characteristics, mental abilities, and personality traits among the peoples of the world. Their zest and zeal reinforced prevailing Western mythologies of racial superiority and the resultant exploitation of nonwhite peoples.

The initial union between psychology and anthropology took place in Germany when P. W. A. Bastain (1871) insisted on the essential connection between psychology and ethnology. (Ethnology is that sub-branch of anthropology concerned with the study of race; it was once considered a field of study so significant that David Wechsler [1939] saw fit to include the word in his IQ test designed to measure an individual's knowledge of general information.) While Bastain was not especially concerned with studying Black people, his interest in ethnical psychology negated earlier views which held "it is not worthwhile to look into the soul of the negro. It is a judgment of God which is being executed that, at the approach of civilization, the savage man must perish."[2] However, at the turn of the twentieth century, increased interest in racial studies began to appear, accompanying the concept of Negritude.[3] Dennett's (1906) perspective was typical of this view:

> I cannot help feeling that one who has acquired a kind of way of thinking black, should be listened to on the off-chance that a secondary instinct, developed by long contact with the people he is writing about, may have driven him to a right, or nearly right, conclusion.[4]

In 1910, Haddon expanded on the term *ethnical psychology* to include the "uncivilized," defining it as "the study of the minds of other races and peoples, of which, among the more backward races, glimpses can be obtained only by living by means of observation and experiment."[5] Haddon's definition was a milestone because it not only cemented the connection between the two disciplines but also suggested a methodological stance as well. Psychology's concern with race was thus legitimized by direction and purpose.

Robert S. Woodworth, then chairman of the anthropology and psychology section of the American Association for the Advancement of Science and later (1914) president of the American Psychological Association, illustrated psychology's concern and interest in studying the comparative nature of humans:

> One of the most agreeable and satisfying experiences afforded by intellectual pursuits comes from the discovery of a clean-cut distinction between things which are superficially much alike. The aesthetic value of such distinctions may even outweigh their intellectual value and lead to sharp lines and antithesis where the only difference that exists is one of degree. A favorite opportunity for this form of intellectual exercise and indulgence is afforded by the observation of groups of men.[6]

Anthropologists, sensing the conflict of shared interest and losing their battle for complete ownership of the study of the races, relinquished a portion of the field to psychologists, who would study the behavior of individuals in carefully defined laboratory or experimental situations. This move consequently justified anthropology's continued research on small communities by means of observation and interview at a face-to-face level. The arrangement was appealing to psychologists, for they viewed themselves as experimental scientists with the accoutrements of a white-coated laboratory milieu.

An early cooperative research effort between psychologists and anthropologists began when the Cambridge Anthropological Society sent an expedition in 1889 to study the mental life of the inhabitants of the Torres Straits:

> For the first time trained experimental psychologists investigated by means of an adequate laboratory equipment, a people in a low state of culture under their ordinary condition of life. The foundations of ethnical experimental psychology were thus laid.[7]

Among the "brass instrument Tarzans" who made this historic trip to the Torres Straits and the Fly River district of New Guinea were anthropologists W. H. R. Rivers and C. S. Myers and psychologist William

McDougall. McDougall went on to promulgate, among other racist views, the dogma of "instincts" in humans. (The instinct theory asserted that inborn and unlearned response tendencies determined social behavior.) The Torres Straits studies were made in the best tradition of Wundtian psychophysics. Hearing, vision, taste, tactile acuity, pain, motor speed and accuracy, fatigue, and memory tests were performed on the unsuspecting, cooperative sepia-skinned villagers. Unsurprisingly, the voices of science concluded that the "wild" natives of the South Pacific did not surpass western man in any trait; rather, the inhabitants were found to be far less intelligent than their examiners. This adventure by the Cambridge Anthropological Society provided an important impetus for American psychologists to seek and study racial variances in humans.

RACIAL DESIGNATIONS

Among other things, anthropology provided psychology with the racial system needed to justify intellectually the existence of differences among human beings. Where early classifications had stemmed from theologically derived doctrines and divided humans into descendants of Shem, Ham, and Japhet, Carl von Linnaeus (1735) made racial distinctions based on color of skin, temperament, customs, and habits (see Table 2.1). This scheme, which designated psychological as well as physical characteristics of the different races, assigned the qualities of capriciousness, negligence, and slowness to Black people. The biblical explanation for racial groupings had presented a major problem of congruence: As the white man explored and plundered new worlds, he claimed that the

TABLE 2.1 Eighteenth-Century Racial Distinctions and Racial Habits Based on Skin Color

Racial Groups	Descriptions
Homo Americanus	Reddish, choleric, erect, tenacious, contented, free; ruled by custom
Homo Europaeus	White, ruddy, muscular, stern, haughty, stingy; ruled by opinion
Homo Asiaticus	Yellow, melancholic, inflexible, light, inventive; ruled by rites
Homo Afer	Black, phlegmatic, indulgent, cunning, slow, negligent; ruled by caprice

Source: Carl von Linnaeus, *Systema Naturae,* 1735.

"discovered" savages were not descendants of Adam and therefore were outside the grace of God. Linnaeus's racial distinctions, therefore, proved advantageous for those seeking to justify the inferiority of the darker races.

Following Linnaeus, a number of racial classifications were made, all of which placed the Black man at the bottom of the human family hierarchy. The relative question of race categorization reached such ridiculous proportions in this country that the U.S. Senate commissioned Daniel and Elnora Folkmar to prepare, for the Immigration Commission, *A Dictionary of Races or Peoples* (see Chapter 1). Under the entry *Negro,* this official government document described the Black man as "belonging to the lowest division of mankind from an evolutionary standpoint." The definition of Negro embraced "Negro, or African (black) whose appearance indicates any admixture of Negro blood . . . whether coming from Cuba, or other islands of the West Indies, North or South America, Europe, or Africa."[8] The term *Negro* was thus considered a racial designation without regard to place of origin, which removed from consideration any ethnic characteristics within the race. From this framework, the role of inferiority was clearly assigned to all Black peoples of the world.

In support of racial classifications, anthropologists contributed many other interesting—and ridiculous—methods for judging variations within Homo sapiens. John Friedrich Blumenbach (1824) developed a method for visually judging cranium variation (Figure 2.1). The *norma verticalis,* or Blumenbach's view, was regarded as an accurate technique by scientists and was performed in the following manner: "the skull was placed between the feet of the observer and after examination from above, classed as oblong, round, and so forth, for the purpose of determining the race to which it belonged."[9] Blumenbach's procedures were also used as a technique for distinguishing those skulls whose previous owners were designated as "civilized" or from those designated as "uncivilized." Several years later similar claims declared that the posterior balance of the skull—its ability to rest on the posterior edge of the occipital hole and the inferior edge of the orbits—was a distinctive sign of the Negro race.[10]

Among the theoreticians who speculated from these views and spun similar webs were F. J. Gall and G. Spurzheim. Their six-volume *Anatomy and Physiology of the Nervous System* (1817) laid the basis for phrenology by asserting that the brain was the organ of the mind. While Gall and Spurzheim accurately speculated that different kinds of behavior were controlled by separate parts of the brain, they mistakenly declared that the external shape of the skull reflected the shape of the brain under-

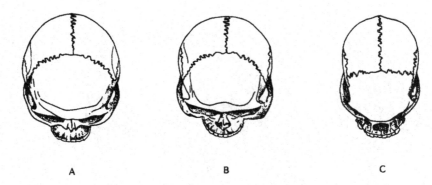

A   B   C

FIGURE 2.1 *Norma Verticalis* or Blumenbach's View for Racial
Identification: (A) Caucasian, (B) Mongol, (C) Negro

neath. Since whites were generally judged to be more intelligent than
Blacks, the Gall and Spurzheim line of reasoning eventually led early
psychologists to conclude that the skull capacities of whites were greater
than the skull capacities of Blacks:

> the skull capacity of modern European whites is 1560 cc., and
> that of European whites of the neolithic period is the same; the
> skull capacity of the mongoloid is 1510 cc., that of the negroes
> of the Pacific Ocean is 1460 cc., and that of African negroes is
> 1405 cc.[11]

As late as 1973, Henry Garrett, a past president of the American
Psychological Association, supported this theory as an argument against
racial integration when he wrote that the Black man's brain "on the
average is smaller . . . less fissured and less complex than the white
brain."[12]

The alleged skull-capacity differences among humans were matched
with studies concerning the shape of the face (Figure 2.2). For example,
Isadore Saint-Hilaire (1847) divided human facial structures into *orthog-
nathic* (oval face with vertical jaws), *eurygnathic* (high cheekbones), and
prognathic (projecting jaws). From these models, it was concluded that
the black race was *prognathous* (forward jawed), the Asian *eurygnathic*
(vertical jawed), and the white race *orthognathus* (upright jawed). In
short, the African was considered more apelike, and therefore inferior, in
comparison to whites. In this regard, even anthropologist Franz Boas,
who later became a leading spokesman for racial equality, wrote the
following:

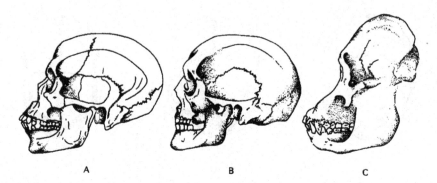

FIGURE 2.2 Skull Shapes: (A) Prognathous Skull of the Negro, (B) Orthognathous Skull of Caucasian, (C) Skull of Orang

Source: A. H. Keane, *Ethnology* (London: Cambridge University Press, 1916), 183.

We find that the face of the negro as compared to the skull is larger than that of the American, whose face is in turn larger than that of the white. The lower portion of the face assumes larger dimensions. The alveolar arch is pushed forward and thus gains an appearance which reminds us of the higher apes.[13]

The intrinsic social bias of physical anthropologists was interwoven throughout these early analyses,[14] and it was not long before the inferior physical status assigned to Blacks was joined with similar analyses along psychological dimensions. An early contention held that "primitive races" could not abstract, inhibit impulses, or choose according to standards of value. Tylor (1916) set a bias for educational psychologists with this observation:

In measuring the minds of lower races, a good test is how far their children are able to take a civilized education. The account generally given by European teachers who have had the children of lower races in their schools is that, though they often learn as well as the white children up to 12 years old, they often fall off, and are left behind by the children of the ruling race.[15]

This view was similar to early animal studies which held that anthropoids also developed physically and mentally at a rate comparable to humans, but ceased to do so beyond the infancy period in humans. Tylor's observations—which were widely accepted during his time—are interesting in that fifty years later the theme of his philosophy was espoused under the banner of "cultural deprivation."

LITERARY AND PHILOSOPHICAL BIASES

The word *race* itself was introduced into the scientific literature by Buffon in his *Histoire naturelle generale et particuliere* (1750).[16] The subjugation of one group of people over another with the element of power to maintain a hierarchical position, is referred to as *racism*.

Centuries of espousing literary and philosophical reasons for this position contributed to "scientific" efforts to maintain the inferiority of darker races. Poets like Rudyard Kipling ("The White Man's Burden," 1899) provided romanticism and justification for racist themes with reference to "those ye better" and the "half-devil and half-child" natives of non-European countries. Philosophers such as Count Arthur Joseph de Gobineau provided the important discourse to "prove" white racial superiority over other groups. De Gobineau (1915), whose racism was distinctly a class concept, annunciated:

> The negroid variety is the lowest and stands at the foot of the ladder. The animal character that appears in the shape of the pelvis, is stamped on the negro from birth, and foreshadows his destiny. His intellect will always move within a very narrow circle . . . The very strength of his sensation is the most striking proof of his inferiority.[17]

De Gobineau's attempt to intellectually justify French colonial rule over North Africa concluded with this analysis: "The black race represents passion and is the source of lyricism and artistic temperament; the yellow man represents utility, order and mediocrity; the white race is the expression of reason and honor."[18]

It is interesting to note that de Gobineau felt that civilization occurred when "races" intermarried. He did not suggest intermarriage between white and Black, however, but the union between various types within the white race (such as Aryan with Mediterranean). He felt that the rise and fall of so-called great civilizations occurred with the mixing of "inferior blood" with "superior blood," thereby causing bastardization" and "decadence." Several decades later, this view served as a philosophical basis for Nazi Germany's race-betterment policy and the subsequent mass extermination of Jews.

The Count's deliverances were joined by overwhelming and amazing scientific attempts to "prove" white superiority. Professional discussions and scholarly papers appeared with the needed consensual validation for white superiority; literally hundreds of research projects were initiated and results published. Scholars of later years would come to view the nineteenth century with embarrassment for its unbelievable conclusions drawn from calibrating brains, skeletons, nerves, limbs, torsos, skulls, and even fetuses of Black people.

NATIVISM: THEMES OF RACIAL DIFFERENCES

Hereditarians believed that "less fit" human races were perishing from the rigors of civilization's struggle and competition. They further believed that this deterioration could be measured and that the results of measurement were predictable. The question of the relative capacities of the races was almost wholly anthropological and philosophical in character; and as such, it held center stage until four separate historical events provided the linkage to psychological theory. These events reinforced nativistic themes by declaring that human differences resulted from innate causes within people rather than from environmental forces in society. In order to understand these influences, let us briefly review each of the four events.

1. Darwin's Origin of Species

When Charles Darwin boarded the *Beagle* in late 1831, the stage had been set by European philosophers who taught that nonwhite races had acquired a permanent inferiority by the inherited consequences of their evolutionary past.[19] In 1859, Darwin's observations and conclusions were published. In *On the Origin of Species by Means of Natural Selection,* his theory "influenced the development of modern psychology as much as any other single event in the nineteenth century. It would be impossible to understand what psychologists today are trying to accomplish or why they go about it as they do unless one first understood something of the importance of evolutionary theory for our contemporary vision of man and his destiny."[20] The survival of the fittest shibboleth maintained that only the strongest and most intelligent individuals would survive the struggles between humans and humans and between humans and the environment. Darwin underscored the appeal for recognizing the importance of individual differences by placing the onus of human plight on humans, rather than on the ills of society. In 1868, Darwin produced a theory of heredity, "Provisional Hypothesis of Pangenesis," in an attempt to account for heritable individual differences.[21] These lines of reasoning led many psychologists to turn their research energies to investigation of sensory and intellectual differences between individuals in order to solve the puzzle of human successes and failures. Darwin's writings further led psychologists to question anew the relationship of humans to "lower" animals and to reexamine the gospel of earlier philosophers, notably Descartes and Lamarck. The comparative nature of psychology nurtured the "white coat" obsession of psychologists in emulating the biological sciences in their study of lower animals via instrumentation, for instance, Yerkes: anthropoids; Thorndike and Guthrie: cats; and the standard bearer of experimental psychologists: rats; yes, even the rat was white!

2. Galton's Eugenics

Sir Francis Galton, an Englishman, interestingly a cousin of Darwin, provided the linkage between scientific naturalism and psychology.[22] Galton's *Hereditary Genius: Its Laws and Consequences* (1869) attempted to illustrate that genius and greatness followed family lines, with his data in hand on the inheritance of coat color in basset hounds.[23] Galton outlined his hereditary laws in *Natural Inheritance* (1899). In 1874, the prolific Galton published *English Men of Science*. (He was not an unduly modest man—his own family was included in this compilation.) Galton tried to show that "great" men inherited not only intellectual ability but also specific types of talents (for literature, medicine, music, and so forth). His intense concern about the importance of inheritance led him to propose a science of heredity, eugenics, which promoted the idea of racial improvement through selective mating and sterilization of the "unfit." Galton stated that

> No more than there is equality between man and man of the same nation is there equality between race and race. This differentiation of men in physique and mentality has led to the slow but still imperfect development of occupational castes within all civilized communities. We may not admit these castes, but they exist nevertheless; probably in a perfectly efficient society, there would always be castes suited to specialized careers—the engineer . . . the actor and the craftsman. Even now we are progressing slowly towards tests for occupational fitness, and eventually that fitness should be intensified by marriage within the caste.[24]

To some psychologists, Galton's eugenics doctrine meant the genetic control of the feebleminded; to others, it meant the genetic control of social undesirables. Each perspective found its own dangerous interpretation. Ironically neither Galton nor his cousin Darwin had any children. (See Chapter 4 for further discussion.)

3. German Psychophysics

While England and France favored deductive and mathematical approaches to science, Germany placed its emphasis on classification and the inductive approach, and it was in Germany that the initial application of experimental method to psychology was made. Leaders included Ernst Weber, Gustav Fechner, Hermann von Helmholtz, and Wilhelm Wundt. The times seemed to favor Germany as the place of origin for experimental psychology because, for nearly a hundred years, German intellectual history had created a scientific temperament better suited to taxonomic description than had developed in France or England.[25]

Physics Envy

In the attempt to create a behavioral science built around theories and laws, psychology emulated the established science of physics. Thus a new creation of scientific psychology came about.

Psychophysics—the study of the effect of physical processes on the mental processes—was the outgrowth of the German contribution to psychological history. Stimulated specifically by the work of Wundt (1879), psychological laboratories began to appear in Europe (most notably in Leipzig) and later in the United States (most notably at Cornell University). Nineteenth-century psychology was a product of the union of philosophy and physiology, which focused on discovering the "structure," or anatomy, of individual conscious processes. Its methodology was called introspection and its problem was to describe the content or structure of the mind in terms of psychological elements and their combinations. The concept, called structuralism, greatly influenced early American psychology and created an enthusiastic interest in the teasing apart of the mind with the "brass instruments" of physiology.

Brass Instruments

The brass instruments were used in psychological research to quantitatively measure human responses to various sensory stimuli (Figure 2.3). Early methods for producing sound made use of small whistles or metal bars. The Galton whistle (a) was activated by squeezing a rubber bulb and was closed by a piston. As the piston was adjusted, the tone of the sound varied. The tuning forks (b), when struck, were designed to sound in unison when an adjustable weight was raised or lowered on one of the forks.

In addition to auditory measurements, the sensory modalities of smell, taste, and skin sensitivity and reaction were subjected to psychological experimentation. The olfactometer (c) was designed to measure the

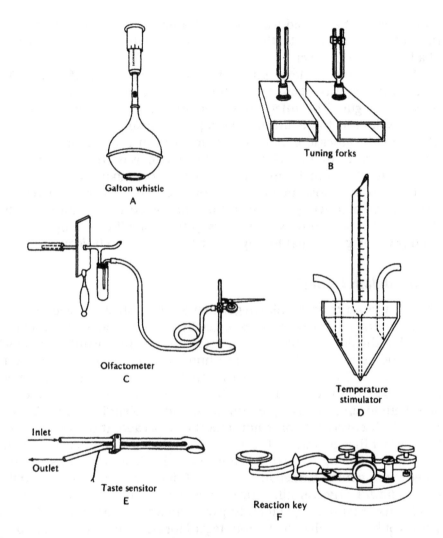

Galton whistle
A

Tuning forks
B

Olfactometer
C

Temperature
stimulator
D

Inlet

Outlet

Taste sensitor
E

Reaction key
F

FIGURE 2.3 Brass Instruments Used for Early Psychological Investigations

Source (a–d, f): E. B. Tichener, *Experimental Psychology* (New York: Macmillan, 1905). Reprinted by permission of the publisher. *Source* (e): T. G. Andrews, *Methods of Psychology* (New York: John Wiley, 1948).

greatest distance that a blindfolded subject could detect the odor from an opened bottle. A valve releasing degrees of the odor was located on one end of the rubber tubing. A forerunner of what was later called the *aesthesiometer* was the *temperature stimulator* (d), which was designed to measure both skin tactile sensitivity and the awareness of temperature differences. Hot and cold water were released through two copper tubes that culminated in a metal tip, and this tip was lightly pressed to the skin of a blindfolded subject.

Measurements of taste sensitivity were frequently performed. The *taste sensitor* (e) was a glass applicator whose aperture was placed on the subject's tongue. The inlet, connected to a system of tubes, allowed various solutions to be directed through the apparatus. The *reaction key* (f) was used to measure individual differences in responding to various sound or light stimuli. This simplistic device was the forerunner of complex reaction timers currently in use in many laboratories.

Later, as brass instrument psychology declined, American psychologists showed a growing interest in the more practical application of the study of conscious processes, thereby placing significant emphases on child psychology, mental testing, and educational psychology.

4. Mendelian Genetics

Though the Austrian monk Gregor Mendel published his scientific inquiry into the genetic differences of garden peas in 1866, it was not until 1900 that the dust was blown off his research and the disturbing parallel was made between agricultural and human inheritance. The time was ripe for the rediscovery of Mendel's work because the excitement generated by Darwin's theory had kept attention focused on outdated models of inheritance, such as "preformation," and "blending inheritance." Mendel's discovery was of major importance because it helped to establish the fact that genetic traits come to the individual in units rather than through a blending of qualities from the individual's ancestors. On the other hand, while Mendelian concepts of dominant and recessive traits were valid for physical differences, they led many researchers to make quick, unsubstantiated parallels to psychological and other nonphysical aspects of human behavior without regard for environmental conditions. It was this framework that encouraged the expansion of hereditarian issues in psychological theory.

AMERICAN PSYCHOLOGY AND RACIAL INVESTIGATION

The events ushered by Darwin, Galton, Wundt, and Mendel, combined with earlier anthropomorphic research, brought about a tremendous interest in measuring human attributes through experimental research in psychology. The popular notion of darker-race inferiority frequently provided grounds for comparing psychological and physical attributes among human beings.

The earliest recorded attempt by American researchers to measure psychological capacities in different races was made in 1881 when C. S. Meyers tested Japanese subjects and proved that the Asians were slower in reaction time than were Europeans. Shortly afterwards, utilizing a popular reaction time device, Bache (1895) tested American Indians and Blacks and concluded that these "primitive peoples" were highly developed in physiological tasks and attributes while "higher" human forms "tended less to quickness of response in the automatic sphere; the reflective man is the slower being."[26] Bache's results are summarized in Table 2.2.

In 1898, the Cambridge Anthropological Society launched its expedition to measure psychological attributes of various races. Large numbers of individual sensory investigations occurred during the early 1900s as a result of the New Guinea expedition; however, none reached the magnitude and fanfare of the "scientific" measurements conducted at the St. Louis World's Fair.

A unique convention was held in 1904, in conjunction with the Louisiana Purchase Exposition (St. Louis World's Fair), during which psychometric and anthropometric studies were conducted on individuals from various parts of the world gathered for exhibition in simulated living conditions. The World's Congress of Races convened at the fair with prominent psychologists in attendance. Professor R. S. Woodworth, Columbia University, led the team in what has been described as a carnival atmosphere. Psychologists at the World's Fair tested the participants, who included Igorots and Negritos from the Philippine Islands, Malayans, Singhalese, Pygmies, and American Indians. This was the first large-scale testing arrangement in the United States.

TABLE 2.2 Group Differences in Reaction Time, 1895

Group	Number of Cases	Auditory R.T.	Visual R.T.	Electrical R.T.
Whites	12	146.9	164.8	136.3
Indians	11	116.3	135.7	114.6
Negroes	11	130.0	152.9	122.9

Source: R. M. Bache, "Reaction Time with Reference to Race," *Psychological Review* 2, (1895): 475–486.

In all, about 1100 individuals were measured and tested; these belonged to 22 groups, and represented 8 distinct ethnic types. One great advantage of our work, especially on its psychometric side, was the testing of all these groups in the same surroundings, with the same instruments and procedure, and by the same experimenters. It is difficult to compare different races of men in their elementary mental characters, when the comparison depends on results got in various parts of the earth and by different men and unlike methods. But when some great agency brings the peoples together into the same surroundings, and within the reach of the same observers, then, if only the observations are well-chosen and accurate, a good basis is afforded for comparative study.[27]

Sensory and pitch discriminations, motor control, illusions, reaction time, and tests of "intelligence" were among the battery of tasks administered to the participants. The "intelligence" tests included the Seguin form-boards, lock test, and marble mazes, all of which represented the state of intelligence testing. The psychologists found what they were predisposed to find that "some of the racial groups who gave the impression of being least intelligent, such as the Negritos and the African Pygmies, behaved a good deal in the same way as the mentally deficient person, making many stupid errors and taking an enormous amount of time."[28] In Woodworth's later autobiographical statement, he reported his reactions to the massive accumulation of data from the World's Fair and the final disposition of the voluminous data.

When the Fair was over, we promptly worked over our data, and reported some of the results of the auditory . . . I gave a general summary of our results and their bearing on the question of racial differences in mental traits. Further than that, the results have never been published, not from any doubt on our part as to their value, but partly because of the unlimited number of fascinating correlations which still remained to be worked out.[29]

A tragic ending occurred when one of the fair's participants, Ota Benga from the Belgian Congo, unwittingly found himself later displayed in a monkey cage at the Bronx Zoo (New York). After a public brouhaha, Ota Benga was released from the zoo. Realizing he could never return to his motherland, Ota Benga later committed suicide in Lynchburg, Virginia.[30] Newspaper accounts reported:

Africans at the 1904 St. Louis World's Fair. Ota Benga is second from left with monkey. Reprinted with permission of the South Caroliniana Library, University of South Carolina.

> When the other natives were returned to their own land from St. Louis he decided to remain behind . . . the homeless pygmy . . . sent a bullet through his heart.[31]

ARCHIVES OF PSYCHOLOGY AND RACIAL STUDIES

Over the following years, a number of psychologists made a series of rapid-fire studies utilizing sensory measurement devices, producing a vast array of impressive statistical tables, curves, ranges, and distributions that gave credibility to the "inferiority" myth. The prestigious *Archives of Psychology*, edited by R. S. Woodworth, included three notable studies that exemplified the obsession of some early psychologists with the study of Black people.[32]

M. J. Mayo's *The Mental Capacity of the American Negro* (1913) based on the grades of 150 white and 150 Black pupils in New York City schools, concluded that "there seem to be statistical grounds for holding to the view of substantial racial equality" between Black and white youngsters.[33] Mayo introduced his study by stating a clear bias: "Among Europeans and their descendants in all parts of the globe there has always existed a feeling of the superiority of the white race. It is a feeling bred in the bone and so strong that it can hardly be eradicated." A few paragraphs later, he continued: "White Europeans always regard their type as ideal—and they have not hesitated to consider wide departures therefore as evidence of inferiority."[34]

Three years later, G. O. Ferguson published *The Psychology of the Negro: An Experimental Study* (1916). This study was considered a classic, by whites, in the study of Blacks. Ferguson's study predicted that

> Without great ability in the processes of abstract thought, the negro is yet very capable in the sensory and motor powers which are involved in manual work. An economy would indicate that training should be concentrated upon these capacities which promise the best return for the educative effort expended.[35]

In accord with the mulatto hypothesis, he, too, felt that mental ability in the Black was proportionate to the amount of "white blood" the Black possessed. As far as emotions were concerned, Ferguson concluded that Blacks were strong and volatile and that "instability of character . . . involving a lack of foresight, an improvidence, a lack of persistence, small power of serious initiative, a tendency to be content with immediate satisfactions, and deficient ambitions" characterized the personality traits of Blacks. He also expressed the theory that "defective morality is a negro characteristic."[36] His statement undoubtedly laid the foundation for other research in the measurement of morality attributes in minority groups.

Race Differences in Inhibition (1923) explored the racist theme: "What is the psychological explanation of the immorality which the Negro everywhere manifests?"[37] Inspired by Ferguson's work, Brenau College (Georgia) psychology professor A. L. Crane stated:

> From the manifestations of immorality among the Negroes, or from their failure to recognize certain social conventions, that the Negro is incapable of morality or of adaptation to the social demand, is a conclusion based upon inadequate evidence. Moral-

ity and social adaptation are the result of the interpretation of the value of a situation, and not a necessary development of inherent capacity."[38]

Crane sought only to substantiate what he was predisposed to prove, that immorality was due to defective inhibition in the American Black. To test his hypothesis, Crane devised a guillotine-like device. A heavy block of wood was dropped from a height above the male subject's hand, which rested on a platform. The subject was told that the block would stop before it hit him, and he was told not to move his hand. The subject did not know that a slight shock would be administered to create the illusion that the block had hit him. The hand movements were electrically recorded. From the research findings, it was clear that the Black research subjects did not trust the equipment or the investigator but appeared to "go along" with the studies. Crane took the study's findings far more seriously than was justified and concluded from his findings that

It does not seem improbable that, in those vocational pursuits which involve great sensory shocks and strains not unaccompanied by danger, the black man should prove more efficient than the white . . . true, considerable persuasion might frequently be necessary to induce the colored man to undertake a dangerous pursuit, but, from the results of this experiment, it appears that it would frequently prove to have been very much worthwhile.[39]

In what must have been acceptable behavior for psychologists during this era, Crane shared his feelings with colleagues in this bit of folksy information:

Only the fellow scientist who has attempted to induce 100 Southern darkies to offer themselves as subject in an experiment of this sort can have any conception of the difficulties involved in actually getting the subjects into the laboratory . . . during the course of the four months in which the writer was attempting to entice negroes into his laboratory, he gladly provided vocal solos for negro churches, harangued Thanksgiving meetings, and delivered formal graduation addresses at negro commencements.[40]

Crane's unprofessional attitude and behavior, mixed with racist condescension, were apparent throughout the study: "It was a never-to-beforgotten experience, the humor and zest whereof, however, more than compensated for the many weary and discouraging hours which it cost to witness a subject fleeing over the hill in fright."[41] Crane's assistants contributed remarks such as "Why you can lead some of those darkies right through the switch room (apparatus) and they'll follow you blindly without ever seeming to think about what the switches might be for."[42]

It was unfortunate that studies such as those by Mayo, Ferguson, and Crane were representative of psychology's investigations into racial differences; they not only provided inaccurate data that led to racist conclusions, but also called into question the intentions of psychological researchers.

NOTES

1. Wundt's laboratory became so overidentified with the gadgets and paraphernalia of structuralism that his detractors caricatured his concept as "brass instrument psychology."

2. H. Burmeister, *The Black Man: The Comparative Anatomy and Psychology of the African Negro* (New York: W. C. Bryant, 1853).

3. *Negritude* refers to positive Black identity and cultural values. During the 1920–1930 era, this was an important literary and philosophical movement, chiefly led by Black intellectuals Aime Cesaire and Leopold Sedar Senghor.

4. R. E. Dennett, *At the Back of the Black Man's Mind* (London: Macmillan, 1906).

5. A. C. Haddon, *History of Anthropology* (New York: Putnam, 1910), 6.

6. R. S. Woodworth, "Racial Difference in Mental Traits," *Science* (February 1910): 171.

7. Haddon, *History of Anthropology*, 104.

8. D. Folkmar and E. Folkmar, *Dictionary of Races or Peoples* (Document No. 662) (Washington, D.C.: Immigration Commission, 1911), 50.

9. J. Barzun, *A Study in Superstition: Race* (New York: Harper and Row, 1935), 35–36.

10. Ibid., 36.

11. G. O. Ferguson, Jr., *The Psychology of the Negro: An Experimental Study* (New York: Science Press, 1916), 27.

12. H. E. Garrett, *How Classroom Desegregation Will Work* (Richmond, Va.: Patrick Henry Press, 1967), 21; *IQ and Racial Differences* (Cape Canaveral, Fla.: Howard Allen, 1973), 14.

13. F. Boas, *The Mind of Primitive Man* (New York: Macmillan, 1922), 73.

14. M. L. Blakey, "Skull Doctors: Intrinsic Social and Political Bias in the History of American Anthropology," *Critique of Anthropology* 7, no. 2 (1987): 7.

15. E. B. Tylor, as quoted by G. O. Ferguson, Jr., in *The Psychology of the Negro: An Experimental Study* (New York: Science Press, 1916), 407.

16. Georges-Louis Leclerc, Comte de Buffon, *Natural History* 4, trans. Barr (London, 1811), 284–285, 291.

17. A. de Gobineau, *The Inequality of Human Races* (New York: Putnam, 1915), 205–211.

18. Ibid., 211.

19. W. B. Provine, *The Origins of Theoretical Population Genetics* (Chicago: University of Chicago Press, 1971), 1.

20. G. A. Miller, *Psychology* (New York: Harper and Row, 1962), 129.

21. Provine, *Origins of Theoretical Population Genetics*, 9.

22. Galton divided races into sixteen defined grades of ability, eight above the median and eight below. The darker peoples of the globe occupied the lower eight grades.

23. In his paper on basset hounds (1883), Galton formulated an interesting algorithm on the law of ancestral heredity. See Provine, *Origins of Theoretical Population Genetics*, 184.

24. F. Galton, "Annals of Eugenics," *Galton Laboratory for National Eugenics* 1, no. 1 (October 1925): 3.

25. D. P. Schultz and S. E. Schultz, *A History of Modern Psychology*, 6th edition, (Fort Worth: Harcourt Brace, 1996) 65–66.

26. M. Bache, "Reaction Time with Reference to Race," *Psychological Review* 2 (1895): 475–586.

27. R. S. Woodworth, "Racial Differences in Mental Traits," *Science* 31 (New York: Science Press, 1910), 7.

28. R. S. Woodworth, *Report on Laboratory Exhibit, Section of Anthropometry and Psychometry*, Louisiana Purchase Exposition, Series III, Subseries XI, Folder 3, (St. Louis, Mo.: Missouri Historical Society, 1905), 203–204.

29. R. S. Woodworth, in *History of Psychology in Autobiography*, ed. Carl Murchison, vol. 2 (Worcester, Mass.: Clark University Press, 1932), 373.

30. "Bushman Shares a Cage with Bronx Park Apes," *New York Times*, Sunday, September 9, 1906, p. 9.

31. "Ota Benga, Pygmy, Tired of America: The Strange Little African Finally Ended Life at Lynchburg, Va.," *New York Times*, Sunday, July 16, 1916, p. 3.

32. This series of studies illustrates the immense attention psychologists spent in comparing psychological differences between whites and Blacks.

33. M. J. Mayo, "The Mental Capacity of the American Negro," *Archives of Psychology* 28 (New York: Science Press, 1913), 17.

34. Ibid., 17.

35. Ferguson, *Psychology of the Negro*, 125.

36. Ibid., 125.
37. A. L. Crane, "Race Differences in Inhibition," *Archives of Psychology* 63 (New York: Science Press, 1923), 15.
38. Ibid.
39. Ibid.
40. Ibid.
41. Ibid.
42. Ibid.

► 3

Psychometric Scientism

In the nineteenth century, the views held by proponents of environmentalist philosophers (John Locke: *tabula rasa,* and John Stuart Mill: associationist psychology), which proclaimed that all individuals were creatures of circumstances and malleable to environmental influences, began to lose ground to the belief that individual abilities were inherited and could be measured by biometrics formulae. The belief that genetic transmission for abilities was precisely what nativistic proponents wanted to hear, with the use of statistical techniques to verify that this view was real, was the seal of approval. Over the years, mathematics has been used to bamboozle many literate scholars and has provided a smoke screen for authenticating seemingly intangible behavioral phenomena. Or, in some cases, gaining an advantage. An example of this was the debate between the great Swiss mathematician Euler and the Voltairians in the court of Russia's Catherine II about the existence of God. With his back against the wall, Euler asked for a blackboard and wrote:

$$(x + y)^2 = x^2 + 2xy + y^2$$

Therefore, God exists.

Unwilling to question the relevance of the formula, which they did not comprehend, and too proud to confess their ignorance of mathematics, Euler's adversaries acquiesced and accepted his argument.[1]

It is of little wonder that the psychological test of mental ability, with its mystical formula, *IQ*, became the tour de force to establish effectively an absolute, objective point of leverage in the scientific debate. By presenting an imposing array of statistics declaring that lower-median IQ scores truly reflected most nonwhite people's abilities, many psychologists inadvertently justified racial prejudice and discrimination as an intellectual necessity. Furthermore, to some of the more zealous founding fathers of the psychometric movement, IQ test scores provided exacting pronouncements of the intellectual inferiority of dark-skinned people. The environmentalist position rapidly eroded as the use of this statistical device became widespread. If Darwin had shown that the fittest survived through evolution of physical characteristics, did not the same laws apply to mental characteristics? If Galton believed that genius-talent was genetically transmitted to leading British families, did not the same logic occur in the attempt to justify lower intellectual talent among the disenfranchised? If European philosophies and religious notions supported the concept of "cursed" people, did not the same wisdom explain the concept of lower intelligence quotients among these people? Without question, in the age of Victorian ethnocentrism, psychometric contentions to support European intellectual superiority were enthusiastically received. Even in its embryonic stage, intelligence tests were regarded as empirical propositions with enormous and inscrutable accuracy. Just what were the theoretical antecedents of psychological tests and measurement techniques that allowed these conditions of faith to develop?

HOW SIGNIFICANT ARE
SIGNIFICANT DIFFERENCES?

Psychologists, obsessed by those things that divided people, ignored those things that could have united individuals and as a consequence placed unnecessary emphasis upon differences between people. The philosophical framework that was set forth to determine degrees to which individuals were dissimilar bolstered the importance of biometric methods for differential psychology. Rather than placing emphasis upon similarity—that is, measurement of the degrees to which individuals are alike—psychologists gave center stage to the quest for measurement of dissimilarities. Differences between people rather than similarity established the precedent for statistics of significance. To appreciate the extent to which statisticians refined this procedure to the microscopic level, one only has to consider that these differences purportedly could be measured to the unbelievable probability of one in thousands. It is highly interesting, if not provocative, that these early statisticians were also prominent members of the Eugenics Education Society, Eugenics Laboratory, and other groups advocating genetic superiority of certain racial inheritance (see Chapter 4). Eugeneticists Karl Pearson (later recognized as the founder of the science of statistics) and Charles Spearman were leading actors who promoted the application of statistics to measure, quantify, codify behavioral phenomena, and differences.

MENTAL TESTS

Though the term *mental test* was employed as early as 1890 by Cattell, it was the later description of mental processes and classifications by French physician Alfred Binet and Victor Henri that served as a framework for theorizing the possibilities of mental measurement. So impressive were Binet's scholarly descriptions (idiot, imbecile, moron, and so forth) that he was quickly deemed the leading innovator in psychometrics. Consequently, in 1904, when the French government formed a commission of physicians, educators, scientists, and public officials to study the problem of teaching retarded children in the Paris public schools, Binet was asked to participate. Teaming with Theophile Simon, a medical doctor, Binet constructed a test of intelligence which, in a few years, played a major role in the attempt to identify intellectual racial differences in the United States. The end result was a psychomedical model of measurement which was touted as scientific from its very beginning—in spite of Binet's own warning of its limitations. Binet had pointed out that while his tests could safely be used to arrive at individual differences, the individuals tested must have had the same, or approximately the same, environmental and educational opportunities. Furthermore, Binet's test, unlike the later revisions, employed simple, everyday problems unrelated to formal classroom instruction. (Examples of these test problems are given in Table 3.1.)

At about the same time, across the English channel, biometrician Charles Spearman (1904) introduced a controversial two-factor theory of intelligence leading to the belief that every mental test measured two components: a *general* factor and a *specific* factor.[2] Spearman's development of factor analysis provided the impetus needed to push forward the theory that a common variance could be found in a matrix of

TABLE 3.1 Sample of Items Used by Binet in the 1908 and 1911 Versions of the Binet-Simon Tests

Age 1 year
Visual coördination of the head and eyes in following an object

Age 3 years
Points to nose, eyes, and mouth
Repeats two digits
Names objects in a picture

Age 4 years
Names a key, knife, and penny
Repeats three digits
Compares two lines

Age 5 years
Copies a square
Repeats a sentence of ten syllables
Unites the halves of a divided rectangle

Age 6 years
Defines familiar words in terms of use
Copies a diamond
Counts thirteen pennies

Age 7 years
Points to right and left ears
Executes three commands given together
Names four colors

Age 8 years
Compares two objects from memory
Counts backwards from twenty
Notices missing parts from pictures

Age 9 years
Gives change from twenty sous
Defines familiar words in other terms than use
Names the months of the year in order

Age 10 years
Copies two drawings from memory
Can tell what is wrong with absurd statements (The body of a girl was found cut in eighteen pieces; they think she killed herself. What is wrong with that?)
Arranges five blocks in order of weight

Age 12 years
Names sixty words in three minutes
Defines three abstract words
Can rearrange a disarranged sentence

Age 15 years
Repeats seven digits
Repeats a sentence of twenty-six syllables
Finds three rhymes for a given word in one minute

Source: James Deese, *General* Psychology. Copyright © 1967 by Allyn and Bacon. Reprinted by permission.

correlations. Therefore, a general, or *g* factor, expressed Spearman's belief that abstract reasoning was positively correlated with verbal knowledge because a single ability ran through both performances (Figure 3.1).

The *g* factor represented broad reasoning and problem-solving abilities. Spearman supported this view by noting that individuals who excel in one area can usually excel in others. Since this analysis did not hold true across the board because even the most capable person may be mediocre in other areas—music, athletics, or business—he suggested that specific, or *s* factors account for specific abilities. Spearman's conception of *g* has been attacked from several fronts, even to the point of labelling it "a falsifiable hypothesis." It is important to note that Spearman began

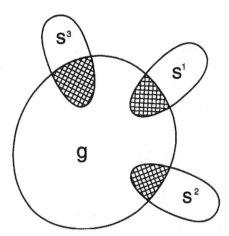

FIGURE 3.1 Spearman's Original Two-Factor Theory. Spearman began with *g* (general capacity) and later discovered he could extract *s*'s (specific intelligences). Thus, Spearman's investigations proceeded from a predetermined idea of a *g* factor then out to *s* factors. Based on this theory, tests of ability correlate because they in part measure an underlying general ability.

with the premise that there was a general factor in intelligence. Therefore, with this mind-set, he was predisposed to "select his tests judiciously" if the prediction was to be successful; and he was also obliged to "doctor up" his correlations by using the dubious "corrections for attenuation," a procedure against which even his friend Karl Pearson protested.[3] In spite of the criticisms, Spearman's *g* factor speculation strongly influenced the conceptualization of intelligence by future psychologists.

Binet's definition of intelligence included "the tendency to take and maintain a definite direction; the capacity to make adaptations for the purpose of attaining a desired end; and the power of auto-criticism."[4] Spearman's concept suggested that Binet's notion of individual learning styles and conditions of affective behavior were not pertinent to the definition; Spearman focused on a narrower aspect of intelligence. As his dichotomous view of intelligence reinforced existing middle-class, Victorian values, it was quickly accepted by those who shared backgrounds emphasizing abstraction and verbalization criteria.

Acceptance of the *g* factor theory encouraged the creation and utilization of verbal- and quantitative-type test items as appropriate measures of "pure intellectual capacity" while deemphasizing the importance of measuring other intellectual qualities.[5] This approach led to unrealistic psychometric evaluation of children whose social class backgrounds, cultures, and life-styles emphasized other values. Arithmetic and vocabulary problems, couched in varying degrees of difficulty and requiring a firm knowledge of the English language, became the ultimate yardstick for measuring the mental abilities of children from oppressed minorities in the United States.

STANFORD-BINET REVISIONS

The Americanization of the Binet-Simon scales occurred at approximately the same time that the *g* factor became entrenched in mental measurement theory. Before the Stanford University revision of the scales gained its overwhelming popularity, the Binet-Simon scales had undergone many dubious translations and revisions: Goddard (1911) and Kuhlmann (1911) in the United States, Ferrari (1908) and Treves and Soffiotti (1909) in Italy, Descoeudres (1911) in Switzerland, Bobertag (1912) in Germany, and Johnson (1922) in England. These and the Stanford revisions were influenced by a unique concept which enabled test results to be interpreted and calculated as a single score: the intelligence quotient (IQ).[6]

$$IQ = \frac{Mental\ Age}{Chronological\ Age} \times 100$$

Binet favored the measure of intelligence as the difference between the mental age and chronological age; William Stern who created the IQ formula in 1912 warned:

> The IQ may be regarded only as a first approximation; it takes on significant value only when the bare quantitative statement is completed by a qualitative diagnosis. To base any pedagogical estimate upon the IQ alone for practical purposes (e.g., assignment to opportunity classes) is indefensible.[7]

Unfortunately, America's educators reified the formula, in the same fashion that the *g* factor had been, and did the opposite of Stern's admonition—declaring major educational decisions based on this score, even to the extent of penalizing the nation's disenfranchised minorities. American test makers not only modified the original intent of the mental tests, but perpetuated the infallibility of the Intelligence Quotient.

LEWIS TERMAN

When Lewis Terman of Stanford University revised the Binet scales in 1916, he directed their use in a manner of which the professor from the Sorbonne had never dreamed. Whatever benefits might have been achieved by revising the Binet test were overshadowed by Terman's bias and his narrow-minded declarations to future psychologists: "(Mental retardation) represents the level of intelligence which is very, very common among Spanish-Indians and Mexican families of the Southwest and also among negroes. Their dullness seems to be racial."[8] Terman further predicted that when future IQ testing of these groups was done, "there will be discovered enormously significant racial differences which cannot be wiped out by any scheme of mental culture."[9]

It is amazing how the Stanford psychologist, later president of the American Psychological Association (APA), reached these conclusions from a scale that was standardized on a sample of approximately 1,000 children and 400 adults—none of them Black. Nevertheless, in the same breath, he called for special education classes and prescribed their content and pedagogy: "Children of this group should be segregated in special classes and be given instruction which is concrete and practical. They cannot master abstractions." Stern, creator of the IQ concept, warned against these interpretations of IQ scores, but Terman's pronouncements reached dangerous proportions: "There is no possibility at present of convincing society that they should not be allowed to reproduce, although from a eugenic point of view they constitute a grave problem because of their unusually prolific breeding."[10] From this perspective, Terman was in agreement with the Galtonian eugenicists and English biometricians.

It was no accident, even beyond Gaussian predictions, that 26 percent of Terman's population had IQs designated below average (often referred to as abnormal).[11] Furthermore, at a time when massive numbers of disfranchised immigrants, laborers, and racial minorities occupied the working-class strata of the U.S. economy, the Terman revision asked for explanations of middle-class proverbs ("He who would eat the kernel must crack the nut," "One swallow does not make a summer"). His test required a child to remember and repeat sentences based on ability to handle the English language ("The red-headed woodpeckers made a terrible fuss as they tried to drive the young away from the nest," "The early settlers had little idea of the great changes that were to take place in this country").[12] It is not too difficult to visualize the minority child struggling not only with pronunciation but repeating words that meant little or were seldom heard in the culture. The ultimate disregard for cultural differences appeared in the task requiring the child to utilize Anglo-Saxon criteria for discriminating between "prettiness" and "ugliness." Not only was this an insensitive exercise, it was damaging to a developing self-image and to a standard of beauty that is subjective for each culture. Increasingly, discussions of social class boundaries were interwoven throughout most theoretical psychology papers of this era. Terman and others (1917) lent early credence to an elitist and segregationist viewpoint when they assigned socioeconomic status categories to IQ scores: very inferior (below 80), inferior (80–90), average (90–109), superior (110–119), and very superior (120 and above). Arguing that IQ scores were primarily due to innate endowments, Terman assigned the following occupational descriptions to his IQ designations:

> Preliminary investigations indicate that an IQ below 70 rarely permits anything better than unskilled labor; that the range from 70 to 80 is preeminently that of semi-skilled labor; from 80 to 100 that of the skilled or ordinary clerical labor; from 100 to 110 or 115 that of the semi-professional pursuits; and that above all these are grades of intelligence which permit one to enter the professions of the larger fields of business. Intelligence tests can tell us whether a child's native brightness corresponds more nearly to the median of (1) the professional classes, (2) those in the semi-professional pursuits, (3) ordinary skilled workers, (4) semi-skilled workers, or (5) unskilled laborers. This information will be of great value in planning the education of a particular child and also in planning the differentiated curriculum here recommended.[13]

The sociopolitical aspect of these classifications clearly indicates the potential power and control inherent in these concepts in mental testing.

With the exception of the gross mental deficiencies discussed by Binet, American psychologists extended the range of classification from idiocy to a vague notion of genius—with various classifications along the way. There were also the American psychologists, led by Lewis Terman, who chorused the blood lineage theme to explain differing scores along the continuum. And it was the educational psychologist Edward Thorndike who announced that intelligence was "roughly" 80 percent genetic, 17 percent based on educational opportunities, and 3 percent accidental.[14] Thorndike's speculations placed an unfair emphasis on the role of heredity; he undoubtedly planted the seed of intellectual bias among prognosticators of Black-white mental abilities.

Throughout this period of intelligence testing, few attempts were made to censure the tests or even to voice skepticism; Terman's views soared as words of great wisdom for neophyte psychologists. As the testing mystique grew, the cloak of secrecy increased. Only "the informed" knew about the IQ formula and its calculation. Individuals submitted to IQ testing but the results were kept under lock and key, protected from unsophisticated eyes. The mental testers, with the sanction of school officials, were given free rein to test any school-age child. Parental consent was unheard of, much less considered a normal condition. There was no code of ethics or standards to check the profession; it was in fact a system in complete control of its subjects.

The 1916 Stanford-Binet scales maintained their dominance in the testing world for 20 years—until the 1937 revision. This revision retained the majority of the old test items but was extended downward to the 2-year-old level and upward to the 22-year-old level. In repetition of the original revision, this version failed to include Black children in its normalization data.

BLACK-WHITE MENTAL TESTING

The earliest effort by U.S. researchers to investigate Black-white differences using intelligence tests was made in 1897 when G. R. Stetson tested 500 African American and 500 European American public school children in Washington, D.C. The test utilized by Stetson consisted of four stanzas of poetry, which the experimenter read aloud and the children were required to repeat.[15] In this exercise, of which little publicity was made, the Black children outperformed the white children. It is interesting to observe that consequently it was determined that the memory technique was not a valid measure of intelligence.

The first reported study using the Binet scales to determine whether racial differences existed was made in Columbia, South Carolina, in 1912. In this study, Josiah Morse of the University of South Carolina directed his graduate student, Alice C. Strong, to measure, with the Goddard revision of the Binet scale, the intelligence of 225 white children and 1,125 Black children. Strong went so far as to divide the Black children into groupings based on the degree of their skin pigmentations: dark, medium, and light-colored. Her purpose for this grouping was "to determine the effect of white blood on intelligence."[16] (This was an effort in support of the mulatto hypothesis, which held that the degree of intelligence increased with the proportion of white blood in Black children. Her findings concluded that "colored children are mentally younger than the White" and that lighter-complexioned Black children obtained higher mental scores. Morse later reported that while the Strong study showed that

> the colored children did excel in rote memory . . . [they] are inferior in esthetics judgement, observation, reasoning, motor control, logical memory, use of words, resistance to suggestion and in orientation or adjustment to the institutions and complexities of civilized society.[17]

Despite this egregious indictment, Morse at least recognized one flaw in the testing instrument when he observed that "the picture tests gave the colored children considerable trouble, probably due to difference in racial esthetics."[18] Later, in a stroke of rare intellectual insight for 1913, Morse noted:

> if Binet and Simon had originally tested southern negro children they would have worked out from the results a scale which would have been different from their present one in several respects, and which when applied to southern white children would be found to be, for the most part, a year or more too young . . . Perhaps some day each branch of the human family will have a Binet scale of its own.[19]

In 1914, B. A. Phillips compared the test scores of 137 white and 86 Black children and then went beyond the mere recording of scores by raising the question of providing separate educational training for Blacks:

> If the Binet tests are at all a gauge of mentality it must follow that there is a difference in mentality between the colored and the white children, and this raises the question: Should the two groups be instructed under the same curriculum?[20]

This analysis was one of the earliest psychological appraisals of intelligence test scores that suggested separate educational programs for Black and white children. Prior to this, evidence supporting the existence of segregated educational programs consisted of philosophical opinions. For example, G. Stanley Hall, the founding father of the American Psychological Association, maintained that

No two races in history, taken as a whole, differ so much in their traits, both physical and psychic, as the Caucasian and the African. The color of the skin and the crookedness of the hair are only the outward signs of the many far deeper differences, including cranial and thoracic capacity, proportions of body, nervous system, glands, and secretions, vita sexualis, food, temperament, disposition, character, longevity, instincts, customs, emotional traits, and diseases. All these differences as they are coming to be better understood, are seen to be so great as to qualify if not imperil every inference from one race to another, whether theoretical or practical, so that what is true and good for one is often false and bad for the other.[21]

With the acceptance of psychology (with its tests of mental ability) as a science, unquestioning credence was given to reports like those of Phillips. Ferguson (1916) echoed a similar contention that Blacks, as a result of recorded IQ test differences, should be trained as manual laborers:

Without great ability in the processes of abstract thought, the negro is yet very capable in the sensory and motor powers which are involved in manual work. And economy would indicate that training should be concentrated upon these capacities which promise the best return for the educative effort expended.[22]

As racist research efforts continued, statistical measures of central tendency evolved into mental percentage comparisons between Blacks and whites. When W. H. Pyle (1915) tested 408 Black children in the Missouri public schools and compared them to white children in the same area, he concluded: "In general the marks indicating mental ability of the Negro are about two-thirds of the whites."[23] The two-thirds statistic was historically significant in that it also supported a political contention that had previously regarded the Black as a "fractionated" man.[24]

CHILD TO ADULT AND INDIVIDUAL TO MASS TESTING

Prior to World War I, fewer than a dozen experimental investigations of the intelligence of Blacks had been conducted; all together fewer than 2,000 Blacks had been studied and nearly all were children in public school settings. The advent of World War I brought about shifts in two directions, from child to adult and from individual to group testing. For example, during the period 1917–1919, group tests developed by a special committee of the American Psychological Association (APA) were administered to over 1.5 million soldiers. Of this number, more than 5,000 Black recruits were tested at Camp Lee (Virginia) alone. The Army Alpha and Army Beta tests formed the first team of the army testing movement.

The Army Alpha, designed for literate draftees, attempted to measure abilities "independent of prior education," and was quickly regarded as a bona fide measure of innate mental ability—even though the test contained general information items that were most certainly culturally laden (Table 3.2).

The Army Beta, extremely difficult to administer, was a nonverbal parallel to the Alpha, containing mazes, picture completions, and geometric constructions. It was created to measure the mental abilities of illiterate and non-English-speaking recruits (Figure 3.2). The Beta's instruction was done by demonstration and with pantomime instructions, in other words, gestures instead of words. Even though reports from several camps felt that the test was not a satisfactory measure for Black recruits because "too large a percentage of the negroes who should make high scores fail in the beta." However, the overwhelming majority of camps praised the test with comments such as "a splendid examination

TABLE 3.2 Sample Items from the Army Alpha Test, 1917

Mathematics
"If it takes six men three days to dig a 180-foot drain, how many will dig it in half a day?"

Synonym—Antonym
Fallacy—Verity (Same/Opposite?)
Innuendo—Insinuation (Same/Opposite?)

Analogies
Lion:animal as rose:smell *or* leaf:plant
Tolerate:pain as welcome:pleasure *or* unwelcome:friend

General Information
The *dictaphone* is a kind of *typewriter, multigraph, phonograph, adding machine?*
Mauve is the name of a *drink, color, fabric, food?*
"Why is wheat better for food than corn?" Because ( ) it is more nutritious; ( ) it is more expensive; ( ) it can be ground finer.

Source: U.S. Government Printing Office, 1918.

FIGURE 3.2 A set of items from the Army Beta Test: Individuals being examined are instructed to determine what is missing or wrong with each of the pictures.

Source: U.S. Government Printing Office, 1918.

for negroes . . . Every negro should be given beta." Several army examiners reported that it was difficult to keep the interest of their Black recruits for "it took all the energy and enthusiasm the examiner could muster to maintain the necessary attention, as there was a decided disposition for the negroes to lapse into inattention and almost into sleep."[25] Nonetheless, thousands of Black recruits were administered the Beta examination. In actuality, tests scores meant very little or nothing to promote army opportunities for the Black recruits because it was the army's intention to draft Black citizens for hard manual labor in labor battalions, butchery companies, grave digging details, and Pioneer infantries.[26] Test scores were just test scores. The Black recruits were experimental subjects for psychological examiners. The naive recruits were unaware that many psychologists who entered the military held racist beliefs, such as the belief that Blacks possessed inferior intelligence. For example, 1st Lt. George O. Ferguson, who wrote *The Psychology of the*

Negro prior to the war, was appointed chief examiner at Camp Lee (Virginia). It was not long before Ferguson tested "negro recruits on the basis of skin color" and compared the intelligence ratings from the lighter and darker groups. His army report, which possessed no military purpose, described the experiment: "In alpha, the lighter negroes obtained a median score of 50; the darker obtained a median of 30. In beta the lighter negroes obtained a median score of 36; the darker obtained a median of 29."[27] Following the war, as a Colgate University professor, Ferguson revealed that his skin color designations in the Camp Lee study were "black," "brown," and "yellow." These results were published in the widely read educational journal *School and Society*.[28] Educational articles published in many academic journals continually focused on the genetic inferiority of Blacks based on the army's test results (Table 3.3). "Bans on interracial marriage, reductions in money spent on black schools, and support for legal segregation would be drawn from these findings."[29] Never fully accepted by the army, the psychological examining units were abolished in 1919; but, the American civilian testing movement was well on its way. Gersh (1981) further reported that

> Membership rolls of the APA increased nearly threefold during the 1920s . . . "serious" psychologists were the ones who had done Army testing—and who later advocated tracking in schools [and] in 1923, 60 percent of the APA membership were involved in testing and by 1927, 23 percent of all American-written articles listed in the *Psychological Index* were on mental development.[30]

TABLE 3.3 Median Alpha Scores for Given Amounts of Education (1916–1918)

Group	0 to 4 Grades	5 to 8 Grades	High School	College
White soldiers				
(Native-Born)	22.0	51.1	92.1	117.8
(Foreign-Born)	21.4	47.2	72.4	91.9
Negro Soldiers				
(Northern)	17.0	37.2	71.2	90.5
(Southern)	7.2	16.3	45.7	63.8
White Officers	112.5	107.0	131.0	143.2

Source: U.S. Government Printing Office, 1930.

POSTWAR PSYCHOLOGICAL MEASUREMENTS

World War I was not only a proving ground for group intelligence tests but also the training ground for psychologists. Majors Lewis Terman and Robert Yerkes; Captains Edwin Boring, Karl Dallenbach, and Albert Poffenberger; Lieutenants Donald Paterson, Arthur Otis, Edgar Doll, and Carl Murchison; and Private David Wechsler were ex-military psychology examiners who continued successfully as civilians. Blacks were not allowed to participate, at any level, in the psychological examining centers. Experiences gained by these psychologists led to the creation of business corporations and university test centers, staffed by ex-army examiners, to create tests to predict and measure intelligence and aptitudes in school children. The same test construction rationale—analogies, pictorial categories, and general information items—were now applied to tests aimed at civilian populations. The United States was inundated by group tests for every educational level: elementary, high school, and college. Products such as the Otis IQ Test, National Intelligence Test, Kuhlmann-Anderson IQ Test, Peterson Rational Learning Test, Pitner-Patterson Series, and the Goodenough Draw-A-Man Test were born. Public school teachers, social workers, guidance workers, and personnel workers became official examiners and interpreters of these tests. Very little debate and few obstacles arose, allowing these tests to be designed, marketed, and placed into use. University classes in tests and measurement became mandatory for educators. These classes emphasized the trilogy of validity, reliability, and usability, suggesting that the existing tests met these criteria. Examiner's manuals became test appendages with displays of statistical data: figures and tables gave the impression of the infallibility of "scientific" quality of the tests.

Grade-level tracking systems, labels, and jargon flowed throughout the manuals. Psychologists and test specialists (often called *psychometrists*), claimed expertise in the human measurement arena. Noninclusion of U.S. minority groups in the test's norms was the rule; whites supplied the standards by which all Americans were measured. In short order, the United States became the world's leader for the test maker-industrial complex. Sadly, in the United States, the losers in the testing world were Black children who struggled to meet a unrealistic standard. They were excluded—victims of poor schools and legalized racial segregation. As with the army recruits, the primary function of the Black child's test scores appeared to be to provide a data base for comparative statistical studies. Black children were joined by other children of color in providing data bases.

THE UNITED STATES INDIAN SCHOOLS

Like Black children, Native American youngsters were easily identifiable and were conveniently segregated. But unlike the monolithic Black schools, reservation schools grouped Indian children along tribal lines that later facilitated intergroup comparisons by researchers.[31] The added variable of language differences offered still another dimension for educational psychologists in their discussions and debates of mental capacities; opinions expressing the need for Native Americans to absorb the white culture in order to improve their "innate inferiority" (as measured by the tests) were frequently discussed.

Some of the principal examples of early testing efforts of Native American children occurred in the mid-1920s. Jamieson and Standiford (1928) administered the National Intelligence, the Pitner Non-Language, and the Pitner-Patterson Performance Tests to a large sample of Ontario Indians and concluded that the observed disparity between verbal and written performance test scores was correlated to the degree of "their contact with white culture."[32] In support of this hypothesis, Hunter (1922) had reported earlier:

> There is a positive correlation between increasing degree of white blood in the American Indian and score on the Otis Intelligence test which would seem to indicate a racial difference probably of intelligence although possibly of temperament.[33]

While a study by Fitzgerald and Ludeman (1926) flatly reported that the Indian child was an inferior being,[34] Hunter, working with Sommermier (1922), tested 711 Native Americans from different tribes who were students at the Haskell Indian Institute (Lawrence, Kansas) and concluded that a correlation of .41 existed between IQ score and degree of white blood.[35] Finally, Garth and others (1927) using the popular National Intelligence Test examining nearly 700 Native Americans in South Dakota, New Mexico, Oklahoma, and Colorado, concluded that significant correlations existed between the degree of white ancestry and IQ test scores.[36]

These studies supported the popular belief that white blood increased the Native American's intellectual capability; however, Klineberg (1928), after testing 100 Yakima Indians in Washington, reported a lack of any conclusive relationship between white ancestry and IQ scores.[37] Klineberg's subsequent research efforts reported similar findings, and it was not long before he was labeled an egalitarian in the human affairs arena. Within a few years, he began to question cultural biases found in IQ tests.

For example, in 1935 he observed that Dakota Indian children considered it to be in bad taste to answer a question in the presence of others who did not know the answer.[38] This observation was soon extended to events in U.S. Reservation school rooms where individual competition was expected to prevail. Porteus (1931) had expressed similar notions while testing indigenous Australians: "the aborigine is used to concerted thinking. Not only is every problem in tribal life debated and settled by the council of elders, but it is always discussed until a unanimous decision is reached."[39] Nevertheless, in spite of Klineberg's and Porteus's findings, there was little visible effort to take cultural factors into consideration in IQ testing.

MEXICAN AMERICANS AND IQ TESTING

Mexican-American children, too, were victimized and frequently labeled "racially inferior" as a result of IQ tests that expected all children to have had the same cultural experiences. Bilingualism was thought to induce a state of mental confusion in these children, and this theory led to the practice of literal translation of the standardized tests from English into Spanish. However, the assumption that Anglo-cultural references were omnipotent and needed only language translation was a major fallacy; little consideration for Mexican-American culture was made during the construction of the tests.

Among those tests translated, the International Group Mental Test (IGMT) gained the most recognition for its use with Spanish-speaking subjects. Beatrice Blackwood (1927) administered the IGMT to 413 Native American and 200 "Spanish-American" children in New Mexico and Arizona in typical fashion for this time.[40] Her purpose was to offer suggestions for the refinement of a "test suitable for primitive conditions" and to determine if any differences existed between the two populations. While she reported no new testing refinement, she concluded that significant IQ differences existed between the Mexican-American and the Native American children.

Among the few voices levied against the acceptance of reports such as Blackwood's was that of George Sanchez, then (1932) Director of the Division of Information and Statistics, New Mexico State Department of Education. He criticized the translated tests because they were "used as actual measures rather than as experimental tools . . . [and] may be still further questioned as to their value in revealing the mental confusion resulting from a 'dual language handicap.' "[41] Sanchez also stressed the importance of the *linguistic* variable, the neglected third factor in the

TABLE 3.4   Studies of Test Results of Spanish-Speaking Children

Student	Date	Measure	Cases[a]	Place
Davenport	1931	Goodenough	420 Ss sibs	Texas
			126 Es sibs	Texas
Delmet	1930	Det. Kdgtn.	341 Ss	Calif.
		Pint. Cun.		
		Pres. Prim.		
		Haggerty In.		
		Otis Grp.		
		Stfd. Ach.		
Fickinger	1930	Pint. Cun.	95 Ss	N. Mexico
		(Eng. & trs.)		
Garretson	1928	N. I. T.	117 Ss	Arizona
		Pantomime	197 Es	Arizona
		Pint. Cun.		
Garth	1923	N. I. T.	307 Ss	Texas
			634 Ind.	Okla. & N. Mexico
Garth	1928	N. I. T.	1006 Ss	Texas, N. Mexico, & Colo.
Goodenough	1928	Goodenough	367 Ss	Calif.
			500 Es	La. & Tenn.
			1590 others	
Haught	1929	Pint. Cun.	All Ss in	N. Mexico
		N. I. T.	4(?) scho.	
		German grp.	systems	
Hughes	1928	Goodenough	440 Ss	Texas
			396 Es	Texas
Knight	1931	Eye-movement	21 Ss	Texas
		(Read.)	Controls Es	Texas
Koch & Simmons	1928	Pant. & 1 of	1492 Ss	Texas
		N. I. T.,	1211 Es	Texas
		Det. 1st Gr., or	613 Negro	Texas
		Pint. Cun.		
Paschal & Sullivan	1925	Perf. Tests	415 Ss	Arizona
		Anthro. Meas.		
Sanchez	1931	Stfd. Ach.	45 Ss	N. Mexico
		Haggerty In.		
Sheldon	1924	Stfd. Binet	100 Ss	N. Mexico
			100 Es	N. Mexico
Sininger	1930	Mon. S. Read.	3336 Ss	N. Mexico
			6563 Es	N. Mexico
Stoltz	1931	Meier-Seashore	82 Ss	Texas
		McAdory	103 Es	Texas
Tireman	1929	Mon. S. Read.	3366 Ss	N. Mexico
			6119 Es	N. Mexico
Wright & Manuel	1929	Stfd. Read.	128 Ss	Texas
		(Eng. & Trs.)	450 Es	Texas
Young	1922	Army Alpha	51 Ss	Calif.
		Army Beta	402 Es	Calif.
			325 others	Calif.

Source: George I. Sanchez, "Group Differences and Spanish-Speaking Children," *Journal of Applied Psychology* 16 (1932): 552–553. Copyright 1932 by the American Psychological Association. Reprinted by permission.

[a] Ss: Spanish-speaking; Es: English-speaking.

heredity and environment debates of the 1920s. His pioneering paper, "Group Differences and Spanish-Speaking Children—A Critical Review," carefully evaluated the large-scale IQ testing of Mexican-American children. Table 3.4 lists the studies on which Sanchez focused his critique. In spite of Sanchez's many criticisms (1932 and 1934), the practice of administering the tests continued.

Although the use of anthropometry in U.S. research declined, physical measurement was often used in conjunction with the IQ testing of Mexican-American children. A case in point was the investigation of nine- and twelve-year-old children in the public schools of Tucson, Arizona. Pascal and Sullivan (1925), after recording an enormous amount of physical data and mental test scores, reported seventeen conclusions, including the following: "Tucson Mexicans who are partially of Indian origin have (a) a lower mental score, (b) a lower social or economic status, (c) a lower school standing in grade, than those Tucson Mexicans who are wholly of white origin."[42] Such studies led many investigators to agree that a definite relationship existed between the proportion of Indian blood in Mexican Americans and their mental test scores. This view in turn supported popular assumptions concerning the importance of "white blood" in Blacks in relation to their IQ test score performances.

THE MULATTO HYPOTHESES

Between 1916 and 1930, Black children were involved in major assessment studies (Table 3.5). Dialectical and cultural differences received little or no consideration; mental test scores of Black and white English-speaking populations were frequently matched and correlated with little regard for those differences, leaving questionable conclusions to be drawn. One outgrowth of these and similar comparisons led to specific issues surrounding what was referred to as the *mulatto hypotheses.*

The mulatto hypotheses were formulated from two perspectives: One held that persons of racially mixed ancestry were inferior to those of "pure" unmixed backgrounds; the other view held that racially mixed persons were superior to those of "pure" backgrounds. For both views, scientific data were recorded. One bizarre study claimed that Black-white offspring in Jamaica were born with the "long legs of the Negro and the short arms of the white, thus putting them at a disadvantage in picking up objects from the ground."[43] This view was studied under a theory of disharmonic results from racial mixing.

Significant numbers of psychological studies during the 1920s and 1930s purported to show a relationship between white ancestry and IQ

TABLE 3.5 Geographical Location of Investigation of Intelligence of Negroes with Standard Tests, 1916–1930

Place	Investigator
Arkansas	Jordan
California	Clark; Goodenough
Florida	McGraw
Indiana	Lenoir; Pressey and Teter
Jamaica, British West Indies	Davenport
Louisiana	Arlitt; Goodenough; Sunne
Mississippi	Boots,
New York City	Klineberg; Murdock
North Carolina	Leggett
Oberlin, Ohio	Wells
Oklahoma	Lacy
South Carolina	Derrick; Strong
South Africa	Loades and Rich
Tennessee	Goodenough; Leggett; Peterson
Texas	Davis; Garth and Whately
Virginia	Ferguson
West Virginia	Klineberg; State Dept. of Education
Wisconsin	Martell

Source: J. St. Clair Price, "Negro-White Differences in General Intelligence," *Journal of Negro Education* (July 1934): 438. Reprinted by permission of the publisher.

test scores of Black children. Klineberg (1931), Eells (1933), and Herskovits (1934) were among the few white scholars refuting these studies by performing and reporting their own research efforts. Herskovits reported the most extensive review on this issue and concluded that "no significant correlations have been made between the amount of Negro blood represented in individuals—whether estimated on the basis on inspection, by the use of genealogies, or by anthropometric measurements—and standing in tests."[44] Yet, in spite of these findings, the mulatto hypotheses continued to maintain widespread support among many researchers.

In order to determine the acceptance level of the mulatto hypotheses among white behavioral scientists, a Howard University professor, C. H. Thompson, queried 169 leading white scholars during the school year 1929–1930.[45] One hundred psychologists were chosen from the membership lists of the Ninth International Congress of Psychology, while educators, sociologists, and cultural anthropologists were selected from random lists.[46] With a 76 percent response rate to the question "Does experimental evidence support or refute the 'mulatto hypothesis'?" Seventy percent of the respondents felt that the evidence was inconclusive.

TABLE 3.6 Conclusions from Investigations of the Relative Inherent Mental Ability of the Negro, 1929–1930

1. Do investigations show the inherent mental ability of the Negro to be inferior or equal to that the White?

Group	Data Inconclusive	Negro Inferior	Negro Equal
Psychologists	64%	25%	11%
Educationists	61	14	15
Sociologists and Anthropologists	57	5	38
Total	62%	19%	19%

2. Does experimental evidence support or refute the "mulatto hypothesis"?

Group	Inconclusive	Supports	Refutes
Psychologists	68%	23%	9%
Educationists	65	10	25
Sociologists and Anthropologists	76	—	24
Total	70%	15%	15%

Source: Charles H. Thompson, "The Conclusions of Scientists Relative to Racial Differences," *Journal of Negro Education* (July 1934): 499, 507. Reprinted by permission of the publisher.

However, the group with the largest percentage supporting the hypothesis were the psychologists. Further analysis of Thompson's data revealed that nearly two-thirds of the total group felt that investigations concerning the "inferiority or equality of inherent black mental ability" were also inconclusive. But, as before, one-fourth of the queried psychologists felt that substantial evidence existed to prove the mental inferiority of Blacks. Interestingly, more than one-third of the sociologists and anthropologists felt that the evidence supported the existence of mental equality between Blacks and whites (Table 3.6). (Also see Appendix B.)

REACTIONS OF BLACK SCHOLARS AND COMMUNITIES

With Black psychologists practically nonexistent during the 1920s and 1930s, it fell to Black educators to protest the unfairness of the psychological testing movement and the mulatto hypotheses. In an autobiographical statement, W. E. B. DuBois stated:

the hurried use of the new technique of psychological tests, which were quickly adjusted so as to put black folk absolutely beyond the possibility of civilization. By this time I was un-impressed. I had too often seen science made the slave of caste and race hate, and it was interesting to see Odum, McDougall and Brigham eventually turn somersaults from absolute scientific proof of Negro inferiority to repudiation of the limited and questionable application of any test.[47]

Among the most vocal critics was Horace Mann Bond, an outstanding twenty-year-old professor at Langston University (Oklahoma). Many of Bond's early criticisms were couched in the form of instruction and warning to Black people to become aware of the conclusions reached by white psychological examiners.[48] He specifically called for active participation against what he called "insidious propaganda . . . which seeks to demonstrate that the Negro is intellectually and physically incapable of assuming the dignities, rights and duties which devolve upon him as a member of modern society."[49] Bond criticized the practice of generalizing from conclusions based on comparisons of unequal social groups: "To compare the crowded millions of New York's East Side with the children of some professorial family on Morningside Heights indeed involves a great contradiction."[50] He felt these interpretations were specially dangerous to the "newly born race consciousness" of Black people and called for immediate actions against these inequities:

The time has passed for opposing these false ideas with science; every university student of Negro blood ought to comprise himself into an agent whose sole purpose is the contravention of such half-truths . . . There is no longer any justifications for the silence of the educated Negro, when confronted with these assertions; and only through his activity and investigation will the truth be disclosed and the ghosts of racial inferiority, mental or physical, set at rest, forever.[51]

In a classic 1927 article, the prolific Bond called the testing of Black children a major indoor sport among white psychologists and outlined rules for the game: "First one must have a *white* examiner; a group of *Negro* children; a test standardized for *white* children tested by white examiners; and just a few preconceived notions regarding the nature of 'intelligence.' "[52] Bond noted that when examining white children the examiner must be careful to establish "rapport" with his subject and that an "esprit cordiale" must exist between himself and the person being

Horace Mann Bond (1904–1972). Dr. Bond, author of numerous books and research articles, became the first Black president of Lincoln University (Pennsylvania) and of Fort Valley State College (Georgia). He was an early critic of psychometric studies that claimed mental inferiority of Black children.

tested. "If this was not done, so long as white children are being tested, the results of the game may not be valid," Bond explained. On the other hand, this was not true, as he noted, when testing Black children. Black children were often criticized for being withdrawn during the testing situation; their docility was assumed to be an inherited trait and of no significance in determining the final test score.

As a result of these feelings, Bond decided to "play the game" of psychometry—with some alterations. He selected Black children from professional homes and middle-class homes, rather than from the laboring-class homes, which were the favorite source of subjects for white psychologists. Using the Stanford-Binet Test, he made special efforts to gain "fullest rapport" during the testing, and he "leaned over backwards" in order to maintain "scientific accuracy." The results were so striking that they even surprised Bond: 63 percent made scores above 106; 47 percent equalled or exceeded IQs of 122; 26 percent made scores over 130. Bond concluded that these exceptional children "were not out of the ordinary . . . the same sort of a group could be selected in any Negro community" provided the same sociocultural background of the subjects existed. Bond's study received no published reaction from white psychologists, but his article did serve notice of the importance of the race of the examiner relative to that of the subject and of social class variables.

In the early 1940s, Allison Davis, a University of Chicago professor and social anthropologist, argued against faulty intelligence testing. The tests, he said, were composed by middle-class professors who used terminology and concepts not comprehended by culturally deprived youth. In 1945, Davis chaired a project designed to investigate social class variables and cultural learning as it bears upon the solution of problems in mental tests. The blue ribbon committee consisted of Kenneth Eells, Robert Havighurst, Ralph Tyler, W. Lloyd Warner, Virgil Herrick, and Lee Cronbach. Davis and his colleagues declaring a series of four interdependent hypotheses.[53]

1. All responses to all items in all tests of general intelligence are inevitably influenced by the culture of the respondent.
2. In a test of general mental ability to be used in the United States, the problems should be selected from the common culture, expressed in cultural symbols common to all native inhabitants of the United States, and selected from that common culture only.
3. In all available tests of general intelligence, however, there are numerous items implying experience that is part of the culture of the higher socioeconomic groups, but not equally a part of the culture of the approximately 60 percent of all Americans who grow up in the lower socioeconomic groups.
4. Therefore, the basic cultural flaws in all available tests of general intelligence may be overcome by including only those problems and symbols that imply experience that is part of the general American culture.

BLACK GRADUATE STUDENTS RESPOND

During the 1930s, a few graduate students began to filter through the northern university training centers. These students became a small legion of protestors, frequently directing their theses, dissertations, and other academic energies toward refuting beliefs of Black mental inferiority. Among these students were Herman G. Canady, master's degree candidate at Northwestern University; Howard H. Long, doctoral candidate at Harvard University; Albert S. Beckham, doctoral candidate at New York University; and Martin D. Jenkins, doctoral candidate at Northwestern University.

Herman Canady's master's thesis (1928) provided critical examination of the importance of the effects of rapport on the IQ—data later regarded a classic in psychological testing. His study in "racial psychology" presented statistical evidence across two dimensions: (1) effects of rapport and (2) race of the examiner. Canady's initial concern regarding these questions was stimulated by an anonymous article of 1916, "Some Suggestions Relative to the Study on the Mental Attitude of the Negro," which questioned the appropriateness of the Binet test for Black children, the unconscious mental biases of the examiners, the tendency of Black children not to "let a white person know anything about him," and the importance of rapport. "It is not too much to say that the mere presence in the room of a member of the dominant race creates an atmosphere in which it is impossible to get a normal response."[54] Inspired by this article, Canady used the Stanford-Binet test on forty-eight Black and twenty-five white children from the elementary schools of Evanston, Illinois. Employing Black and white examiners, he set about testing the assumption that "if it is true that a white examiner cannot gain the full cooperation of Negro children because of racial barriers, it might also be true that a Negro examiner would encounter the same difficulty in testing white children."[55] His results showed that the testing environment was in jeopardy under both reversed-examiner conditions, indicating the influence that rapport played on the testing situation.

Howard H. Long's dissertation (1933) at Harvard explored the relationship between IQ test scores of poor and middle-class Black children. Long's study underscored the inappropriateness of utilizing white socioeconomic classification schemes (SES) for describing all Black populations. Most important was his research data that illustrated the wide range of intellectual ability found in Black children.[56]

Albert S. Beckham's dissertation (1933) compared IQ test results of Black children from the public schools of Washington, D.C., Baltimore, and New York City.[57] He produced evidence showing that median IQ scores of Black children from these major cities fell squarely into the range of average intelligence. Beckham's investigation countered evidence by white psychologists which had shown that the Black child was at least ten points below the white child in IQ score level.

Martin D. Jenkins's dissertation (1935) was an important socio-psychological study of Black children with superior intelligence. He showed that the proportion of gifted Black children was about the same as that for gifted white children, provided that equal educational opportunities were provided.[58] Jenkins, later president of Morgan State University, reported testing a Black girl with a Stanford-Binet IQ score of 200.[59] This research was significant because it provided authenticated data that counteracted popular beliefs of Black inferiority and underlined, again, the importance of testing rapport.

INTELLIGENCE TESTING AND THE COURTS

The Stanford-Binet was contested in several court cases in which institutionalization of a patient was the issue. A precedent was established in 1916 when New York Supreme Court Justice Goff "refused to accept the Binet test as sufficient ground for committing a delinquent girl to an institution for the feebleminded."[60] Goff's comment that standardizing the mind was as futile as attempting to standardize electricity, drew the disdain of many test followers. While the Binet test encountered early legal difficulties, it gained popularity and met little resistance among educators, who used its results for the assessment and assignment of school children. Not until many decades later was the question of the validity of intelligence tests contested.

It was not until the late 1970s that the use of psychological tests in California was found to be in violation of Title VI of the Civil Rights Act (1964) by a federal court. Judge Robert Peckham ruled that standardized intelligence tests are racially and culturally biased, have a discriminatory impact against Black children, and have not been validated for the purpose of essentially permanent placements of Black children into educationally dead-end, isolated, and stigmatizing classes for the so-called educable mentally retarded. (See Chapter 8 for further discussion.)

WECHSLER-BELLEVUE SCALE

Fortunately, just when clinical psychology was emerging as an accepted profession, the Wechsler-Bellevue Scale (1939), derived chiefly from World War I testing protocols, was developed chiefly for the measurement of adult intelligence. Within a short time, the Wechsler-Bellevue and its later revisions became the leading psychological tests of intelligence and a standard instrument in public mental hospitals, child-guidance clinics, and veteran's hospitals. The tests not only combined Binet and performance-type items for ability assessment, but also used the pattern of scores as a guide for other clinical purposes. Wechsler also rejected the mental age concept of former tests in favor of point scales, which allowed test scores to be contrasted with "normed" scores with age as the only criterion.

Wechsler defined intelligence as the "aggregate or global capacity of the individual to act purposefully, to think rationally, and to deal effectively with his environment."[61] He did not use Blacks in his normed test data; rather, the test was standardized on 670 white children and 1,081 white adults. In justifying the population he used, Wechsler frankly discussed the issue of racial norms and his solution: "Thus, we have eliminated the 'colored' vs. 'white' factor by admitting at the outset that our norms cannot be used for the colored population of the United States."[62] Obviously psychologists and educators paid little heed to this statement; for many years the tests were used indiscriminately in the mental measurement and other clinical diagnoses of minority-group populations.

PERSONALITY TESTING OF MINORITY GROUPS

Widespread personality stereotyping had categorized the Black American as easy going and happy, the Mexican-American as hot-blooded and excitable, and the Native American as stolid and savage. These minority groups were generally classified as lazy. Psychologists attempted to measure these and other personality attributes by using temperament and personality tests of the late 1920s. The leading tests during this era included the Pressey X-O Tests, Downey-Will Temperament Test, Carnegie Test, Woodworth-Matthews Questionnaire, Thurston Personality Schedule, and Allport Ascendence-Submission Test.

As early as 1922, psychologist June Downey felt that "in racial psychology important results may be expected to follow temperamental testing."[63] She believed the results of mass temperamental testing would determine whether different personality characteristics could be attributed to racial groups. In subsequent years, much effort was expended in an attempt to detect and measure these characteristics. Sunne (1925) compared personality test results of Black and white teenagers and reported that "Negroes were slower in movement than the whites, that they have a slightly greater inertia, greater motor impulsion and the same interest in detail, volitional perseveration, and coordination of impulses, and less motor inhibition."[64]

In 1927, Garth studied "170 full blood Indians" from the United States Indian Schools at Santa Fe and Albuquerque, New Mexico, and Rapid City, South Dakota. He compared their Will-Temperament Test scores with scores made by Blacks in a previous study. He concluded that the Native Americans were less speedy in decision making and exhibited more motor inhibition than the Blacks.[65] McFadden and Dashiell (1923) administered the Downey-Will Temperament Test to an equal number of Black and white high school and college students and concluded that only minor differences existed between the groups.[66] Hurlock (1930) reported no significant difference of personality traits when the Downey Test was administered to 110 white and 101 Black seventh- and eighth-grade students.[67] In the same study, she analyzed most of the previous major attempts to measure Black-white personality differences and questioned the practicality of attempting to measure these differences. In support of the Hurlock Study, Cooper, a white professor in a Black college, administered (1929) the Allport Ascendance-Submission Reaction Study to large numbers of Black college students and found no racial differences, concluding that "this test disproves the traditional view that the Negro is innately more submissive than the white man."[68]

As test data disagreements began to plague the area of personality assessment, doubts of test validity and reliability arose. No two tests seemed to measure the same thing. Moore and Steele (1934) reported that they found little correlation between the results of any two tests.[69] With the added possibility of individuals "faking" answers, it was apparent that paper-and-pencil personality tests were in jeopardy from several perspectives.

In the early 1930s, a new technique of personality assessment appeared, the Rorschach ink blot technique, later to be classified as a *projective technique*. The first published research in the United States involving this test appeared in 1930; within eight years nearly 150 articles had been published on its clinical applications. Standardization was an immediate problem, however, and relatively few studies were made evaluating the test's reliability or validity. With the Rorschach's dependence on psychoanalytic theory for interpretation, there was some question of its validity for individuals who had been systematically excluded from equal participation in the majority culture; nevertheless, most psychologists viewed the test as a promising instrument because of its relative independence of language and other culturally restricted content. In reality, the test was far from being "culturally free"—the Freudian-based philosophical underpinnings were biased, and the psychologists who administered and interpreted the tests were not culturally free.

Before long the Rorschach technique was joined by other projective devices. For instance, rather than rely on ambiguous stimuli to elicit examinee responses, as on the Rorschach, the Thematic Apperception Test (TAT) consisted of thirty pictures of people in a variety of situations. The process of identifying the hero (called "needs") and the environmental forces (called "press") in the stories created by minority examinees called for abilities more often found lacking in the background of white clinicians. In 1971, Robert Williams, a Black psychologist, created a counterpart of the TAT in his Themes Concerning Blacks (TCB). The TCB was used on hundreds of clients establishing a set of standards that were far more appropriate for Blacks, in that themes were based on environments familiar to most Blacks.[70] (See Chapter 8.)

RACE STUDIES AND ANTI-SEMITISM

As European anti-Semitism simmered in the pre–World War II period, several American professional organizations began to issue disclaimers for "misinterpretation" of their racial-difference data. In several instances, claims of Jewish "racial" inferiority had been gleaned from psychological studies of the 1920s and 1930s conducted in this country. Frequent references to these studies by the Nazis became a source of embarrassment and shame. Consequently, the Council of the Society for the Psychological Study of Social Issues (SPSSI) published an "official protest against the non-scientific interpretations of American findings."[71] This statement declared in part: "In experiments which psychologists have made upon different peoples, no characteristic, inherent psychological differences which fundamentally distinguish so-called 'races' have been disclosed." The statement, directed at the Nazi call for the maintenance of an "Aryan-pure race" and the categorization of a "Jewish race," concluded, "there is no indication that members of any group are rendered incapable by their biological heredity of completely acquiring the culture of the community in which they live."[72] The statement included no specific reference to minorities in the United States. (See Appendix A.)

The World War II German "race betterment" movement with its belief that a "super race" could be bred was a derivative of an insidious entanglement between nativistic psychology and the "science" of eugenics.

NOTES

Chapter Epigraph: W. E. B. DuBois, *Dusk of Dawn* (New York: Harcourt, Brace and Co., 1940), 99–100.

1. S. Andreski, *Social Sciences as Sorcery* (London: Andre Deutsch, 1972), 127.

2. The assumption held by psychologists and the general public, that intelligence was innately determined, influenced leading assessment theorists during this era. L. Terman and later army psychologists constructed their tests following this principle.

3. R. E. Fancher, *The Intelligence Men: Makers of the IQ Controversy* (New York: W. W. Norton, 1985).

4. L. J. Cronbach, *Essentials of Psychological Testing* (New York: Harper and Row, 1949), 200.

5. The contemporary concept of fluid or analytic ability, as expressed in Raven's Progressive Matrices Test, is an extension of the *g* factor.

6. W. Stern, *Über Psychologie der Individuellen Differenzen* (Leipzig, 1900), 46.

7. Ibid., 146.

8. L. M. Terman, *The Measurement of Intelligence* (Boston: Houghton Mifflin, 1916), 92.

9. Ibid., 92.

10. Ibid., 93.

11. Sharing the same broad academic discipline with clinical psychologists, educational psychologists interchangeably used jargon from the clinical setting. In this way, many educational psychologists regarded themselves as clinicians with access to medical diagnoses. The frequent use of Freudian jargon and psychiatric terminology by psychometrists was common. These tandem boundaries led educational psychologists to speculate frequently in areas of psychiatry and genetics with less than adequate backgrounds in these disciplines. With a partisan cohort, they were rarely challenged on the appropriateness and accuracy of their conclusions. Recently, educationalists speculating in genetics have experienced far more criticism and are unable to receive wholehearted endorsement of their pronouncements.

12. L. Terman and M. Merrill, *Measuring Intelligence* (Boston: Houghton Mifflin, 1937), 122–123.

13. L. Terman, *Intelligence Tests and School Reorganization* (New York: World, 1923), 27–28.

14. E. L. Thorndike, *Human Nature and the Social Order* (New York: Macmillan, 1940). Many years have passed, and educators are still attempting to estimate the percent of variance that genes and environment may affect IQ test scores.

15. G. R. Stetson, "Some Memory Tests of Whites and Blacks," *Psychological Review* 4, (1897): 285–289.

16. A. C. Strong, "Three Hundred Fifty White and Colored Children Measured by the Binet-Simon Measuring Scale of Intelligence," *Pedagogical Seminary* 20. (1913): 485–515.

17. J. Morse, "A Comparison of White and Colored Children Measured by the Binet Scale of Intelligence," *The Popular Science Monthly* 84 no. 1 (January 1914): 75–79.

18. Ibid., 77.

19. Ibid., 79.

20. B. A. Phillips, "The Binet Test Applied to Colored Children," *Psychological Clinic* 8 (1914): 190–196.

21. G. S. Hall, "The Negro in Africa and America," *Pedagogical Seminary* (1905): 358.

22. G. O. Ferguson, Jr., *The Psychology of the Negro: An Experimental Study* (New York: Science Press, 1916), 125.

23. W. H. Pyle, "The Mind of the Negro Child," *School and Society* 1 (1915): 358.

24. Article 1, Section 3, of the Constitution of the United States in discussing tax apportionment declared that free persons, including indentured servants, would be counted as a whole and that the vast majority of Blacks would be considered three-fifths of a person.

25. R. Yerkes (Ed.), *Psychological Examining in the United States Army*, National Academy of Sciences, Vol. XV, (Washington, 1921), 706.

26. E. J. Scott, *American Negro in the World War*, (Washington, D.C.: Underwood and Underwood, 1919) 35.

27. R. Yerkes (Ed.), *Psychological Examining in the United States Army*, 736.

28. G. O. Ferguson, "The Intelligence of Negroes at Camp Lee, Virginia," *School and Society* IX, no. 233 (June 14, 1919): 721–726.

29. D. Gersh, "The Development and Use of IQ Tests in the United States from 1900 to 1930" (Unpublished Dissertation, State University of New York at Stony Brook, 1981), 102.

30. Ibid.

31. Since there were no post-high school programs for Native Americans, the U.S. government made provisions for individuals to attend the all-Black Hampton Institute (now University) in Virginia. This practice continued until the early 1940s.

32. E. Jamieson and P. Standiford, "The Mental Capacity of Southern Ontario Indians," *Journal of Educational Psychology* 19 (1928): 536–551.

33. W. S. Hunter, "Indian Blood and Otis Intelligence Test," *Journal of Comparative Psychology* 2 (1922).

34. J. A. Fitzgerald and W. W. Ludeman, "Intelligence of Indian Children," *Journal of Comparative Psychology* 6 (1926).

35. W. S. Hunter and E. Sommermier, "The Relation of Degree of Indian Blood to Scores on the Otis Intelligence Test," *Journal of Comparative Psychology* 2 (1922): 257–277.

36. T. R. Garth, "The Will-Temperament of Indians," *Journal of Applied Psychology* 11 (1927): 512–518.

37. O. Klineberg, "An Experimental Study of Speed and Other Factors in 'Racial' Differences," *Archives of Psychology* 93 (1928): 111.

38. O. Klineberg, *Race Differences* (New York: Harper and Row, 1935), 367.

39. S. D. Porteus, *The Psychology of a Primitive People* (New York: Longmans, 1931), 438.

40. B. Blackwood, "A Study of Mental Testing in Relation to Anthropology," *Mental Measurement Monographs* 4 (December 1927): 113.

41. G. I. Sanchez, "Group Differences and Spanish-Speaking Children—A Critical Review," *Journal of Applied Psychology* 16 (1932): 549–558.

42. F. C. Paschal and L. R. Sullivan, "Racial Factors in the Mental and Physical Development of Mexican Children," *Comparative Psychology Monographs* 3 (October 1925): 46–75.

43. C. B. Davenport and M. Steggerda, "Race Crossing in Jamaica," *Publication, Carnegie Institution of Washington, D.C.* 395 (1929): 469–471.

44. M. J. Herskovits, "A Critical Discussion of the 'Mulatto Hypotheses,' " *Journal of Negro Education* 3 (July 1934): 401.

45. C. H. Thompson, "The Conclusion of Scientists Relative to Racial Differences," *Journal of Negro Education* 3 (July 1934): 494–512.

46. For a complete listing of these psychologists, see Appendix.

47. W. E. B. Dubois, *Dusk of Dawn* (New York: Harcourt Brace, 1940), 99–100.

48. Rarely was any form of scholarship, let alone criticism from Black psychologists considered. This academic racism led Black scholars to publish their own journals and to establish other media of communication. A leading periodical of this era was *The Crisis*, edited by W. E. B. DuBois at Fisk University.

49. H. M. Bond, "Intelligence Tests and Propaganda," *The Crisis* 28, no. 2 (June 1924): 61.

50. Ibid., 64.

51. Ibid., 64.

52. H. M. Bond, "Some Exceptional Negro Children," *The Crisis* 34 (October 1927): 257–280.

53. K. Eells, A. Davis, R. Havighurst, et al., *Intelligence and Cultural Differences* (Chicago: University of Chicago Press, 1951), 6–7.

54. Anon., "Some Suggestions Relative to a Study of the Mental Attitude of the Negro," *Pedagogical Seminary* 23 (1916): 199–203.

55. H. G. Canady, "The Effect of 'Rapport' on the IQ: A New Approach to the Problem of Racial Psychology," *Journal of Negro Education* 5 (1936): 209–219.

56. H. H. Long, "Analyses of Test Results From Third Grade Children Selected on the Basis of Socio-Economic Status," Unpublished Doctor's Dissertation, Harvard University, 1933.

57. A. S. Beckham, "A Study of the Intelligence of Colored Adolescents of Different Socio-Economic Status in Typical Metropolitan Areas," *Journal of Social Psychology* 4 (1933): 70–91.

58. M. D. Jenkins, "Socio-Psychological Study of Negro Children of Superior Intelligence," *Journal of Negro Education* 5 (1936): 175–190.

59. P. Witty and M. Jenkins, "The Case of 'B'—A Gifted Negro Girl," *Journal of Social Psychology* 6 (1935): 117–124.

60. "The Binet Test in Court," *Eugenical News* (August 1916): 55.

61. D. Wechsler, *The Measurement of Adult Intelligence* (Baltimore: Williams and Wilkins, 1939), 3.

62. Ibid., 109.

63. J. E. Downey, *The Will-Temperament and Its Testing* (Yonkers, N.Y.: World, 1924).

64. D. Sunne, "Personality Tests—White and Negro Adolescents," *Journal of Applied Psychology* 9 (1925): 256–280.

65. T. R. Garth, "The Will-Temperament of Indians," *Journal of Applied Psychology* 11 (1927): 512–518.

66. J. H. McFadden and J. F. Dashiell, "Racial Differences as Measured by the Downey Will-Temperament Test," *Journal of Applied Psychology* 7 (1923): 30–53.

67. E. B. Hurlock, "The Will-Temperament of White and Negro Children," *Pedagogical Seminary* 38 (1930): 91–99.

68. P. Cooper, "Notes on Psychological Race Differences," *Social Forces* 8 (1929): 426.

69. H. Moore and I. Steele, "Personality Tests," *Journal of Abnormal and Social Psychology* 29 (1934–1935): 45–52.

70. R. Williams, "Testing Minority Patients," *Washington University Alumni Magazine* (St. Louis, 1971): 77–78.

71. M. Van de Water, "Racial Psychology," *Science-Supplement* 30 (September 1938): 7–8, 71.

72. "Statement on Racial Psychology by the Society for the Psychological Study of Social Issues," (Washington, D.C.: American Psychological Association (SPSSI), 1938).

▶ 4

Psychology and Race

Archaeological remains from the First Dynasty (circa 3500 B.C.)—inscriptions, tomb-paintings, and artifacts—indicate that games of probability based on random events occupied the attention and amusement of the Egyptians. These games of chance were played by tossing an astragalus (knuckle bone) to begin the random events.[1]

There is no evidence that these games ever included or speculated on human conditions; however, in another time and place—during the nineteenth century in England—random chance was developed into the "science" of probability and statistics. Philosophical ideas and statistical evidence commingled to infer and predict human destiny based on mathematical curves. Values from the elite social class were palmed off on the lower classes in order to determine the degree to which the groups differed. In short order, the practice of group comparison became widespread and regarded as scientific explorations. Scholars, with personal agendas, became so involved with their quasi-scientific comparisons, that on occasion they deliberately manipulated data in order to obtain results that fulfilled their expectations. These practices were successful because the majority of people had no idea or cared little about what the numbers meant. And, since most of these scholars were of the British elite and leisure class, they had full reign creating philosophies to reflect their chauvinistic worldviews. Little wonder, then, that the anxious use of applied mathematics, under these scenarios, led to surreptitious nipping and tucking of data sets.

Egyptian tomb painting showing a nobleman in afterlife using an astragalus in a board game

Source: Ancient Egyptian Paintings. Nina M. Davies, compiler (Chicago: University of Chicago Press, 1936), pl. XCV. Courtesy of the Oriental Institute of the University of Chicago.

SUSPICIOUS STATISTICAL SHENANIGANS

While suspected data tampering in selected research findings has occurred throughout the ages, this practice mushroomed during the nineteenth century. The anthropometric era of body measurements employed the simplistic tape measure, caliper, and weight scales as the basic technology for comparative data gathering. Few doubts were raised about these findings by peer researchers. As other professionals joined in the cavalcade of comparative data gathering, data was collected without interference or outside verification of the findings. In some cases, blatantly fraudulent data-tampering deeds were noted particularly in the arena of human cranial measurements.

Craniologists, usually medical doctors, set about their task of collecting and measuring skulls from as many different races as they could secure. Robert Bean so convinced himself that Blacks were inferior to whites, that his experimenter bias allowed his enthusiasm to affect his vision and he recorded measurements which supported his belief that Blacks did not possess the cranial capacity to house sufficient cerebral matter necessary for higher intellectual thought and reasoning. When Dr. Bean's calculations appeared too good to be true, he drew the suspicion of others, most notably his ex-professor, Franklin P. Mall.[2] Professor Mall, awed by Bean's "perfect" statistical correlations, attempted to replicate his ex-student's measurements. In short order, Mall revealed that Bean had unequivocally massaged his measurements in favor of European skulls, that is, larger cranial capacity. An earlier craniologist, Samuel Morton, not only had measurement problems, he was ghoulish: He had a collection of over a thousand human skulls in his home at the time of his own demise. His mathematical results were basic and straightforward: Europeans were superior and Africans were inferior. According to Gould (1981) who reworked Morton's data, "Morton's (Crania) summaries are a patchwork of fudging and finagling in the clear interest of controlling a priori convictions." Gould, however, vindicates Morton's motives by kindly stating, "I find no evidence of conscious fraud; indeed, had Morton been a conscious fudger, he would have not published his data so openly."[3]

Even the country gentleman Francis Galton's statistical techniques left a legacy of faulty and suspect procedures. This comes as no surprise since Galton was more of a philosopher-thinker than a scientist. He was frequently guilty of "experimenter expectancy" in his zest to subordinate the "ragged and dangerous" underclass and to glorify those he considered to be superior.

The marriage of statistics with philosophical ideas was legitimate, but the union opened the door to questionable scientific practices. Inventor and philosopher Charles Babbage (1830) summarized the situation in his "Reflections on the Decline of Science in England."[4] Even though he, too, was a man of the leisure class, he excoriated the general lack of "checks and balances" to keep philosophers and "wanna be" scientists aboveboard when calculating their statistics, and in an effort to expose fraudulent experimenters, he developed a list of techniques for bending data. "Trimming," Babbage wrote, "consists of clipping off little bits here and there from those observations which differ most in excess from the mean, and sticking them on to those which are too small." Trimming was considered to be a general practice by many Victorian-age scientists. Babbage considered the "cooking" of data far more detrimental to science as he defined the term, "an art of various forms, the object of which is to give ordinary observations the appearance and character of those of the highest degree of accuracy." In explaining the technique of scientific cooking, Babbage said, "If a hundred observations are made, the cook must be very unlucky if he cannot pick out fifteen or twenty which will do for serving up."[5] As statistical sophistication increased so did the difficulty of detecting such trickery. And, since it was rare for scientists and researchers to examine one another's raw data, conditions of faith bolstered by "scientific" mind-sets were accepted as the gospel truth.

In spite of questionable theories concerning the nature of intelligence, twentieth century psychologists pushed forward with IQ tests that were based on unproven and highly debatable concepts. Convinced of the validity and reliability of the g factor in intelligence, psychologists continue to support unitary test scores based on the two-factor theory. (See Chapter 3.) As aggregate scores of non-European populations consistently occupied the lower stratum of racial comparisons, doubts of the g factor's validity were never mentioned; rather, most psychologists steadfastly supported the theory and its results. Unfortunately with no recognized ombudsmen to argue for a reexamination of the theory, IQ test scores became a scientific Mason-Dixon Line for racial demarcations.[6] Other concerns such as the quest for culture-free items, cultural specific items, and test item screening committees removed the heat from the g factor.

By the mid-twentieth century, the crown jewel of studies supporting the hereditarian view of intelligence was propelled during the investigation of identical twins reared apart from each other who were administered IQ tests to determine if intellectual differences could be noted. While recognizing the uniqueness of identical twins, most psychologists recognized that results obtained with them do not necessarily generalize to other groups of people. Far too many intervening variables confound any parallels drawn from these studies. Even when separated early in life, twins most often are assigned by adoption agencies to similar environments; this factor alone falsely inflates the apparent role of genetic factors. Nonetheless, distinguished British psychologist, Sir Cyril Burt, the father of British educational psychology, amassed the largest IQ database of identical twins in the scientific world that was used to supported the role heredity played in intelligence. Burt argued that 80 percent of intelligence is inherited and that an individual's environment has relatively little effect on intelligence. Burt's findings influenced generations of psychologists until Princeton psychologist Leon Kamin and University of Hull (England) psychologists Ann Clarke and Michael McCaskie uncovered evidence that indicates that Burt worked backwards from his conclusions and changed or invented his raw data to make it fit his answers. Their investigations were provoked in part by the fact that three differ-ent studies produced results that were identical to three decimal places, a possibility (that) defies odds of millions to one unless Burt tampered with his original observations.[7]

Further investigations claimed that Burt had adjusted the twins' IQ scores, social classes, and sample sizes and had obfuscated other data. There was even doubt concerning the existence of some of his twins and belief that his collaborators were figments of his imagination. The so-called scientific proof supporting hereditarian sources of intelligence suffered an irreparable setback as a result, but hard-core supporters of the hereditarian viewpoint refuse to relinquish the validity of Burt's studies and continue to support the validity of identical twin comparisons as measured by two-factor IQ tests. In addition, academicians drew parallels between laboratory animals and humans in the quest to discover genetic factors in intelligence.

WHITE RATS AND MAZES

The belief that lower animal intellectual talents could be compared with human multifaceted skills undergirded a number of twentieth century psychological assumptions and theories. For example, in 1927, the first extensive psychological experiment in behavior genetics was begun at the University of California at Berkeley. Robert Choate Tryon, then an associate professor of psychology, designed an elaborate selective breed-ing experiment to produce a line of maze-bright and a line of maze-dull rats.[8] The year before, the first study of sibling resemblance in laboratory rats had been conducted by Stanford University psychology student Mildred Burlingame.[9] While Burlingame's study was based on a short-term series of maze-running tasks performed by albino rats, Tryon began with a "parental" generation of male and female albino rats and con-ducted his experiment over decades. The primary aims of Tryon's ex-periment were to establish under environmental control a maze-bright and a maze-dull strain of rats to determine the nature of the genetic determiners at work, to discover the constancy of this psychological difference throughout a large range of the rats' lifespan, and to find important biological and psychological correlates of the difference in this maze ability.[10]

Tryon's automatic mechanical device, which delivered the animals into the maze, claimed to control any intervening variables in environmental conditions. In order to offset calculation errors, electric recorders were used. In 1940, Tryon reported findings concluding that "proof of inheritance of individual difference in maze ability" was found.

As a result of this evidence, many leading researchers and large numbers of laymen quickly inferred that maze running by white rats was directly related to general intelligence in human beings, and that these abilities were Mendelian dominant. Moreover, it was felt that Tryon's study produced evidence substantiating inherited intellectual differences in human beings across racial lines. But in 1949, L. V. Searle reported contradictory findings after testing Tryon's strains of rats on learning tests other than maze-running ability (discrimination of distance, angles, and brightness). He illustrated that the so-called bright rats were not bright on everything and that the dull rats were not dull on everything.[11] This evidence should have undercut the parallel drawn between maze running in rats and general intelligence in human beings—that is, intelligence is a multifaceted function beyond simplification of a few factored variables.

Oddly enough, Searle's study has not received the recognition it deserves from the profession. His work points out the inconsistencies and errors of hereditary determinations of intelligence, and suggests an alternative view that offers a more compelling, less deterministic, perspective on the field.

If scientific evidence could be shown to support the cause of hereditarian views, some advocates pushed for the control of reproduction through the removal of "inferior" groups of people.

PSYCHOLOGY AND EUGENICS

Perhaps it was the significance and importance of heredity, birth control, and sterilization found in the earliest writings of Western philosophy and religion that influenced the deterministic bias found in some perspectives. In the Republic, Plato (427–347 B.C.) suggested that in order to improve the human species, "the best men must cohabit with the best women in as many cases as possible and the worst in the fewest, and that the offspring of the one must be reared and that of the other not, if the flock is to be as perfect as possible."[12]

Mention of the significance of heredity can be found in biblical verse. In the New Testament, reference to heredity was made when Jesus delivered the immortal Sermon on the Mount and warned of false prophets who appear in sheep's clothing:

> Even so every good tree bringeth forth good fruit; but a corrupt tree bringeth forth evil fruit.
> A good tree cannot bring forth evil fruit, neither can a corrupt tree bring forth good fruit.—Matthew 7:17–18

A recommendation for birth control appeared in the early writings of economic theory in the eighteenth century, when Thomas Malthus held that if the world's population were allowed to reproduce at a constant rate, many people would face the prospect of malnutrition or starvation. The Malthusian Doctrine suggested the necessity for controlling human growth in relation to world economic growth.[13]

During the nineteenth century, Darwinian concepts of natural selection and survival of the fittest became shibboleths for generations of advocates of birth control measures and other "race betterment" philosophies. (See Chapter Two.) Darwin's cousin, Francis Galton, coined the term *eugenics* in 1883 and defined it as "the study of the agencies under social control that may improve or impair the racial qualities of future generations either physically or mentally."[14] In *Hereditary Genius: Its Laws and Consequences* (1869), Galton expressed a platonic belief that "it would be quite practical to produce a highly gifted race of men by judicious marriages during several consecutive generations." As a mechanism to popularize and expand this notion, Galton established the Eugenics Society of Great Britain in 1908 and the following year published the *Eugenics Review,* a monthly journal that served as the chief medium of communication for eugenicists throughout the world.

Similar efforts aimed at race betterment were initiated in other countries settled by peoples of western European descent. In the United States, the movement grew with the establishment of the American Eugenic Society in 1905.[15] Henry Laughlin, one of its founders, proudly declared that "the English-speaking people seem to take the lead in the study of human breeding, just as they have in the production of superior domestic animals . . . the English are, in truth, the world's most skillful breeders."[16] Figure 4.1 illustrates the "idealized man" as perceived by eugenicists at the beginning of the twentieth century.

Charles B. Davenport, another leading figure in the eugenics movement in the United States, offered a parallel and a prediction: "Man is an organism—an animal: and the laws of improvement of corn and race horses hold true of him also. Unless people accept this simple truth and let it influence marriage selection, human progress will cease."[17]

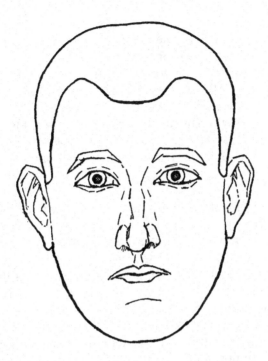

FIGURE 4.1 The idealized man of colonial ancestry, drawn to scale from Ales Hrdlicka's studies. The outline of the face is almost oblong; the head is high and "well-developed," which was supposed to denote "superior intelligence." Eugenicists strived to maintain this type in the U.S. population.

Source: Paul Popenoe and D. Johnson, *Applied Eugenics* (New York: Macmillan, 1920), 425. Reprinted by permission of the author.

CARNEGIE STATION FOR EXPERIMENTAL EVOLUTION

In Washington, D. C., steel magnate Andrew Carnegie established the Carnegie Institution for Experimental Evolution in 1904 and placed Davenport in charge. This was the first formal eugenics organization in North America. Under the auspices of the institution, the Carnegie Station for Experimental Evolution was established at Cold Spring Harbor, New York. Davenport was also placed in charge of this operation.

Eugenicists, following the "rediscovery" of Mendel's laws of heredity in 1900, placed extreme faith in the concept that "like produces like." Unfortunately, the theory was interpreted to mean that superior reproduces superior, inferior reproduces inferior, and the criminal reproduces the criminal. The purpose of the Carnegie Station, then, was to expand the study of hereditary traits in plants and lower animals to include humans. In 1910, with funds donated from the E. H. Harriman family, the Eugenics Record Office was established as an adjunct to the Eugenics Section of the American Breeders Association.[18] The establishment provided eugenicists with the facility and funds needed to document and maintain files on human traits. One of the largest centers of its kind in the world, the Eugenics Record Office proclaimed ten ambitious purposes:

1. To serve eugenical interests in the capacity of repository and clearinghouse.
2. To build up an analytical index of the traits of American families.
3. To study the forces controlling and the hereditary consequences of marriage-matings, differential fecundity, survival, and migration.
4. To investigate the manner of inheritance of specific human traits.
5. To advise concerning the eugenical fitness of proposed marriages.
6. To train field workers to gather data of eugenical import.
7. To maintain a limited field force actually engaged in gathering data for eugenic studies.
8. To cooperate with other institutions and with persons concerned with eugenical study.
9. To encourage new centers of eugenics research and education.
10. To publish the results of researchers and to aid in the dissemination of eugenical traits.[19]

A unique aspect of the Eugenics Record Office programs was the system of record keeping for family histories. It employed a catalog analysis of human traits based on an elaborate, expansible decimal system:

    0—General traits
    08—General diseases
    09—Occupations
    1—Integumentary system
    2—Skeletal system
    25—Muscular system
    3—Nervous system
    35—Criminality
    4—Mental traits
    43—Movements
    5—Sense organs

6—Nutritive system
7—Respiratory system
8—Circulatory system
85—Lymphatic system
9—Excretory system
94—Reproductive system[20]

Each trait was assigned a numerical rating, for example:

The number "4598" represents ability at chess playing, the "4" standing for mental traits, "45" for special mental ability, "459" for special ability in athletic or other games, "4598" for special ability in chess playing.[21]

The Trait Book, published by the Record Office, was designed to standardize record keeping for the growing number of eugenic field workers. (Catalog-analysis information for Section 4, "Mental Traits," was coordinated by the well-known psychologists E. L. Thorndike and R. M. Yerkes.)

An important program within the Record Office was a two-month training course for prospective field workers, taught by C. B. Davenport and H. H. Laughlin, and designed to provide laboratory and clinical studies in human heredity and instruction in making firsthand pedigree studies (Figure 4.2 shows one of the training charts used). Between 1910 and 1918, nearly two hundred people were trained in these courses. The graduates scattered across the United States and the Caribbean Islands, performing and reporting their field-work findings to the Record Office. Some returned to colleges and universities to spread to their students the techniques and philosophies of eugenic investigation.

Psychology courses often became vehicles for eugenics propaganda. One graduate of the Record Office training program wrote, "I hope to serve the cause by infiltrating eugenics into the minds of teachers. It may interest you to know that each student who takes psychology here works up his family history and plots his family tree."[22] Harvard, Columbia, Brown, Cornell, Wisconsin, and Northwestern were among the leading academic institutions teaching eugenics in psychology courses. But the profession of psychology served the eugenicists' cause in a far more important way than merely being an outlet for its propaganda. Psychology made its chief contribution by providing much of the philosophical discussion purporting to validate the existence of "fine-lined" individual differences. While psychology's measuring devices conveniently labeled these mental variations, its developmental theories helped guide the eugenicists from theoretical positions to applied programs.

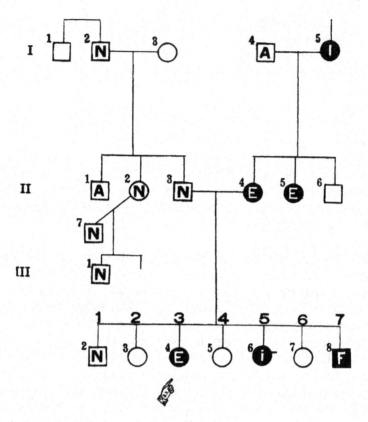

FIGURE 4.2 Example of a simple pedigree chart and (opposite) key

Source: C. B. Davenport, *The Family-History Book,* Eugenics Record Office Bulletin No. 7, September 1912, pp. 96, 100.

APPLIED EUGENICS AND EUTHENICS

The assertion that individuals and groups of people were either "desirable" or "not desirable" led to two applied lines of approach to the concept of increasing the "quality" of human beings. These were *eugenics* and *euthenics*. Eugenic programs were concerned with the control of individual heredity while euthenics programs sought control of the environment.

Due to the conservative view to attribute positive outcomes and traits to internal causes rather than any external sources, eugenic programs were by far the more popular and more expansive attempts at race betterment. On the other hand, euthenics advocates were small in

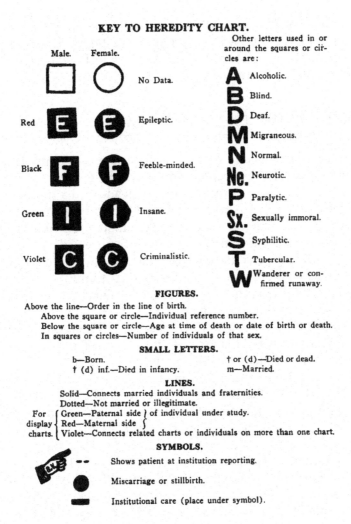

KEY TO HEREDITY CHART.

Male.	Female.		Other letters used in or around the squares or circles are :
☐	○	No Data.	**A** Alcoholic.
Red	**E**	**E** Epileptic.	**B** Blind.
			D Deaf.
Black	**F**	**F** Feeble-minded.	**M** Migraneous.
			N Normal.
Green	**I**	**I** Insane.	**Ne.** Neurotic.
			P Paralytic.
Violet	**C**	**C** Criminalistic.	**Sx.** Sexually immoral.
			S Syphilitic.
			T Tubercular.
			W Wanderer or confirmed runaway.

FIGURES.
Above the line—Order in the line of birth.
Above the square or circle—Individual reference number.
Below the square or circle—Age at time of death or date of birth or death.
In squares or circles—Number of individuals of that sex.

SMALL LETTERS.
b—Born.   † or (d)—Died or dead.
† (d) inf.—Died in infancy.   m—Married.

LINES.
Solid—Connects married individuals and fraternities.
Dotted—Not married or illegitimate.
For display charts. { Green—Paternal side } of individual under study.
Red—Maternal side
Violet—Connects related charts or individuals on more than one chart.

SYMBOLS.
Shows patient at institution reporting.
Miscarriage or stillbirth.
Institutional care (place under symbol).

number and correspondingly less vocal in their influence, while the eugenicists, large in number, were very vocal. Both were quick to point to the results of warfare, in which the strongest and healthiest young men were eliminated. Consequently, both groups advocated peace programs and armed forces composed of volunteers rather than conscripts.

Eugenicists were middle-class white professionals, including a large number of college and university teachers, researchers, and administrators. The movement against the "socially unfit" made many connections and allies with those against the "racially unfit." Psychologists unwittingly contributed to both views by calling attention to individual differences found through army testing in World War I and by the announcement of "discovered" racial differences in IQ scores. When eugenicists took the lead and proposed a number of programs to carry out their mandate of race betterment, it was to be expected that psychologists would be in the vanguard.

FINDINGS OF THE RESEARCH COMMITTEE

Fearful that natural selection would not operate to accomplish the survival of the fittest, the research committee of the eugenics section of the American Breeders Association unanimously adopted a resolution establishing a group of scholars to "study the best practical means, so far as the innate traits are a factor, of purging the blood of the American people of the handicapping and deteriorating influences of . . . anti-social classes."[23] Leading representatives from the fields of psychology, sociology, and anthropology, as well as from medicine and law, were called to membership in this committee. Psychology's role was to provide analyses of the "standards and tests for determining the types of mental degenerates and defectives proposed for sterilization."[24] Additionally, psychologists were charged with analyses of the effects of sterilization on the "mental processes, industry, habits of life, and sex instincts." Sociologists were to be concerned, among other things, with methods of reaching "defectives and potential parents of defectives not in institutions." For discussion purposes, this committee utilized an interesting classification of social misfits: (1) the feeble-minded, (2) the pauper, (3) the inebriate, (4) the criminalistic, (5) the epileptic, and (6) the insane.

One outgrowth of the committee's report was the suggestion of a number of remedies for "purging the blood of the race" in which defective strains were found. These suggestions included segregation, birth control, rewards for parenthood, restrictive marriage laws, eutelegenesis (artificial insemination), and sterilization.

Segregation called for the separation of men and women confined to institutions, such as mental hospitals, prisons, and other restricted settings, in order to prevent the inmates, characterized as socially undesirable, from reproducing.

Birth Control procedures were encouraged to reverse the alleged trend of larger families being produced by "lower economic status" and "lower IQ groups"; free clinics and supplies were to be provided to specially selected groups.

Rewards for parenthood meant the offering of bonuses to parents of "superior ability" as an inducement; financial assistance resembling scholarships would encourage select groups to have as many children as they wanted. For example, during pre-World War II, eugenicists in the United States discussed a plan to offer "cash grants to pilots of the Army Air Corps, who were not reproducing their 'superior stock' due to a lack of income."[25]

Restrictive marriage laws and customs were designed to prevent consanguineous matings, which would increase the number of persons homozygous for recessive genes (those designated as negative); legal restrictions and taboos were created to decrease "socially inadequate and unfit" reproductions. Restrictions prohibiting marriage between whites and Blacks drew support from this philosophy. (See Appendix C for a compendium of miscegenation laws in the United States.)

Eutelegenesis. Since the "pure sire method" was considered the most advanced technique for animal breeding, eugenicists suggested the extensive use of selected sires for artificially inseminating prospective human mothers. This process was called *eutelegenesis.*

Sterilization was the leading remedy of those suggested; its appeal, both abroad and in the United States, is a matter of record, noticeably among a number of state judicial and legal organizations advocating race betterment philosophies.

STERILIZATION LAWS

"Whereas, heredity plays a most important part in the transmission of crime, idiocy, and imbecility"—thus began the text of the first state law permitting mental institutions to perform sterilization operations upon inmates. This Indiana law (1907) stimulated concerted efforts by other state governments to enact and enforce similar sterilization procedures. The state of Washington (1909) followed Indiana with similar legislation as a part of its criminal code, making it clear that sterilization would also be a form of punishment for those guilty of "carnal abuse of a female person" or those classed as "habitual criminals." California (1909) enacted laws to permit "asexualization of inmates" at state hospitals, the Sonoma State Home, and state prisons.

By 1930, twenty-four states had sanctioned sterilization as an eugenic measure, and over 10,000 individuals were sterilized under the provisions of these laws (Table 4.1). (*Vasectomy,* the excision of the vas deferens, and *salpingectomy,* the cutting of the oviducts, were the primary surgical procedures.) California, using the Stanford-Binet Intelligence Test as the primary psychometric measure of mental deficiency, led the nation with 6,787 court-ordered sterilizations. By 1935, sterilization laws had been passed in several European countries: Switzerland, Denmark,

TABLE 4.1 States Having Sterilization Laws and Number of People Sterilized by January 1, 1930

State	Number of persons sterilized		
	Males	Females	Total
Alabama	32	12	44
Arizona	0	0	0
California	3,636	3,151	6,787
Connecticut	7	193	200
Delaware	171	107	278
Idaho	0	0	0
Iowa	43	14	57
Indiana	120	3	123
Kansas	414	243	657
Maine	4	8	12
Michigan	62	326	388
Mississippi	0	0	0
Montana	27	33	60
Nebraska	109	199	308
New Hampshire	4	57	61
North Carolina	2	1	3
North Dakota	22	17	39
Oregon	257	393	650
South Dakota	19	42	61
Utah	43	36	79
Virginia	94	274	368
Washington	1	8	9
West Virginia	0	0	0
Wisconsin	35	270	305
Total (24 states)	5,134	5,743	10,877

Source: Progressive Labor 9, No. 1, April 1973, p. 95.

Germany, Sweden, and Norway. By 1945, more than two-thirds of the United States had passed some form of sterilization law and nearly 44,000 such operations had been performed.

The constitutionality of the sterilization laws was debated from the beginning. These laws were often confusing because the distinction between sterilization for eugenic purposes and sterilization for punitive reasons was vague; the laws presented a conglomeration of racial and eugenic phraseologies that were open to subjective interpretations; and many of the statutes considered sterilization a sanitary measure to be determined by authorities and not requiring due process of law. Consequently, court cases were debated at all levels of jurisdiction. For example, in 1912 a suit was filed in New Jersey challenging the right of state institutions to sterilize mentally deficient patients. The court later ruled in favor of state institutions performing such operations. In *Buck v. Bell* (1927), argued from a Virginia statute which permitted the sterilization of an institutionalized, feeble-minded white woman, the U.S. Supreme Court ruled that sterilization was not a violation of due process and equal protection of the laws of the Fourteenth Amendment.[26] The *Buck v. Bell* decision became a major precedent for future litigation, encouraging advocates of enforced sterilization procedures.

Not only were attempts made to sterilized the so-called feeble-minded, but also similar efforts were made to identify and describe families with a predominance of labeled intellectual defect, pauperism, and crime. In an effort to document and thus verify the popular adage, "like father, like son," the family history method of investigation grew to become a leading technique in research efforts. Since it was clear that large groups of European descendants were unsuccessful in the quest for achievement in the land of opportunity, they were quickly labeled "white trash," regardless of the reasons for their plight. The cause for this failure was identified as degeneration.

"DEGENERATE" FAMILIES

The earliest "degenerate" family pedigree was published by Richard L. Dugdale in 1875 and followed up by Arthur H. Estabrook in 1915 under the auspices of the Eugenics Record Office. This family, called the Jukes, became a eugenic cause celebre for those who argued in support of theories of the inheritance of mental and social defects—in spite of Dugdale's warning of "environmental considerations."[27] The family was alleged to have produced many offspring classified as "immoral," "harlots," "lechers," "paupers," "drunkards," "fornicators," "murderers," "rapists," and "thieves." The Industrial Revolution scattered the Juke families from Connecticut to Minnesota in search of new employment opportunities. It was at this point that Estabrook, with the financial assistance of a Carnegie grant, traced the families noting their social and mental conditions. The original investigation by Dugdale was from a sociological stance, whereas Estabrook's follow-up emphasized only the genetic aspect of inbreeding.

In 1897, eight-year-old Deborah Kallikak (a fictitious name created by Henry Goddard from the Greek *kalos*, "good," and *kakos*, "bad") was committed to the Vineland (New Jersey) Training School for Backward and Feebleminded Children. Shortly after her commitment, Goddard, who had established a research department at Vineland, began a number of family history research ventures. With a team of researchers, an extensive investigation was launched into Deborah Kallikak's family history. The results of this study were documented as proof-positive supporting the bad seed concept because the family was purported to consist of two branches, one "normal" and the other "degenerate."[28]

The investigation claimed to produce documentary evidence that Martin Kallikak, a Revolutionary War soldier, fathered both good and bad progeny as a result of his involvement with a feebleminded tavern girl and his later marriage to a "good" Quaker girl (Figure 4.3). Goddard reported finding 480 descendants, of which 143 were feebleminded, 33 were sexually immoral, 24 were alcoholics, and many others were brothel keepers and criminals.

A number of family histories were published during this period that followed the Kallikak format and claimed to document extensive pedigrees of degeneracy. These investigations played an important role in biasing scholars, as well as the general public, toward the "bad seed" philosophy. Among these popular studies were the following: the *Ishmaelites* (Estabrook), the *Dack Family* (Finlayson), *The Hill Folk: Report on a Rural Community of Hereditary Defects* (Danielson and Davenport), and the *Mongrel Virginians* (Estabrook and McDougle). However, it was the study of the Kallikak family that achieved prominence and provided material for frequent lectures and subject matter for many basic psychology courses.

While the theme of family degeneracy was a popular subject, it was probably not a major influence in the decision by American psychologists to support eugenic programs. Several outstanding psychologists of this period did contribute leadership and intellectual support to the race-betterment movements, however, these advocates strongly influenced generations of students, colleagues, and other followers. Among these leaders were G. Stanley Hall and Edward L. Thorndike.

EUROCENTRISM: CYCLE OF SCIENTIFIC RACISM

The continuous flow of Eurocentric meandering supporting the intellectual superiority of whites has been more than a nuisance for Blacks. Required to expend an inordinate amount of intellectual and emotional strength in responding to these critics, Blacks sapped much of their energies, which should have been directed elsewhere. Almost as certainly as the changing of the seasons, contributions to scientific racism have recurred throughout the twentieth century. Like salmon returning to their spawning ground, Eurocentric psychometricians and their mettle swam against the tide by cyclically reviving national conscience and furious debate with their sordid schemes of racial intelligence superiority.

MARTIN KALLIKAK

FIGURE 4.3 The influence of heredity as demonstrated by the "good" and the "bad" fictionalized Kallikaks. Note the "bad" are drawn with thick lips, pronounced features, and horns.

Source: Henry E. Garrett, *General Psychology* (New York: American Book Company, 1955), 65. Reprinted by permission.

Each prophet proclaimed the same message: Black people occupy the bottom rung of the mathematically useless intelligence quotience ladder, and social programs—designed by spendthrift liberal agendas—are unable to narrow the gap. The primary reason for social stratification, they claim, is genetic difference. These prophets appeared before and after the *Brown* (1954) decision, which signaled the end to racially segregated public schools; psychology's scientific racists fought hard to provide statistical evidence to prevent racial integration in the public schools. During the 1960s, eminent psychologist Henry Garrett's tract "How Classroom Desegregation Will Work" supplied weak comparative IQ test data between whites and Blacks and cranial capacities to argue for the end of compensatory education programs such as Head Start and Follow Through. Fortunately, Garrett's attempts resulted in negligible consequences.

The decade of the 1970s saw the reemergence of these counterbalancing psychologists seemingly bent on undoing social progress by again mismeasuring intelligence, thus, reifying the hypothetical construct of the *g* factor. In 1969, Berkeley educational psychologist Arthur Jensen strode into prominence just as the United States was establishing federally financed compensatory programs designed to prepare disadvantaged children for increased learning opportunities. His 1969 article "How Much Can We Boost IQ and Scholastic Achievement" was aimed toward discrediting the purpose of such programs by revitalizing the tired racist theme that inheritance accounts for 80 percent of the variability in intelligence. Although Jensen attracted a following of supporters, Illinois professor Jerry Hirsch examined Jensen's research and "uncovered literal misrepresentations of a kind and to an extent that erodes all confidence in it (and in him) as a reliable source of information."[29] Hirsch further questioned the derivation of Jensen's formula for estimating broad heritability. "He did not say how this formula is derived. It has no theoretical justification nor does it estimate heritability broad or narrow."[30]

Jensen's speculations were supported by physicist William Schockley who advanced a bizarre cash payment plan to Black people with IQs below 100 who would voluntarily submit to sterilization operations:

> [If] a bonus rate of $1,000 for each point below 100 IQ, $30,000 [were] put in trust for a 70 IQ moron of twenty-child potential, it might return $250,000 to taxpayers in reduced cost of mental retardation care.[31]

Generally regarded as an eccentric, Schockley defended his thesis with a straight-faced demeanor. Like his friends, he drew upon studies comparing the intelligence quotients of identical white twins separated at birth and subsequently reared in different environments. These studies reported that the measured IQs were similar in identical twins regardless of environmental differences. Schockley advocated a national genetics control program to counteract what he termed "dysgenics, a retroactive evolution through the disproportionate reproduction of the genetically disadvantaged."[32] According to this view, the reported lower IQ scores of Black Americans are due to inheritance rather than to environmental factors.

While many Americans viewed the passing of the Garrett-Jensen-Schockley era with relief, the concept of the genetically disadvantaged comprising "a class of people deficient in [higher IQ scores] and increasingly doomed to labor, if they find work at all" served as a precursor for Richard Herrnstein and Charles Murray's *The Bell Curve: Intelligence and Class Structure in American Life*, published near the end of the twentieth century. These authors produced data from racially biased scientists supporting what they claimed is a "taboo fact that intelligence levels differ among ethnic groups . . . already well-known and widely discussed among psychometricians and other scholars."[33] Lamentably, *The Bell Curve* falls in line with earlier racially categorized statistics ignoring social-environmental factors such as income. *The Bell Curve* served up an "old wine from a new bottle" utilizing data from racially biased researchers who received financial support from questionable funding resources.

THE PIONEER FUND

Harry Laughlin, in 1904, was on the receiving end of steel magnate Andrew Carnegie's financial support for the Eugenics Society; in 1910 he was in a similar position when the Harriman family contributed toward the establishment of the Eugenics Record Office; in 1937 he was in a similar position when textile tycoon Wickliffe Draper became the major contributor to the Pioneer Fund. This largess became a conduit for the purpose of funding professors and other researchers to "improve the character of the American people" through race betterment principles and to encourage the procreation of "white persons who settled in the original 13 colonies prior to the adoption of the constitution and/or related stocks."[34] Over the next thirty years, the Pioneer Fund provided financial assistance to a number of academics whose research was directed toward establishing a hereditarian point of view. With assets in the millions of dollars, the Pioneer Fund supported, and continues to support, a number of racial studies in the United States and in Ireland. Recipients include the American Immigration Control Federation; the Foundation of Human Understanding; Richard Lynn, professor of psychology at the University of Ulster; Hans Eysenck's Institute of Psychiatry at the University of London; and Seymour Itzkoff of Smith College.[35] Among the most outlandish studies supported by the Pioneer Fund is one by psychology professor J. Phillipe Ruston of the University of Western Ontario who "focused for years on proving that the bigger one's brain and the smaller one's genitals," the greater one's intelligence.[36] Ruston's work leaves one wondering about his inspiration. Nonetheless, in spite of the obstacles and stereotypes presented by deterministic research studies, the promise of the psychology discipline to understand, predict, and control behavior was interpreted as a vitally useful and important subject matter area by the emerging Black academic world.

BLACK AMERICANS AND PSYCHOLOGY

Conclusions reached by eugenicists were declared invalid or meaningless or just ignored by Black professors and other professionals, and the reasoning was obvious. Eugenicists were correctly viewed as white supremacists using the concept of genetics as their weaponry against Black people. During this period, a sense of helplessness prevailed among Black academicians whose voices of dissent were simply ignored and made little or no impact on the white research community. The white academic community was indifferent to the remarks of Black scholars. While the armchair speculations made by eugenicists were discussed by Black scholars, psychological science—sans eugenics indoctrination—was the thrust in the training of prospective Black teachers, ministers, and physicians, who were desperately needed in the neglected Black community.

Part Two will focus on the role of psychology in America's historically Black colleges and of the individuals who helped to shape the field of psychology into useful tools for the betterment of the country.

NOTES

1. *Ancient Egyptian Paintings.* Nina M. Davies, compiler (Chicago: University of Chicago Press, 1936), pl. XCV.
2. S. J. Gould, *The Mismeasure of Man* (New York: W. W. Norton, 1981), 80.

3. Ibid., 54.

4. C. Babbage, *Reflections on the Decline of Science in England and on Some of Its Causes* (London: B. Fellowes, Ludgate Street, 1830), 174–190.

5. Ibid.

6. Mason and Dixon's line is usually thought of as the land survey that divides the North and the South in the United States. Actually it is the east-west boundary line that separates Pennsylvania from Maryland and part of West Virginia. Before the Civil War, the southern boundary of Pennsylvania was considered the dividing line between the slave and nonslave states.

7. C. Harris, "3 Say Briton Falsified Data on IQ," *Washington Post*, October 29, 1976, sec. A20. A number of excellent discussions are available on this subject. See L. Kamin, *The Science and Politics of I.Q.* (Lawrence Erlbaum: Potomac, Md., 1974).' Arthur Jensen defended Burt in "Did Sir Cyril Burt Fake His Research on Heritability of Intelligence? Part II," *Phi Delta Kappan*, 1976, 491–492.

8. R. C. Tryon, "Genetic Differences in Maze Learning in Rats," *Intelligence: Its Nature and Nurture*, National Society for the Study of Education, Thirty-Ninth Yearbook, Part I (Bloomington, Ill.: Public School Publishing Company, 1940), 111–119.

9. M. Burlingame and C. P. Stone, "Family Resemblance in Maze-Learning Ability in White Rats," *Nature and Nurture, Their Influence Upon Intelligence*, National Society for the Study of Education, Twenty-Seventh Yearbook, Part I (Bloomington, Ill.: Public School Publishing Company, 1938), 89–99.

10. Tryon, "Genetic Differences in Maze Learning," 112.

11. L. V. Searle, "The Organization of Hereditary Maze-Brightness and Maze-Dullness," *Genetic Psychology Monograph* 39 (1949): 279–325.

12. Plato, *Republic*, trans. Paul Shorey, The Loeb Classical Library (New York: Putnam, 1935), 30.

13. T. R. Malthus, *An Essay on the Principle of Population* (London: J. Johnson Company, 1803).

14. A. H. Hersh, "Eugenics," *The Encyclopedia Americana* 10 (Danbury, C.T.: Grolier, 1996), p. 567.

15. Madison Grant, Irving Fisher, Fairfield Osborne, and Henry Crampton joined Laughlin in establishing the American Eugenic Society. These men felt that the white race was superior to other races and that the "Nordic" white was superior to other whites.

16. H. H. Laughlin, "Report No. 1," vol. 1 (Cold Spring Harbor, N. Y.: Eugenics Record Office, June 1913).

17. C. B. Davenport, *Heredity in Relationship to Eugenics* (1911; reprinted New York: Arno, 1972).

18. The American Breeders Association (later called the American Genetics Association) was organized to bring together animal and plant breeders to realize the importance of the laws of heredity. The committee on eugenics of this

organization included psychologists Robert M. Yerkes, Harvard University; Madison Bentley, Cornell University; and psychiatrist Adolf Meyer, Johns Hopkins University.

19. Laughlin, "Report No. 1."

20. C. B. Davenport, *The Trait Book,* vol. 6 (Cold Spring Harbor, N.Y.: Eugenics Record Office, 1912), 3.

21. Laughlin, "Report No. 1."

22. D. W. LaRue, "Teaching Eugenics," *Eugenical News* (August 1917): 62.

23. During this era, social misfits were classified as the *5 Ds:* dependent, a tramp or pauper; defective, manic-depressive or the senile dement; deficient, idiot or imbecile; delinquent, thief or truant; and degenerate, sadist or moral imbecile.

24. H. Laughlin, "Report of the Committee to Study and to Report on the Best Practical Means of Cutting Off the Defective Germ-Plasm in the American Population. 1. The Scope of the Committee's Work." *Bulletin 10A,* (Cold Spring Harbor, N.Y.: Eugenics Record Office, 1914), 7.

25. S. Kuhl, *The Nazi Connection: Eugenics, American Racism, and German National Socialism* (New York: Oxford Press, 1994), 83.

26. *Buck v. Bell,* Superintendent, 274 US 200, United States Supreme Court, 1927.

27. R. L. Dugdale, *The Jukes: A Study in Crime, Pauperism, Disease, and Heredity* (New York: Putnam, 1910), and A. H. Estabrook, *The Jukes in 1915* (Washington, D.C.: Carnegie Institution, 1916).

28. H. H. Goddard, *The Kallikak Family: A Study in the Heredity of Feeblemindedness* (New York: Macmillan, 1912).

29. J. Hirsch, "To 'Unfrock the Charlatans,' " *Sage Race Relations Abstract 6,* no. 2 (May 1981): 1–62.

30. Ibid.

31. Kuhl, *The Nazi Connection,* 7.

32. *U.S. News and World Report,* "Is Quality of U.S. Population Declining?" (November 22, 1965). Report based on symposium, Genetics and the Future of Man (1965) held at Gustavus Adolphus College (Minn.) from William Schockley, "Population Control or Eugenics."

33. R. Herrnstein and C. Murray, *The Bell Curve: Intelligence and Class Structure in American Life* (New York: Free Press, 1994), dust jacket.

34. J. Mercer, "A Fascination With Genetics," *The Chronicle of Higher Education* (December 1994): A28. (For an excellent discussion of the Pioneer Fund, see Hirsch, "To 'Unfrock the Charlatans,' " 13.)

35. Ibid., A28.

36. Ibid., A29.

▶ Part II

Psychology and Psychologists

Chapter 5
The Psychology of Survival and Education

Chapter 6
Black Psychologists: Training, Employment, and Organizations

Chapter 7
Production of Black Psychologists in America

Chapter 8
Francis Cecil Sumner: Father of Black American Psychologists

► 5

The Psychology of Survival and Education

The struggle to secure a formal education has been a long and arduous path. Unlike other immigrants to this country, the African came to America not to escape oppression and to seek life, liberty, and the pursuit of happiness but to be oppressed and enslaved. The stigma that had been attached to blackness provided the psychological fuel to support this injustice—slavery. Africans were brought to the New World in the early 1500s by Spanish colonists from the West Indies to establish sugarcane plantations on the southeastern coast of North America. However, disease and other ill fortunes forced most of these slaves and Spaniards to return to Hispaniola. Almost a hundred years later, in 1619, "a dutch man of warre docked at Jamestown, Virginia and sold twenty negars" as servants to English colonists—marking the African diasporic struggle for existence in the New World.

Nearly two centuries later, as the cotton gin was perfected, the demand for slaves rose dramatically, and what had been a small band of African servants grew to a magnitude of over four million throughout North America.

THE PSYCHOLOGY OF SURVIVAL

As enslaved Africans increasingly became the vital cog in the Southern capital economy, their presence posed an immediate need to maintain them as a subjugated workforce. Both physical and psychological subjugation were necessary because of their sheer numbers—more often than not, the Black population exceeded the white population. Since the slaves were cast as beasts of burden with no emotional needs, the stage was set for complete bondage. While the process of destroying cultures, personal identities, languages, self-esteems, and self-concepts continued, the Africans were referred to as "bucks," "wenches," and "pickaninnies." As an institution, slavery was designed to bring about the loss of self-identity and to create a people whose physical and emotional needs could only be met by their subjugators. The pathological acceptance of the master's value system totally devalued the slave. Family units were ignored; the male slave was least likely to receive emotional reciprocity from the master thereby fostering self-hatred and frustration. It was literally impossible for a slave to assume minor dignity or authority among his peers except as an entertainer or preacher. He was sold, bartered, and traded without consideration of significant others; even in sickness, the slave's utilitarian value was the foremost concern. The slave was treated in the same fashion as a veterinarian would tend a farm animal. As a house slave, the male could only assume positions as valet, carriageman, butler, or handyman. Demasculinization was the result. On the other hand, while the Black woman possessed little or no opportunity for emotional reciprocity, she was often regarded as property to be used in any manner—by the master. The rape of a Black woman (by anyone other than the slave master) was considered a crime only because it involved trespassing and destroying personal property.[1] Black women often became sexual objects for the disposal by white men. House slaves became nursemaids and surrogate parents for many of the master's children—relegating the slave's own children to lesser care.[2] The field slave was simply a tool for labor and was most exposed to extreme hardships and labor. The destruction of the emotional life of the field slave was severe, and conditions for mere survival were harsh. Any form of disobedience could lead to violent repression for both males and females—thereby holding the slaves in complete psychological bondage. With the destruction of the slave's security, psychological well being, and other human needs, the slave was left with only three major options: (1) to psychologically identify with the slave master, (2) to escape from the slave master, or (3) to physically attack or fight the slave master.

IDENTIFICATION WITH THE SLAVE MASTER

Identification with the oppressor was a chief survival technique as slaves incorporated the values and attitudes of the slave master. In this manner, sharing in the master's triumphs or failures, slaves avoided feelings of incompetency because the master's actions became a substitute for their own. If the master was happy so was the slave; and on the other hand, if the master was sad so was the slave. Thus, the slave was able to resolve conflicts vicariously through identifying with the oppressor. Identification was a form of self-defense in situations where the slave felt utterly helpless and unable to rectify his or her own needs with reality. With the destruction of the self, a complete acceptance of inferiority evolved. What could have been considered deleterious activities were consciously incorporated into normative behavior. For example, feeling fully inferior, the slave would acquiesce by removing his hat in the presence of a "superior" individual or step from the pathway of a "superior." No disagreement would be expressed nor would the slave's own concerns supersede the concerns of the "superior." Here was the birthing ground of the stereotypical "Uncle Tom" and "Sambo." Finally, identification became a successful mechanism for survival under conditions that would not allow any other reaction. Before the end of the nineteenth century, these cases of obsequiousness would be viewed as negative and undesirable by naive individuals.

FLIGHT AND ESCAPE REACTIONS

Celestial navigation provided a road map to freedom for escaping slaves: "Follow the North Star—Follow the Drinking Gourd," (the Big Dipper). These became symbols for freedom.[3] As escape routes became more exact and effective, an Underground Railway created safe havens for sequestering fugitive slaves on their way north. Spirituals contained secret codes for escaping and negotiating conduits to freedom. Harriet Tubman, an escaped slave, the most heroic "conductor" who made numerous trips into the deep South, is said to have sung this song in shadowy corners of the night, conveying to slaves her presence and for them to prepare for the trip to freedom:

> Go down Moses! Way down in Egypt Land
> And tell old Pharaoh . . .
> To let my people go.[4]

Reactions from Slave Owners

Supporters of slavery struggled to explain why slaves were running away (besides the obvious explanation). They attempted to prove scientifically that their earlier exhortations of the happy slave were truthful and that the South was a "rightful" milieu and that servitude was the rightful condition for the African. One such medical authority went so far to declare that the "Negro's brain froze in a cold climate, inducing insanity" and urged, "out of kindness to the Negro, that he be kept in the South."[5] These supporters of slavery felt that servitude fulfilled God's designated role because the African was cursed to be a submissive "knee bender" requiring the control of others.[6] As frustrated slave owners searched to explain why supposedly contented and happy slaves would want to run away or escape bondage, accusations were leveled at the border state slave owners, claiming that they created the problem by being too lenient, treating them as equals, and "making little or no distinction in regard to color." The Underground Railroad's success made it clear that discontentment among slaves was widespread and that the escapes would continue, regardless of these speculations.

Psychological Diagnoses for Runaway Behavior

Physician Benjamin Rush, one of the signers of the Declaration of Independence and later called the Father of American Psychiatry, asserted that the African possessed illnesses that were peculiar to the Negro race of humanity. This set the stage for another physician, Dr. Samuel Cartwright, to make remarkable claims that the slave's running away indicated a mental disorder called *drapetomania,* which he said was common to Blacks and to cats. In discussing "diseases peculiar to the African," Cartwright utilized the language of science and offered the following advice to prevent slaves from running away.

> Before negroes run away . . . they become sulky and dissatisfied. The cause of this sulkiness and dissatisfaction should be inquired into and removed, or they are apt to run away or fall into the negro consumption. When sulky and dissatisfied without cause, the experience of those on the line and elsewhere was decidedly in favor of whipping them out of it, as a preventive measure against absconding, or other bad conduct. It was called whipping the devil out of them.[7]

In what could have qualified as entries in a racist "Diagnostic and Statistical Manual (DSM) for Mental Disorders," Dr. Cartwright offered hope to the slave master: "With the advantage of proper medical advice, strictly followed, this troublesome practice that many negroes have of running away, can be almost entirely prevented, although the slaves be located on the borders of a free State, within a stone's throw of the abolitionists.[8] Cartwright's solution promised that

> If treated kindly, well fed and clothed with fuel enough to keep a small fire burning all night, separated into families, each family having its own house—not permitted to run about at night, or to visit their neighbors, or to receive visits, or to use intoxicating liquors, and not overworked or exposed too much to the weather, they are very easily governed—more so than any other people in the world.[9]

Not satisfied with drapetomania, Cartwright labeled another disease: *Dyaesthesia Aethiopis,* or "Hebetude of Mind and Obtuse Sensibility of Body-Called by Overseers, 'Rascality,' " which affected "free negroes" more than slaves. Here, he reasoned slaves would contract this disease if they were treated as free men. He described the symptoms as behaviors of careless movements that involved

> stupidness of mind and insensibility of the nerves induced by the disease. Thus, they break, waste and destroy everything they handle—abuse horses and cattle—tear, burn or rend their own clothing, and paying no attention to the rights of property, they steal . . . they wander about at night, and keep in a half-nodding sleep during the day. They slight their work—cut up corn, cane, cotton or tobacco when hoeing it, as if for pure mischief.[10]

Similar to the hope he held for curing drapetomania, Cartwright felt that this *dyaesthesia Aethiopis* was easily curable if his instructions were followed:

> the skin is dry, thick and harsh to the touch, and the liver inactive. The liver, skin and kidneys should be stimulated to activity, and be made assist in decarbonising the blood. The best means to stimulate the skin is, first to have the patient well washed with warm water and soap, then to anoint it all over with oil, and to slap the oil in with a broad leather strap then to put

the patient to some kind of work in the open air and sunshine, that will compel him to expand his lungs, as chopping wood, splitting rails or sawing with the cross-cut or whip saw . . . such treatment will, in a short time, effect a cure.[11]

Following Thomas Szasz's (1970) critique and guidelines, the rationale for supporting drapetomania and *dysaethesia Aethiopis* had extreme importance and relevance to the occurrence of racism and mental health because (1) it augmented the use of authority and vocabulary of medical science to dehumanize Black people; (2) it helped generate language and reasoning to justify coercive control of individual behavior; and (3) the omission of this knowledge from textbooks and other pedagogy undermined efforts to understand the bases of racism in psychology and psychiatry.[12]

AGGRESSIVE REACTIONS

As the Black population increased, so did the number of slave revolts. Two prominent examples were Denmark Vesey's insurrection in South Carolina in 1822 and Nat Turner's revolt in Virginia in 1831. Nat Turner, by all accounts, was a brilliant slave preacher who sharpened his early reading skills through "sabbath schools" and Bible study. Denmark Vesey, likewise an intelligent man, acquired his basic skills in much the same way as Turner. Because leadership in these insurrections was traced to literate slaves, harsh laws forbidding the instruction of Blacks in reading, writing, and arithmetic were enacted as defensive measures throughout the South. These laws, later called the Black Codes, had statutes which specifically prohibited the education of slaves, and any white person convicted of teaching Blacks faced heavy fines and imprisonment while the slave faced cruel punishments.[13] Many of the restrictions against the education of slaves were directed against slave masters who advocated educating slaves so as to increase their economic efficiency. In other instances, these codes were directed toward zealous abolitionists who taught slaves to read English in order for them to read their Bibles. (A number of extremely talented Africans in the United States were noted during this era, for instance, Phyllis Wheatley and Benjamin Banneker, who removed doubts that Africans were not literate or intelligent.) The hysteria of this era eventually led to paranoic monitoring of slaves' leisure activities to the point that only oral communication was allowed among slaves. This latter restriction was often carried to incredible extremes: In Mississippi, for example, slaves were prevented from beating drums or blowing horns for fear of secret messages being transmitted.

While there were many instances where slaves and southern freedmen (such as in Charleston, S.C.) were formally educated or secretly taught at night under the direction of friends and sympathizers, the restriction on educational pursuits in the nineteenth century caused slaves to regard reading and writing as forbidden fruit. The *Black Codes* all but removed any hope for the majority of slaves to acquire formal education. Even in the North, while many freedmen managed to obtain limited schooling, frequently they faced possibilities of physical harm. In a number of instances, prejudice against freedmen trying to secure an education led to acts of violence on the part of "loyal white citizens." Historical accounts reveal many cases in which Black children were stoned on their way to and from schools and their teachers publicly whipped. While teaching materials were scant in the makeshift freedmen schools, publications of northern tract societies, Bibles, miscellanies from New England attics, and similar materials substituted for textbooks and other conventional teaching aids. In a few cases, freedmen sailed to England and Scotland to become college educated while some attended open-door liberal American institutions. Berea College (Kentucky) and Oberlin College (Ohio) were prime examples of the liberal schools of this period. In 1862, John Brown Russworm at Bowdoin College (Maine), Edward Jones at Amherst College (Massachusetts), and later Mary Jane Patterson at Oberlin became the first Blacks in the United States to receive college degrees. By the time of the Emancipation Proclamation, approximately forty Black men and women had managed to earn college degrees.

During the Civil War, the combination of warfare and the quest for learning by Black soldiers produced some memorial scenes:

Passing through a sally-port at Fort Hudson, a few days since, near that rugged and broken ground made memorable by the desperate charge of the colored regiments, June 14th, 1863, I met a corporal coming in from the outworks with his gun upon his shoulder, and hanging from the bayonet by a bit of cord a Webster's spelling-book. Already, hundreds in every regiment have learned to read and write. In almost every tent, the spelling-book and New Testament lie side by side with weapons of war. The negroes fight and the negroes read.[14]

In the months and years that immediately followed the war, formal schools for Black people were created and higher education for the exslaves began.

THE EMERGENCE OF BLACK COLLEGES

Following the war, the old secret night schools for slaves were converted to open day schools as federal efforts, missionary associations, and aid societies vigorously began to establish learning centers for the "Black refugees" or, as the freed slaves were referred to by the military, "contrabands of war." (Prior to the Emancipation Proclamation, freed slaves were referred to as "contraband.") A number of these schools were established by the all-white American Missionary Association and the Freedmen's Aid Society of the Methodist Episcopal Church staffed with teachers who were missionaries of these benevolent and religious orders. In 1854, Lincoln University in Pennsylvania became the first American institution for Blacks chartered to grant higher degrees. Two years later, Wilberforce University was established in Ohio. In the next fifteen years, Shaw University (1865), Fisk University (1866), Talladega College (1867), Howard University (1867), Tougaloo College (1869), and Benedict College (1871) were all founded. In 1866, Missouri became the first state to establish a separate public college for Blacks. By 1885, Atlanta had become the home of five Black institutions: Morehouse College, Clark College, Spelman College, Morris Brown College, and Atlanta University.[15]

The federal government's land grant provisions (Morrill Acts 1862, 1890)[16] established state-supported institutions; thus, with the addition of the Black religious denominations more Black colleges were created. These schools were colleges or normal schools in name only because they provided education at the primary level only. Not until after World War I, did these colleges begin to enroll students at the collegiate level.[17] In 1928, the Southern Association of Colleges and Secondary Schools decided to rate Black institutions elevating the status and acceptance of the Black colleges.

By 1940, more than one hundred Black colleges and universities were located in seventeen southern states, enrolling most of their students from the South's segregated public school system (Table 5.1). Serving purposes unprecedented in the annals of formal education in the United States, these physically inadequate colleges embarked on a mission to train needed professionals for Black communities. Often located in the same vicinity as a large, well-to-do, all-white college, the

TABLE 5.1   Establishment of Black Colleges and Universities (1854–1935)

Institution	Location	Year Founded
1. Lincoln University	Chester County, Pa.	1854
2. Wilberforce University	Wilberforce, Ohio	1856
3. Atlanta University	Atlanta, Ga.	1860
4. Shaw University	Raleigh, N. C.	1865
5. Virginia Union University	Richmond, Va.	1865
6. Fisk University	Nashville, Tenn.	1865
7. Lincoln University	Jefferson City, Mo.	1866
8. Howard University	Washington, D. C.	1867
9. Talladega College	Talladega, Ala.	1867
10. Morehouse College	Atlanta, Ga.	1867
11. Johnson C. Smith University	Charlotte, N. C.	1867
12. Saint Augustine's College	Raleigh, N. C.	1867
13. Roger Williams University	Nashville, Tenn.	1867
14. Storer College	Harper's Ferry, W. Va.	1868
15. Hampton Institute	Hampton, Va.	1868
16. Straight College	New Orleans, La.	1868
17. New Orleans University	New Orleans, La.	1869
18. Tougaloo College	Tougaloo, Miss.	1869
19. Claflin University	Orangeburg, S. C.	1869
20. LeMoyne College	Memphis, Tenn.	1870
21. Allen University	Columbia, S. C.	1870
22. Benedict College	Columbia, S. C.	1870
23. Barber-Scotia College	Concord, N. C.	1870
24. Leland University	Baker, La.	1870
25. Clark University	Atlanta, Ga.	1870
26. Alcorn A. & M. College	Alcorn, Miss.	1871
27. Knoxville College	Knoxville, Tenn.	1872
28. Brewer Junior College	Greenwood, S. C.	1872
29. Wiley College	Marshall, Texas	1873
30. Alabama State Teachers College	Montgomery, Ala.	1874
31. Alabama State A. & M. Normal	Huntsville, Ala.	1875
32. Arkansas A. M. & N. College	Pine Bluff, Ark.	1875
33. Morgan College	Baltimore, Md.	1876
34. Philander Smith College	Little Rock, Ark.	1877
35. Western University	Kansas City, Kans.	1877
36. Jackson College	Jackson, Miss.	1877
37. State Normal School	Fayetteville, N. C.	1877
38. Tillotson College	Austin, Texas	1877
39. Selma University	Selma, Ala.	1878
40. Lane College	Jackson, Tenn.	1878
41. Voorhees N. & I. School	Denmark, S. C.	1879
42. Tuskegee N. & I. Institute	Tuskagee, Ala.	1881
43. Spelman College	Atlanta, Ga.	1881
44. Southern Christian Institute	Edwards, Miss.	1881
45. Bettis Academy	Trenton, S. C.	1881
46. Morristown N. & I. College	Morristown, Tenn.	1881
47. Bishop College	Marshall, Texas	1881
48. Paul Quinn College	Waco, Texas	1881
49. Paine College	Augusta, Ga.	1882
50. Livingstone College	Salisbury, N. C.	1882
51. Edward Waters College	Jacksonville, Fla.	1883
52. Swift Memorial College	Rogersville, Tenn.	1883
53. Virginia State College	Petersburg, Va.	1883
54. Arkansas Baptist College	Little Rock, Ark.	1885

Continued

TABLE 5.1 *Continued*

Institution	Location	Year Founded
55. Morris Brown College	Atlanta, Ga.	1885
56. Natchez College	Natchez, Miss.	1885
57. Kittrell College	Kittrell, N. C.	1885
58. Shorter College	North Little Rock, Ark.	1886
59. Princess Anne Academy	Princess Anne, Md.	1886
60. Rust College	Holly Springs, Miss.	1886
61. Mary Allen Seminary	Crockett, Texas	1886
62. Prairie View State College	Prairie View, Texas	1886
63. Florida A. & M. College	Tallahassee, Fla.	1887
64. Guadalupe College	Sequin, Texas	1887
65. St. Paul N. & I. College	Lawrenceville, Va.	1888
66. Virginia College & Seminary	Lynchburg, Va.	1888
67. State Normal School	Elizabeth City, N. C.	1889
68. Georgia State Ind. College	Savannah, Ga.	1890
69. Coleman College	Gibsland, La.	1890
70. Stowe Teachers College	St. Louis, Mo.	1890
71. State College for Colored Youth	Dover, Del.	1891
72. The A. & T. College	Greensboro, N. C.	1891
73. West Virginia State College	Institute, W. Va.	1891
74. Florida N. & I. College	St. Augustine, Fla.	1892
75. Fort Valley N. & I. School	Fort Valley, Ga.	1893
76. Texas College	Tyler, Texas	1894
77. Brick Junior College	Bricks, N. C.	1895
78. State A. & M. College	Orangeburg, S. C.	1895
79. Kentucky State Ind. College	Frankfort, Ky.	1896
80. Colored A. & N. University	Langston, Okla.	1897
81. St. Phillips Junior College	San Antonio, Texas	1898
82. Central City College	Macon, Ga.	1899
83. Samuel Houston College	Austin, Texas	1900
84. Miles Memorial College	Birmingham, Ala.	1902
85. Coppin Normal School	Baltimore, Md.	1902
86. Bethune Cookman College	Daytona Beach, Fla.	1904
87. Georgia N. & A. College	Albany, Ga.	1905
88. Louisiana N. & I. College	Grambling, La.	1905
89. Morris College	Sumter, S. C.	1905
90. Butler College	Tyler, Texas	1905
91. Mississippi Industrial College	Holly Springs, Miss.	1906
92. Jarvis Christian College	Hawkins, Texas	1909
93. West Kentucky Ind. College	Paducah, Ky.	1910
94. Maryland Normal School	Bowie, Md.	1911
95. Lincoln Institute	Lincoln Ridge, Ky.	1912
96. Tennessee A. & I. College	Nashville, Tenn.	1912
97. Cheyney Training School	Cheyney, Pa.	1913
98. Southern University	Scotlandville, La.	1914
99. Xavier University	New Orleans, La.	1915
100. Bluefield St. Teachers College	Bluefield, W. Va.	1921
101. N. C. College for Negroes	Durham, N. C.	1925
102. Winston-Salem Teachers College	Winston-Salem, N. C.	1925
103. Bennett College	Greensboro, N. C.	1926
104. Houston Junior College	Houston, Texas	1927
105. Dunbar Junior College	Little Rock, Ark.	1929
106. Miner Teachers College	Washington, D. C.	1929
107. Louisville Municipal College	Louisville, Ky.	1931
108. Dillard University	New Orleans, La.	1935
109. State Teachers & Agri. College	Forsyth, Ga.	Unknown

smaller and poorer Black college struggled to provide an adequate environment of higher education. Clearly the Black schools with their limited facilities, understaffed, inadequately funded, were never intended to be on a par with the white institutions: Financial contributions were grossly inadequate in supplementing the intentionally meager state appropriations. As the number of professional Black faculty became increasingly available, they replaced the white missionaries and professors. With growing student enrollments, these teachers faced heavier teaching loads, lower salaries, and fewer benefits compared to their counterparts in the white schools.[18] Yet, in spite of these debilitating circumstances, Black colleges became the spawning grounds for teachers and other professionals who otherwise would have been uneducated.

TEACHING PSYCHOLOGY IN BLACK COLLEGES: SIMILARITIES, NOT DIFFERENCES

Most of the subject matter taught during the early days of the Black colleges consisted of classical discourses. Very little attention was paid to the teaching of science; "the Latin, Greek, geometry, logic, and philosophy already stereotyped in white colleges of the South became the curricula of the Negro colleges."[19] But Black communities' urgent need for elementary and secondary school teachers, preachers, and trade workers led to a type of academic training that deemphasized psychology's brass instrument curriculum and stressed the applied aspects of psychology. This had a direct effect on the content of psychology courses; the German influence in American psychology (which had created the preoccupation with laboratory research in reaction time, "just noticeable differences," and memory exercises) was virtually ignored in the Black schools for more relevant subject matter. So, while white institutions provided for psychology to be taught as a laboratory science and made strenuous efforts to make psychology emulate the "hard" sciences, Black institutions were forced to narrow the discipline to practical applications.

A most important aspect in the teaching of psychology in the Black colleges was the deemphasis on the alleged hereditarian basis for differences in intelligence among individuals, races, and social class—points often stressed in mainstream colleges and universities. While the white schools, particularly at the graduate level, were busily delineating and "splitting the differences" between the IQ scores among various races, Black schools were emphasizing the very opposite stance, that is, the

Psychology Club at Wilberforce University in 1914. Nearly forty students were members of this club, which pre-dated the formation of *Psi Chi*, the National Honor Society of Psychology in 1929.

Source: The Tawana Remembrancer, Wilberforce, Ohio, vol. 1, no. 1 (1914): 55.

similarities between people. It was common for the nearly one hundred black psychology professors and several hundred teachers of education to stress that humans, regardless of race, are far more alike than unalike and that IQ is affected by normal environmental variations. Thus, they emphasized that lack of educational equity and opportunity provide for measurable IQ differences between people. This philosophy was important because it removed the deficit stigma attached by group differences as often discussed by mainstream psychologists and emphasized the inequities found in educational opportunities for Black people. As psychometric research continually bombarded the general and collegiate audiences with the dubious information that Blacks were at least one standard deviation below the mean IQ scores of whites, many professionals contested these findings gained from tests that were considered inaccurate. These concerns were most often discussed in magazines and periodicals read by Blacks and rarely read by whites. Not only were these concerns and the teaching of psychology in Black schools of little significance to mainstream psychologists during this era, this neglect continues as witnessed by historical accounts of psychology. The teaching of psychology in America's Black colleges was strangely ignored; it was a period that did not exist in the eyes of white historians—a period in the "twilight zone." What is true are the results: Hundreds of thousands of students were trained in the psychology classrooms of Black colleges and they eventually staffed America's racially segregated schools.

Following World War I, enrollments in these colleges dramatically increased. By 1933, more than 38,000 students were receiving collegiate instruction, and 97 percent of these students were in colleges in Southern states.[20] It is estimated that between 1920 and 1970, the nation's Black colleges produced more than 1,300 baccalaureate degree holders who each eventually earned a doctorate degree.[21] When factored into the mass equation, hundreds of thousands of Black Americans were trained in these colleges, and in their own unique way, psychology professors taught the science of human behavior both traditionally and nontraditionally. Records indicate that the level of interest in psychology among Black students was quite evident as psychology clubs were organized in many Black schools. It is difficult to imagine any collegiate institution having more profound impact upon its student body than the early Black colleges.

The assignment of psychology courses within departments of education became a frequent practice in both Black and white schools. By the late 1930s, only four Black schools offered psychology as an undergraduate major, a situation that not only limited the opportunities for Blacks to earn a degree in the subject but also directly influenced the popularity of educational psychology. With the emphasis on educational psychology, instruction in experimental psychology and statistical methodology courses was lacking in most programs.

West Virginia State College, an early leader in educational research efforts, initiated a number of interesting investigations during the 1930 to 1940 period among which were a series of studies designed to survey the "status and curricula offerings and aspects of curriculum in colleges for Negroes." The first of these studies was "Psychology in Negro Institutions," in which Herman G. Canady, chairman of West Virginia's psychology department, set out to obtain information concerning: (a) the status of psychology in the curriculum, (b) the nature of the introductory course in psychology, (c) undergraduate courses in psychology, (d) provisions for laboratory work, (e) library equipment, (f) teaching personnel, and (g) research in psychology in America's Black colleges. Canady's data were derived from analyses of questionnaires sent to fifty Black colleges in 1936. Canady's survey revealed that only fourteen institutions, out of the total of fifty, had departments of psychology and that only four of these schools offered psychology as a major subject. In spite of this lack of formal attention to the field, psychology courses were popular with many Black students. Several studies corroborated this finding in appraisals of the popularity of various courses[22] (Table 5.2).

Typically, the colleges surveyed by Canady emphasized basic and applied courses in psychology. These courses were usually one semester in duration and were taught by the lecture-discussion method. Few practical courses existed and laboratory courses were rare, although most professors at these schools indicated they would have offered laboratory experiences if the equipment and space were available.[23] Canady also reported that a total of twenty-eight different courses in psychology were taught during the 1940s (Table 5.3). He specifically drew attention to the absence of certain courses:

> It is of interest to note the larger number of courses of an applied nature and the relatively few in pure and theoretical psychology; also, that no institution offers a course in race psychology and that no institution offers a course with the distinct title of "The Psychology of the Negro."[24]

It appears that Canady had called for the first Black psychology course as early as the 1930s.

TABLE 5.2 Choice of Significant Subjects or Activities Expressed by Undergraduate and Graduate Students in Black Colleges (1936)

Significant Subject	Atlanta		Fisk		Hampton		Howard		Prairie V.		Va. State		Xavier		Total	
	U.G.	G.	U.G.	G.	U.G.	G.	U.G.	G.	U.G.	G.	U.G.	G.	U.G.	G.	U.G.	G.
Social Science	18	24	18	11	7	9	38	27	—	1	6	3	—	1	87	76
Education	10	6	12	15	6	10	21	23	3	3	3	3	3	4	58	64
Science	13	10	9	7	6	7	15	10	—	—	1	1	—	—	44	35
English	10	8	3	3	12	1	9	11	—	—	—	—	3	5	37	28
Research	—	4	—	4	—	5	—	5	—	—	—	1	—	—	—	19
Miscellaneous	1	1	—	2	3	1	4	6	4	2	—	—	4	—	16	12
Psychology	2	2	3	—	3	—	7	4	—	—	—	—	—	1	15	7
Mathematics	3	1	—	—	3	—	5	4	—	—	—	—	—	—	11	5
Foreign Language	2	1	—	—	—	—	5	2	—	—	1	—	1	—	9	3
Music	1	—	3	3	2	—	2	—	—	—	—	—	1	—	9	3
Social Work	—	—	—	—	—	—	—	7	—	—	—	—	—	—	—	7
Business Administration	4	4	1	—	—	1	1	1	—	—	—	—	—	—	6	6
Agriculture	—	—	—	—	—	—	—	—	3	1	1	—	—	—	4	1
Home Economics	—	—	1	—	—	—	2	—	—	—	—	—	—	—	3	—
Library Science	—	—	1	2	—	—	—	1	—	—	—	—	—	—	1	3
Rural Work	—	—	—	—	—	—	—	—	—	3	—	—	—	—	—	3
Total	64	61	51	47	42	34ᵃ	109	101	10	10	12	8	12	11	300	272

Source: Fred McCuistion, *Graduate Instruction for Negroes in the United States* (Nashville: George Peabody College for Teachers, 1939), 79. Reprinted by permission.
ᵃSummer session only

TABLE 5.3 Courses Offered in Psychology in Black Institutions (1936)

Name of Course	Times Offered
Educational Psychology	41
General Psychology	40
Child Psychology	30
Social Psychology	22
Adolescent Psychology	22
Abnormal Psychology	14
Experimental Psychology	7
Statistical Methods	5
Applied Psychology	4
Psychology of Religion	4
Psychological Test	3
Differential Psychology	3
Race Psychology	2
Genetic Psychology	2
Business Psychology	2
Psychology of Learning	2
Recent Schools of Psychology	2
Clinical Psychology	2
Elementary Psychology for Nurses	1
Medical Psychology	1
Legal Psychology	1
Psychological and Psychiatric Social Work	1
Psychology of Personal Adjustment	1
Psychology of Selling and Adjusting	1
Mental Psychology	1
Human Behavior	1
Nations Psychology	1
Comparative Psychology	1

Source: H. G. Canady, "Psychology in Negro Institutions," *West Virginia State Bulletin* 3 (June 1939).

LIBRARY AND RESEARCH FACILITIES IN BLACK COLLEGES

The construction of physical plants and provisions for general library holdings were greatly enhanced through donations by Northern philanthropists. Notable in these efforts was Julius Rosenwald, executive officer of Sears and Roebuck Company in Chicago, who began in 1911 by providing funds to assist in the construction of buildings and libraries at Black schools.[25] The Rosenwald funds not only drew attention to and greatly stimulated the development of libraries at Black colleges, but also played an important role in the formal training of librarians and psychology professors at the graduate level (see Chapter 6). Around 1915, the Carnegie Corporation earmarked funds specifically for the development of libraries and library services in a number of Black schools. However, even with this financial assistance, library facilities continued to be grossly inadequate in meeting the needs of the students.

A total of twenty-six different psychology periodicals were subscribed to by Black college libraries. The most popular journals were the *American Journal of Psychology, Journal of Social Psychology, Journal of Educational Psychology*, and *Mental Hygiene*. The less popular journals, even though subscribed to, were the *Journal of Comparative Psychology, Journal of Genetic Psychology*, and *Psychological Bulletin*.[26]

Only eight psychology professors (three of whom were white) out of a total of eighty-eight psychology professors in the Black colleges reported having published research during the period 1931 to 1936.[27] The heavy commitment to teaching responsibilities and the lack of graduate training undoubtedly contributed to this situation. (Table 5.4 describes

TABLE 5.4 Major Fields of Graduate and Undergraduate Training and Highest Degree Held by Psychology Instructors in Black Colleges (1936)

Major Field of Training	No. of Instructors	Highest Degree Held			
		Ph.D. Ed.D.	M.A. M.S.	B.A. B.S. Ph.B.	B.D.
Psychology	20	5[a]	13	2	
Ed. Psychology	7	2	5		
Education	38	5	28	5	
Philosophy	5	2	2		1
Sociology 7) Theology 1)	10		8		
Relig. Ed. 1) Spanish 1)					
Dept. Omitted	2		2		
Degree Omitted	6				
Totals	88	16	58	7	1
Trained in approved fields	27	7	18	2	

Source: H. G. Canady, "Psychology in Negro Institutions," *West Virginia State Bulletin* 3 (June 1939).
[a]Three of these are white.

the educational training of the professors by listing their highest degree held in 1936.)

Employment Opportunities in Psychology

The limited number of Black role models in psychology and a lack of encouragement from the employment field presented a persistent problem in the recruitment of students for careers in psychology. In order to offset the lack of information about employment opportunities, college catalogs frequently described employment possibilities, but this practice provided inadequate answers to questions of whether job opportunities for Black graduates existed and what specific areas of psychology offered the best chances for jobs.

Lily Brunschwig, one of the few white psychology professors in Black colleges during the late 1930s, called attention to the growing interest her undergraduate students had expressed in choosing psychology as a career. In 1939, to gain information about employment opportunities, she dispatched a questionnaire to Black psychologists and other Blacks trained in the field of psychology. She asked, "What vocational opportunities are or will be available for Negro students wishing to prepare for psychology as a career?" While her study was not intended to provide a complete census of Black psychologists, it did offer an interesting sample of the activities of Black professionals trained in psychology at that time (Table 5.5).

By far the largest number of psychologists who took part in the Brunschwig study described themselves as teachers of psychology.[28] (This finding was to be expected; college teaching was the chief avenue of

TABLE 5.5 Major Activities of Black Psychologists (1940)

Activity	Number of Individuals
Teacher of Psychology—Full Time	8
Teacher of Psychology—76 to 95% of the Time	8
Teacher of Psychology—51 to 75% of the Time	16
Teacher of Psychology—10 to 50% of the Time	14
Psychological Research: School Psychologist	6
Clinical or Consulting Psychologist	1
Psychologist in Nursery School	1
Vocational Guidance, Student Personnel	0
Administrator, College or High School	3

Source: Lily Brunschwig, "Opportunities for Negroes in the Field of Psychology," *Journal of Negro Education* (October 1941): 666. Reprinted by permission of the publisher.

employment in all fields for the highly trained Black.) Of the total number in the Brunschwig study, only seven were engaged in activities such as research, clinical work, and school psychology. The study did note that a substantial representation of Black women had found employment in the profession of psychology at that time. (This was to be expected; a larger number of Black women graduate from college than Black men.) An interesting sidelight of this study was the inclusion of a statement from a young Black psychologist who had secured employment in the face of "vigorous discouragement."

In reply to your letter and questionnaire regarding vocational opportunities for Negroes in the field of psychology, I can sum up my own opinions by saying that Negroes who think of psychology in terms of their life work are preparing for a nonexistent field. But I say, go on and prepare for it. The demand for real psychology will inevitably develop—and it should begin within the next few years . . . The trick in securing work in psychology lies in keeping body and soul together until a job breaks. I did it by three years of social work. Then, in the summer of 1938 I learned that the new director of the clinic of [ ] might receive favorably an application from me. There were many difficulties involved in the acceptance of my application. There had never been a Negro in the clinic; there were white boys as well as Negro boys to be tested; they were not sure that a Negro could adjust to the social conditions of the institution; they were not certain that a Negro employee would be received as apartment mate by a white employee; and so on . . . Finally, all mental resistance to my application was broken down and I came to intern . . . After interning from October to June, I was offered my present position. The vacancy thus created in the clinic made it possible for another Negro to intern. A third Negro, from Howard University, worked under my direction last summer. So this institution may be considered one place where there are opportunities for internship.

One of your questions deals with opportunities for advancement in the field. They are not too good. And this is not a racial problem. The psychologists who are making money are those who have left the field of applied psychology . . . I'd say that opportunities are better for Negroes than for whites, but that isn't saying much. We have white interns now who float from one institution to another as interns—some with three years of experience. There are too many white psychologists for the present demand; Negroes have no place in psychology, as was pointed out to me some time ago, because jobs have not yet opened in Negro institutions. When there are jobs, and this should be rather soon, they will go to those who are prepared for them.[29]

The immediate employment picture was dismal, but prospects for the future expressed by many of the professionals were encouraging, leading Brunschwig to conclude that "vocational opportunities for Negro psychologists will increase" in spite of the "period of social change and uncertainty."[30] Chapter 6, "Black Psychologists: Training, Employment, and Organizations," focuses on seemingly insurmountable odds and problems in training early Black psychologists—the curricula, and the formation of organizations to promote concepts and objectives of Black psychologists in the United States.

NOTES

1. J. H. Franklin, *From Slavery to Freedom: A History of Negro Americans,* 3rd ed. (New York: Knopf, 1967), 188.

2. J. O. Killens, *Black Man's Burden,* (New York: Trident, 1965).

3. "Foller de drinkin' gou'd," were lyrics in a slave song which instructed slaves to follow the stars that formed the Great (Big) Dipper, a route that led to the head waters of the Tombigbee River (Mississippi and Alabama) over the divide and up the Tennessee River to "the grea' big un" (the Ohio River), leading them to freedom. While this was an accurate map, slave bounty hunters ("bushwackers") also learned of the route and often intercepted slaves around Shawneetown, Illinois. This increased the need for the "Underground Railroad" to dodge the bushwackers.

4. As a child, Harriet Tubman (1830–1913) was struck by an overseer, fracturing her skull and causing symptoms of narcolepsy for the rest of her life. In spite of this condition, which caused her to walk with a cane, and with a price on her head, dead or alive, she led more than three hundred slaves to freedom with a rifle always at her side. She boasted, "My train never ran off the track, and I never lost a passenger." Ms. Tubman, without a doubt, was Black America's first hero.

5. S. A. Cartwright, "Essays, being inductions drawn from the Baconian philosophy proving the truth of the Bible and the justice and benevolence of the decree dooming Canaan to be servant of servants; and answering the question of Voltaire: 'On demande quel droit des estrangers tel que les Juifs avaiant sur le pays de Canaan!' " From a series of letters to the Rev. William Winans by Samuel Cartwright . . . Vidalia, La., 1863. In one of these essays, Cartwright explained, "By the discovery of America Japheth became en-

larged as been foretold 3800 years before. He took the whole continent. He literally dwelt in the tents of Shem in Mexico and Central America. No sooner did Japheth begin to enlarge himself, and to dwell in the tents of Shem, than Canaan left his fastnesses in the wilds of Africa, where the white man's foot had never trod, and appeared on the beach to get passage to America, as if drawn whither by an impulse of his nature to fulfill his destiny of becoming Japheth's servant."

6. S. A. Cartwright, "Diseases and Peculiarities of the Negro Race," *New Orleans Medical and Surgical Journal* 7 (1851): 691–715.

7. S. A. Cartwright, "Diseases and Peculiarities of the Negro Race," *DeBow's* 11 (September 1851): 332.

8. Ibid., 671-715.

9. Ibid., 332.

10. Ibid., 334.

11. Ibid., 335.

12. T. S. Szasz, *The Manufacture of Madness; A Comparative Study of the Inquisition and the Mental Health Movement.* (New York: Harper and Row, 1970), 188–189.

13. Early education of Blacks during the 1700s was limited to a few scattered schools. The Society for the Propagation of the Gospel in Foreign Parts established a school for Blacks in Charleston, South Carolina, in 1745 and another in North Carolina in 1763. The New York African Free School, established by the Society in 1786, became the first public school for Blacks. Other schools were established in Henrico County, Virginia; Washington, D.C.; Georgetown; Cincinnati; and New York City.

14. M. F. Armstrong and H. W. Ludlow, *Hampton and Its Students* (New York: Putnam, 1875), 121.

15. Many of the private Black colleges were named after white benefactors and role models, for example, Howard, Wilberforce, Hampton, Spelman, Lincoln, Fisk, and so forth.

16. The first and second Morrill Acts established land-grant colleges in the Southern states that maintained a dual-racial based system of schools. The first Morrill Act (1862) provided for agricultural and mechanical colleges but did not provide for a division of federal funds. As a result of this omission, the Black colleges were severely underfunded. For further discussion see D. O. W. Holmes, *The Evolution of the Negro College* (New York: Arno, 1969), 150–156.

17. Enrollments in these colleges increased at the collegiate level following World War I. For further discussion see "Survey of Negro Colleges and Universities," United States Department of the Interior, Bureau of Education Bulletin (1928), 7.

18. For an interesting account of the plight of Black professors during the 1930s see A. P. Davis, "The Negro Professor," *The Crisis* (April 1936): 103–104.

19. F. McCuistion, *Graduate Instruction for Negroes in the United States* (Nashville, Tenn.: George Peabody College for Teachers, 1939), 12.

20. H. Rose, "Negro Educators in Academic Marketplace," *The Journal of Negro Education* vol. XXXV, no. 1 (Winter 1966): 18–26.

21. Ibid.

22. H. G. Canady, "Psychology in Negro Institutions," *West Virginia State Bulletin* 3 (June 1939).

23. Ibid., 168.

24. Ibid., 168.

25. E. R. Embree and J. Waxman, *Investment in People: The Story of the Julius Rosenwald Fund* (New York: Harper and Brothers, 1949), 60.

26. H.G. Canady, "Psychology in Negro Institutions," 168.

27. Ibid.

28. L. Brunschwig, "Opportunities for Negroes in the Field of Psychology," *Journal of Negro Education* (October 1941): 664–676.

29. Ibid., 675.

30. Ibid., 676.

▶ 6

Black Psychologists
Training, Employment, and Organizations

While Europe served as the training area for many early white psychologists, the United States was the spawning ground for Black psychologists. Hall at Clark, Cattell at Columbia, and Tichener at Cornell received their early psychological training with open arms at Leipzig, Germany; each of these scholars became leaders in psychology and actively engaged in research, publishing, and the training of psychologists. On the other hand, Black scholars such as Sumner at Howard, Eagleson at Spelman, and Canady at West Virginia State were trained at universities in the United States under difficult circumstances. These students received few encouragements, no university assistantships, no student appointments; survival became a matter of solving challenges quite unlike those of their white counterparts.

Success for Blacks seeking to attain graduate-level training was largely a matter of good fortune and the ability to negotiate often lonely campuses with confrontational environments.[1] Being accepted into these schools would appear to present insurmountable barriers but fortunately a few northern white universities did accept and even encourage the enrollment of Black graduate students by allowing their entrance examinations to be administered at Black colleges. Clark University in Massachusetts, under the leadership of G. Stanley Hall, was one of those northern universities. Clark not only enrolled Black graduate students during this era but also graduated more Black scholars in the behavioral sciences than all other white colleges combined. In attendance at Clark during the 1915 to 1920 period were Howard Long (M.A., psychology, 1916), Francis Sumner (Ph.D., psychology, 1920), J. Henry Alston (M.A., psychology, 1920), E. Franklin Frazier (M.A., sociology, 1920), and Thomas Brown (Ph.D., sociology, 1920). The atmosphere in other universities was not as conducive to encouraging Blacks to enroll; their enrollments reflected as much. Since the majority of Black college graduates lived in the South and southern white universities denied them admission, it is obvious why the total number of enrolled Black graduate students, during this era, was limited. Geography was a major independent variable in determining whether an individual could attend graduate school, thereby creating a negative correlation between the distance a Black college graduate lived from the school and the probability of attendance. Also, policies at most northern colleges required graduates from Black colleges to complete an extra undergraduate year—earning a second degree to validate their abilities—at the white universities. Most importantly, when the decision was made to attend graduate school, the cost of out-of-state fees, tuition, relocation, and minimal living maintenance forced many potential Black graduate students to either alter their goals or delay training for many years until they had acquired sufficient money. This delay elevated the median age of Black graduate students, especially those from the South, ten to fifteen years above that of their white counterparts. Even as late as the 1950s, the ages of Black psychologists holding the doctorate degree ranged from thirty-one years of age to sixty-four years of age; the median age was forty-three years.[2] Over 75 percent obtained a doctorate eight years or more after their first degree—more than one-half obtained it ten years after. See Table 6.1.

A more tragic result of this situation was that many Black college graduates lowered their ambitions or abandoned professional aspirations altogether in favor of employment that offered dependable wages, retirement programs, and fringe benefits. Post office and railroad jobs became premium occupations, outside of public school teaching, in the Black communities. Waiting on tables was frequently performed by highly trained Blacks at resorts and on most of the first-class trains, for instance on the New York Central's Twentieth Century Limited, Union Pacific's Sunset Limited, and Louisville and Nashville's Hummingbird's dining room coaches. Positions of cook and waiter were staffed by Black high school teachers, principals, and college professors. Also, it was not uncommon to witness college graduates employed as Pullman sleeping

TABLE 6.1   Age Ph.D./Ed.D. Degree Awarded

Age of Recipient	Frequency
45	1
43	1
40	1
38	1
37	1
36	1
34	2
32	3
31	3
30	3
26	3
25	2
N=22	

Range of ages at time of award of doctorate degree.

car porters or railway baggage handlers (Red Caps). The lack of financial funds was the major barrier for potential Black graduate students.

PHILANTHROPIC FOUNDATIONS

Federal and state assistance were nonexistent and the promise of academic assistantships impossible; it fell upon help from private benevolent organizations to establish funds for financial assistance. The Peabody Education Fund, the Duke Endowment, and Rockefeller's General Education Board were major private foundations established for education in general and were shared by some Black Americans; however, several private foundations were devoted exclusively to the educational needs of Black Americans: the John F. Slater Fund, Daniel Hand Fund, Anna T. Jeanes Fund, and Rosenwald Funds. Beginning in 1928, the Rosenwald largesse developed into an oasis for extremely talented, financially stranded graduate students. See Table 6.2.

The Julius Rosenwald Foundation

The Rosenwald Funds provided real opportunities for the crème de la crème Black graduate students to receive monies in order to graduate from northern universities. Only requiring recommendations from ex-professors, this source was the most desired conduit for financial assistance for Black scholars of every discipline. Not only were the Rosenwald

TABLE 6.2 Sample of Rosenwald Fund Recipients, 1930–1948

Name	Field	Year
Anderson, Marian	Music-Voice	1930
Bond, Horace Mann	Education	1931, 1932
Botemps, Arna	Creative Writing	1938
Clark, Kenneth B.	Psychology	1940
Clark, Mamie Phipps	Psychology	1940, 1941, 1942
Davis, Alonzo J.	Psychology	1939
Davis, Allison	Anthropology	1932, 1939, 1940
Drake, St. Clair	Anthropology	1935, 1936, 1937, 1946
Drew, Charles	Medicine	1931
Dunham, Katherine	Anthropology	1935, 1936
Ellison, Ralph	Creative Writing	1945
Franklin, John Hope	History	1937, 1938
Frazier, E. Franklin	Sociology	1944
Greene, Lorenzo J.	History	1934, 1940
Hurston, Zora N.	Anthropology	1935
Johnson, James Weldon	Creative Writing	1928, 1930, 1931
Julian, Percy	Chemistry	1934, 1935
Logan, Rayford	History	1944
Long, Herman H.	Psychology	1942
Morton, Mary A.	Psychology	1937
Quarles, Benjamin	History	1937, 1945
Snowden, Frank W.	Literature	1938

Source: Data from E. Embree, and J. Waxman, Investment in People (New York: Harper and Row, 1949), 89.

Funds concerned with the training of Black scholars, but also the Foundation made giant steps in virgin territory when it attempted to facilitate racial integration in all-white colleges and universities by encouraging these institutions to hire Black professors. In 1945, the Foundation mailed more than 500 letters to universities offering information concerning the hiring of qualified Black professors. It is important to note that in the early 1940s, there was not one Black professor teaching in these schools and clearly the white schools would not hire any without the prodding of an outside power structure. Only 160 schools responded to the Foundation's questionnaire, and half of these responses were in the category "We are placing this list (of Black Ph.D. professors) in our files for future reference."[3] With no offers for jobs and negative responses from the college presidents, some type of forced intervention was necessary in order to open the employment doors for Black Americans. Not until decades later when the Federal government legally mandated affirmative action did any behavior changes occur. The college presidents responding to the Rosenwald questionnaire clearly indicated that to hire a Black professor, to them, would be unfair to white people because this action would take the place of hiring a white professor. This reflected a concept that all such jobs should be held by white professors, regardless of the qualifications of the Black Americans. Fear of negative community reactions also was considered a reason why some of these schools did not hire Black professors. One college president volunteered to circulate the Foundation's letter to his staff, even though he felt that Black professors would not fill any needs for his university.

The possibility of hiring Black professors in the all-white schools was so dismal that in 1941 the Fund agreed to pay the salary of Harvard-trained anthropologist, Allison Davis, if the University of Chicago would appoint him to the faculty. Thus when Davis was appointed to the University of Chicago in 1941, he became the first Black faculty member to be appointed to a major white university on a full-time basis.[4] In an interesting follow-up study, a twenty-year comparison of hiring practices was made by the Southern Education Reporting Service (SERS) with questionnaires addressed to presidents of the same 179 institutions. See Table 6.3. In 1968, historian Gilbert Belles concluded "there is enough evidence to conclude that faculty desegregation at white colleges is still far from commonplace."[5]

TABLE 6.3 Comparison of the Rosenwald Fund Survey of Negro Faculty at Selected White Institutions, 1945–47, and the Southern Education Reporting Service Survey of the Same Institutions, 1967–68

	1945–47	1967–68
Number of institutions contacted	600	179[a]
Number replying	179	138
Per cent response	29.8	77.1
Number of respondents supplying complete information	178	130
Number of respondents reporting Negro faculty members	42	79
Per cent reporting Negro faculty members employed	23.6	60.7
Total number of Negro faculty members reported	75	785
Total number of all faculty at institutions supplying information for the survey (approximate)	40,000	60,000
Per cent of Negroes on the faculties of all institutions supplying information for the survey	.002	.013
Estimated number of Negroes in the U. S. having completed five or more years of college	3,550[b]	194,000[c]

Source: "Negroes Are Few on College Faculties," *Southern Education Report* (July/August 1968): 23–25. Chart reprinted by permission of the author, A. Gilbert Belles.
[a]The institutions represented by this number are the same ones which replied to the 1945–47 survey.
[b]An estimate made by Fred G. Wale of the Rosenwald Fund in 1947.
[c]Estimated by the U. S. Bureau of the Census, as of March, 1966.

The Rosenwald Foundation was clearly in the forefront of private sector's struggle for equal opportunity in academia. The Rosenwald Foundation terminated in 1948.

EMPLOYMENT IN THE BLACK COLLEGE

Following practices in the white institutions, psychology courses became integral parts of the curricula in the struggling Black colleges, especially in the training of teachers. Every Black college provided at least one course in psychology as early as 1906. Formally trained psychologists, both Black and white, were at a premium at this time—the hope of staff-trained psychologists to become professors was dim. Most of the psychology teachers held degrees in education, religion, sociology,and physics. Even when job opportunities were available in academia, the prospect of struggling to earn an advanced degree in order to become a professor was further dimmed by poor salaries, heavy teaching loads, little job security, or meager retirement plans. In 1936, one professor, A. P. Davis, offered this frustrating view:

> [The Black college professor] is criminally underpaid. Having slaved at the most menial and humiliating work for a period of five to ten years in order to get his degrees from a high-priced northern university, he comes out finally with a body often impaired in health and practically always a large debt to repay . . . money he has had to borrow to supplement that which he so painfully earned. He is then ready to go to work; and if he is fortunate enough to get a position, he can look forward to an average salary of less than two thousand dollars a year . . . He teaches from eighteen to twenty-one hours a week . . . and has been educated above his means, because the average American white man of his economic status would have not gone as far in education as he has.[6]

Davis continued to paint a disheartening picture:

> Lack of money, over-work and other unpleasant factors make it practically impossible for him to do anything outstanding in the field of pure scholarship. He cannot buy books on a large scale himself, and he cannot get them at his school libraries, because there are no really adequate libraries in the Negro schools. Probably the worst handicap of all is the lack of a

scholarly atmosphere about him. There is no incentive, and, of course, no money for research in most schools.[7]

Charles R. Drew, the famed physician-researcher, expressed his feelings about the difficulties of the Black scholar during the 1930s in these terms:

> While one must grant at once that extraordinary talent, great intellectual strength and unusual opportunity are necessary to break out of this prison of Negro problem . . . the walls here in America are at times too thick to breach and too high to climb. The atmosphere of racial prejudice and discrimination contributed much to the absence of blacks in graduate schools.[8]

Employment in Clinical Psychology and Research

On rare occasions the Black psychologist found employment in the private sector. Beyond the Black colleges and universities, the government services provided the few avenues for employment. The military was perhaps the first large recognized body to designate individuals as clinical psychologists. In 1944, 244 enlisted men were appointed as officers in the army and were given short, intensive courses in clinical psychology. Of this number, five were women and one was Black. The Federal Civil Service was next; in 1946 two Black clinical psychologists were appointed to the Veterans Administration program.[9] One was in the Philadelphia Regional Office, and the other was at the VA Hospital in Tuskegee, Alabama. In a survey taken in 1945, approximately one-half of Black clinical psychologists were employed in the Veterans Administration. Probably one other indication of Black early participation in clinical psychology was the acceptance of a Black to what was called "the first Post Doctoral Seminar in Clinical Psychology" which was held at the University of Michigan."[10]

Similar to the situation in the Black colleges and universities, a number of Blacks without doctorates, no doubt, were employed at many state, private, and federal institutions. In research positions, Blacks were slowly being appointed in various federal agencies principally located in the Washington, D.C. area. For example, in 1955, Alvin Goins was appointed to the Naval Research Laboratory (Washington, D.C.) as an experimental psychologist working in the area of physiological and engineering psychology. Goins's appointment in the burgeoning field of human factors represented a breakthrough in civil service appointments. Although Blacks were slowly integrating the federal government professional labor force as psychologists they were often in solo situations in each agency. With their presence being known, however, the appearance of Black psychologists made the nation aware of their abilities and availability.

BLACK PSYCHOLOGISTS ORGANIZE

During the twentieth century, Black psychologists formally organized on two occasions: once in 1938 at Tuskegee, Alabama, and again in 1969 at San Francisco, California. On each occasion the impetus was due to dissatisfactions with traditional professional approaches to the problems of Black Americans and their communities. This lack of appropriate attention paid to the problems of Black American youth and to the necessary vocational direction and guidance for their successful employment led Herman Canady of West Virginia State College to begin a vigorous effort to organize Black professionals in psychology.

Blacks Interested in Psychology

Even though a small number of Black psychologists held membership in the American Psychological Association (APA), the agenda of the APA was far removed from discussions concerning the needs of the Black people. This was an era of comparative psychology when the problems of Black Americans were viewed only in relationship to white Americans. Southern chapters of the National Educational Association (NEA) had refused to admit Black teachers, thus bringing about the formation of the powerful all-Black, American Teachers Association (ATA). The ATA, originally called the National Association of Teachers in Colored Schools, was formed in 1904 and grew into an extremely effective voice for Black teachers. The majority of Black psychologists were educators, so they were members of this organization. Herman Canady's effort to organize Black psychologists was in conjunction with the 1938 ATA annual convention held at Tuskegee Institute. For years, annual meetings of the ATA found psychologists in caucuses, discussing common interests and concerns. During this era, the motivation of Black psychologists toward unfair and unequal treatment was straightforward; they held little hope for an integrated workforce. It was within this context that Black psychologists organized. Professor Canady mailed "A Prospectus of an Organization of Negroes Interested in Psychology and Related Fields" to ATA members who were interested or worked in the area of psychology. See Figure 6.1.

Name	Psychology Section of A.T.A., or ????
Major Objective	To advance, promote and encourage the teaching and application of the science of psychology and related fields, particularly in Negro institutions.
Specific Purposes	To set up qualifications for teachers of psychology in Negro institutions and to maintain a list of institutions that meet the standards determined by the association.
	To assist Negro institutions in the training and selection of psychologists.
	To bring to the section outstanding persons of the nation for general and specific enlightenment on current trends in psychology, cognate subjects and in research techniques.
	To discuss outstanding research efforts in Negro institutions and elsewhere.
	To offer counsel and advice to members of the association in selecting and conducting research programs.
	To assist in securing financial aid for members who are working on projects which call for expenditures which exceed the resources of the average individual.
	To stimulate the study and research of psychological problems as a basis for understanding behavior problems of Negroes.
	To create genuine interest in scientific psychology in institutions of higher learning for Negroes.
	To keep members in touch with major studies, surveys, etc., being carried on in the country in which trained and qualified Negroes might participate.
	To represent to research workers and teachers of other subjects the highest ideals of both synthetic and analytic research.
	To look forward to the publication of a quarterly having some such title as Human Psychology, or Racial Psychology, or etc.
Membership	Membership shall be open to persons who are interested in the teaching, application and advancement of the science of psychology and related fields.
Officers	There shall be three officers: namely, Chairman, Vice-Chairman, Secretary.
Meeting	Meeting shall be held at the time and place of the convening of A.T.A., or ????

FIGURE 6.1 A Prospectus of an Organization of Negroes Interested in Psychology and Related Fields

During the 1938 ATA convention at Tuskegee, a two-day program allowed psychologists to discuss the proposed formation of their group and to contribute to the convention's theme, "The Negro Youth Looks at Occupations in America." See Figure 6.2.

Enthusiasm was evident: It was unanimously voted to organize the group. Division 6, Department of Psychology of the ATA, was established. Herman G. Canady was elected chairman; Howard H. Long, vice chairman; and Oran W. Eagleson, secretary. Unfortunately, the beginning of World War II redirected attention away from the ATA effort, but

---

AMERICAN TEACHERS' ASSOCIATION
Tuskegee Convention of July 26–29, 1938

Program of the Psychology Section for Wednesday Afternoon,
July 27, 1938 2:15–4:15 p.m.

CONVENTION THEME:
THE NEGRO YOUTH LOOKS AT OCCUPATIONS IN AMERICA

Part I (60 minutes)

Presiding: Herman G. Canady, Department of Psychology, West Virginia State College, Institute, W. Va.

Topic: *Consideration of the Prospectus of the Psychology Section and the Formation of a Permanent Organization*

Part II (60 minutes)

Presiding: Dean J. Otis Smith, Alcorn A & M, Alcorn, Miss.

Topic: *Psychology in Negro Institutions—Undergraduate and Graduate Curricula*
(This Discussion will concern itself with personnel, courses, equipment and library facilities; also, the problems of instruction and the improvement of the teaching of psychology.)

Speakers: Herman G. Canady, Department of Psychology, West Virginia State College, Institute, W.Va.
Dr. F. C. Sumner, Department of Psychology, Howard University, Washington, D.C.

FIGURE 6.2 Program for 1938 American Teachers' Association Convention

approximately thirty years later a revitalization of Black psychologists occurred due to the rising tide of discontentment with what was regarded as a form of exploitation of the Black community by white researchers and the malaise of the American Psychological Association (APA) to the issues of Black Americans.

AMERICAN TEACHERS' ASSOCIATION
Tuskegee Convention of July 26–29, 1938

Program for the Psychology Section for Thursday Afternoon,
July 28, 1938 2:15–4:15 p.m.

CONVENTION THEME:
THE NEGRO YOUTH LOOKS AT OCCUPATIONS IN AMERICA

Presiding: Dr. Oran W. Eagleson, Department of Psychology, Spelman College, Atlanta, Ga.

Topic   *The Services of Psychology to Education and the Social Order*
(This involves primarily a consideration of the application of psychology to the solution of many of the social, educational and political problems of the Negro. Consideration might also be given to the following questions: To what extent would research in psychology in Negro institutions serve as a basis for understanding behavior problems of Negroes? What are some psychological problems that need investigation?)

Panel Jury: (1) *To Education,* Dr. Martin D. Jenkins, Dean, Cheyney Teachers' College, Cheyney, Pa.
(2) *To Vocational Guidance,* Dr. Charles L. Cooper, Department of Industrial Education, A & T College, Greensboro, N.C.
(3) *To the Public School,* Dr. Howard H. Long, Assistant Superintendent of Schools, Washington, D.C.
(4) *To Student Personnel Work,* Dr. Ambrose Caliver, U.S. Office of Education, Washington, D.C.
(5) *To Medicine,* Dr. George Branche, U.S. Veterans Hospital, Tuskegee, Ala.
(6) *To the Social Sciences,* Dr. Bertram W. Doyle, General Secretary, Board of Education, C.M.E. Church, Nashville, Tenn.

FIGURE 6.2 *Continued*

The Association of Black Psychologists

As three decades passed, the feeble attention of the APA to a myriad of social issues—minority representation on APA committees, lack of Blacks hired by the APA central office, poor representation of Black graduate students in the nation's training pipelines, and questionable theoretical underpinnings in psychology directed toward minority groups—contributed to the discontentment of a newer generation of Black psychologists. The APA had literally set itself up for what was later to occur—other than Kenneth Clark, APA president-elect for 1969, and Martin Jenkins, president of Morgan State College, Black psychologists and their concerns were practically invisible in the APA philosophies and power structure.

When APA's Division 9, The Society for the Psychological Study of Social Issues (SPSSI), presented to the APA administration in 1963 a proposal to study the training and employment needs of Blacks in psychology a sigh of relief was sounded by Black psychologists and an ad hoc Committee on Equality of Opportunity in Psychology (CEOP) was established to (1) explore the question of equal opportunity hiring practices relative to Black psychologists in professional and academic positions, (2) examine recruiting and selection of students for training in psychology, and (3) determine steps that may provide training and exchange opportunities for teachers and scholars in Black colleges and universities. The formal organizational structure appeared to bog down, however, and not much progress was made until 1967 when the following recommendations were made:

1. The APA should encourage effective measures to acquaint undergraduates in the Black colleges with the career possibilities for Blacks in psychology.
2. The APA should adopt appropriate measures to increase the participation of Black psychologists in the APA.
3. The Equal Opportunities Committee should obtain existing comparable statistics for non-Black psychologists so that comparisons can be made with Black populations and additional information be obtained with somewhat greater certainty.

National Association of Black Psychologists

Judging from the long delays the APA had exhibited in approaching these problems and with the appearance that these recommendations could dissipate in the revolving committee processes, Black psychologists were primed for confrontations. Thus, while the genesis of the resulting organization appeared to be the result of a spontaneous firestorm, it was decades of smoldering that had finally ignited the psychologists' fuse—San Francisco was the tinderbox when approximately 200 Black psychologists attending the 1968 APA convention met following meetings of a smaller cadre of Black psychologists the previous evening in a hotel room.

Who Was in the Room?

The names of the individuals who initiated the call for the historic meeting have been a matter of much discussion. The issue became, not who was in the room, but rather, who was not in the room. Upwards to seventy-five people claim to have been in the small hotel room in early September 1968. Joseph White, in discussing the atmosphere during this time, commented

> When we got to San Francisco it was like a conscientiousness floating around . . . people started talking in the hallways and then someone said, let's meet in my room or Bob William's room . . . I can't remember, but the central topics of the meetings were plain and simple: We were dissatisfied with psychology's exploitations and the white definitions for behavior that placed Blacks in a negative light. We were determined to construct some new definitions and terminologies . . . we were mainly dissatisfied with the APA because of the lack of graduate students in the nation's psychology programs . . . also, the APA had taken no stand on the social revolution that was going on . . . all around them.[11]

After deciding to call a meeting of the larger body of psychologists at the convention, a mailing list was created and the group organized as the National Association of Black Psychologists. Charles Thomas and Robert Green were elected as co-chairs and Ernestine Thomas as Secretary. Immediate concerns were voiced: (1) The APA must racially integrate its own workforce; (2) The APA should facilitate the entry of more Blacks into the nation's graduate schools; (3) The APA should monitor their journals so that racist themes would be eliminated; and (4) The APA should establish a program within which minority concerns about psychology could be expressed. A press release in September, 1968, summarized the initial thrust of the National Association of Black Psychologists:

> The Association of Black Psychologists was formed as a national organization during the San Francisco meeting of the American Psychological Association in September, 1968. More than 200 Black psychologists who hold positions in various academic, public, industrial, and governmental programs met to develop a nation-wide structure for pooling their resources in meeting the challenge of racism and poverty. The Association charged that APA through inadequate positive measures condoned the white racist character of the American Society and failed to recognize the new Black movement as the most promising model for solving problems stemming from the oppressive effects of American racism.
>
> Members of the Association have pledged themselves to the realization that they are Black people first and psychologists second. Accordingly, they will not continue to ignore the exploitation of the Black community by those elements of society who maintain traditional patterns of operation or who are unable to create meaningful alternative modes of affirmative action.
>
> The Association has local, state, and regional divisions. The formation of these groups is to develop and implement activities which include calling a halt to the abuse of Black communities by white researchers who use data taken from such communities to advance themselves professionally and economically while those studied continue to exist as a powerless people. ABP also will address its attention to increasing the number of Black students and professionals in psychology. Moreover, it will press for improving the training and certification of psychologists who seek to work with minority groups in some enabling capacity.
>
> As educated Black people, the membership assumes a primary responsibility for engaging in critical thinking about the relationships between Black people and the society in which they live. And from such activities, by whatever means necessay, bring about the elixir in our society which every white group accepts as a birthright but continues to be wanting among Black people. Accordingly, we are pledged to effect change in those areas in which the American Psychological Association has been insensitive, ineffectual, and insincere.[12]

A dramatic "wake-up call" for the APA occurred during the 1969 APA convention when a group of Black students interrupted George Miller's presidential address with an appeal for Black concerns and the APA's cooperation for an increased production of Black psychologists. So effective was this drama that the APA Council of Representatives shortly agreed to recognize the Black Students in Psychology Association (BSPA), their concerns, and their organization. A joint committee composing of representatives of the APA, Association of Black Psychologists (ABPsi), and BSPA later met in 1969 with Robert L. Williams, then chair of ABPsi, arguing for a moratorium against the use of culturally biased tests and for increasing the number of Black graduate students in psychology. These arguments laid the foundation for an open forum at the 1973 National Conference of Levels and Patterns of Training in Professional Psychology (Vail, Colorado) in laying out important concepts for graduate program accreditations, ethical issues, and the need for increasing the enrollment of ethnic graduate students in training programs.

TOWARD A BLACK PSYCHOLOGY

A 1970 *Ebony* magazine article, "Toward a Black Psychology," described a new concept, the psychology of Blacks, by presenting a picture of Black family life, Black dialect, and Black philosophical ideas that had not been widely acknowledged or discussed before.[13]

The author, University of California at Irvine professor Joseph White, wrote: "It is difficult, if not impossible, to understand the life-styles of black people using traditional theories developed by white psychologists to explain white people." This public questioning of "time-honored" theories set the stage for the establishment of a philosophical basis for what White termed, "Black Psychology." This label disturbed many white and some Black traditionalists because it was viewed as dichotomizing psychology into white and Black categories—causing many discussions of what Black Psychology was and what it was not. These discussions resulted in a sounding board to reject racial concepts dating from the eighteenth century to the present. As such, it stimulated a host of discussions ranging from "Black Studies in Psychology" to the "Role of the Negro in American Psychology." As the Black Psychology movement gained its early momentum, psychological terminologies were utilized not only as a protest against previous inequities but also as a matter of necessity to describe unique conditions

Joseph L. White (1932–). Dr White propelled the Black psychology
movement through his seminal essays, "Guidelines for Black Psychologists,"
and "Toward a Black Psychology," during the late 1960s and early 1970s.
His critiques of traditional psychological practices introduced an era of
psychological theories and practices geared toward Black Americans and
their communities.

frequently found in the Black experience not accounted for by traditional psychology. *Nadinolization, negromachy, nigrescence, weusi anxiety,*
and *materialistic depression* were among the new descriptive and diagnostic coinages of the 1970 era.

Within a decade, the ABPsi began to place major emphases on
"Africentrically-principled discourses and spiritual rejuvenation," with
cultural themes emanating from the African religions and philosophies.
West African dress and motifs became popular among the attendees
with Egyptology a special interest among many psychologists in showing African connections to psychology as related to American Black
people, the diaspora, and psychology. Georgia State University's Asa

Hilliard's theme, *Return to the Source* (1972), became a rallying point for the recognition of the African continent as a significant historical contributor to civilization.[14] Clinical psychologist Na'im Akbar emerged as a pioneer in the development of an African-centered approach to psychology.[15] Along with Wade Noble's *African Psychology* (1986) and Joseph Baldwin's *The African Personality in America* (1992), other examples of African-centered philosophies in psychology became known.[16] In a later call for expansion and possible international connections for American Black psychologists, Daudi Azibo forecast that "perhaps it will not be too long before continental and other diasporic African psychologists can effectively link with African (American) psychologists under the revitalized nascent, Africentrically-rooted African psychology."[17] Nigerian-based scholar, Amina Mama, however, contests the unitary African worldview stance embraced by "the diaspora-based Afrocentric school of black intellectuals." In her book, *Beyond the Masks* (1995), she takes the view that neither Eurocentric nor Afrocentric philosophies "can withstand the paradigm shift heralded by post-structuralism and by the demise of the grand old frames of reference, a demise that heralds our entry into the post-colonial era that will end the twentieth century."[18] However, Africentric bases of psychological principles are seen in diasporic research studies seeking to establish credibility for twenty-first century Black psychology.[19]

TOWARD TRADITIONAL PSYCHOLOGY

The twentieth century was a period when modern psychology and Black American psychologists developed, nurtured, and matured and produced significant research for the understanding and betterment of Black Americans. It is interesting to realize that the most significant utilization of psychological science for public policy was the outgrowth of two Black Americans. No one can match the profound effects that Kenneth and Mamie Clark's "The Development of Consciousness of Self and the Emergence of Racial Identification in Negro Pre-School Children," (1939) and "Skin Color as a Factor in Racial Identification of Negro Pre-School Children" (1940) research findings had upon American society. Their investigations on racial identification (the doll studies) played a pivotal role when the Supreme Court agreed to hear appeals from lower court decisions on school racial segregation. In the Court's decision to reverse the "separate but equal" doctrine and declare school racial segregation unconstitutional, the Court concluded that "To separate them [Black children] from others of similar age and qualifications solely because of their race generates a feeling of inferiority as to their status in the community that may affect their hearts and minds in a way unlikely ever to be undone."

This statement not only signaled an end for education's apartheid system in the South, but also brought to recognition psychology's contributions toward producing significant social change in this country. There is no doubt of the impact of the Clarks' work for the betterment of American society.

In addition, Kenneth Clark's work with Gunner Myrdal (*An American Dilemma,* 1944), followed by Clark's *Prejudice and Your Child* (1963), *Dark Ghetto* (1965), and *Pathos of Power* (1974), places him in the forefront of social psychology. *Dark Ghetto* was translated into six foreign languages and distributed throughout the world. In 1968, *Black Rage,* written by Black psychiatrists, William H. Grier and Price M. Cobbs, was the first book to reveal the full dimensions of the inner conflicts and desperation of Black American life. This book served as a precursor for later studies on racism, prejudice, and coping styles that dominated the interests of Black researchers. Textbooks by Dalmas Taylor, *Psychology: A New Perspective* (1975), William Cross, *Shades of Black* (1991), Adelbert Jenkins, *Psychology and African Americans* (1995), and James Jones, *Prejudice and Racism* (1996), are examples of scholarly studies in the traditional mode. Finally, research studies concerning bicultural evolution and models of racial identity development maintained a focus for many professors and students pursuing advanced degrees (Thomas, 1971; Cross, 1973; Helms, 1990; and Parham, 1993).

The next chapter focuses on the numerical output of early psychologists, the early holders of psychology doctorates, and the academic sources of doctorate holders in psychology for the first half of the twentieth century.

NOTES

1. Black students enrolled in northern white universities were faced with harsh psychological realities—often viewed as outsiders—not belonging to the academic milieu. Many were not welcomed in the university dining halls or cafeterias, prohibited from joining organizations, and did not participate in most social functions. Sadly, some were allocated special tables in the dining halls and other campus locations. Without many friends, these students learned parts of the campuses to avoid or frequent.

2. J. Morton, "Negro Psychologists," Unpublished Manuscript, 1945, Evanston, Ill.

3. A. G. Belles, "The College Faculty, the Negro Scholar, and the Julius Rosenwald Fund," *The Journal of Negro History* vol. LIV, no. 4 (October, 1969): 384.

4. Ibid. Allison Davis was born in Washington, D.C. and earned degrees from Williams, Harvard, Howard, and Chicago. He also studied at the London School of Economics. In the 1940s, he argued that Black children were being held back and that their educational potential was untapped because of faulty intelligence testing. He attacked the assumption that children from poor families were intellectually inferior to their upper income contemporaries. His efforts prompted several urban school systems to discontinue the use of intelligence tests. He was the author or coauthor of ten books. In 1995, Dr. Davis was commemorated on a U.S. postage stamp for his contributions to anthropology, education, and psychology.

5. A. G. Belles, "Negroes Are Few on College Faculties," *Southern Education Report* (July/August 1968): 23–25.

6. See A. P. Davis, "The Negro Professor," *The Crisis* (April 1936): 103–104 for an interesting account of the plight of Black professors during the 1930s.

7. Ibid.

8. C. R. Drew, "Negro Scholars in Scientific Research," *Journal of Negro Education* 35 (1950): 135–136. This excerpt is part of an address delivered before the Annual Meeting of the Association for the Study of Negro Life and History, New York City, October 30, 1949.

9. Morton, "Negro Psychologists."

10. Ibid.

11. From a taped interview conducted by the author with Joseph White at Irvine, California, on August 3, 1995. According to Professor White, "In the first room, I think there might have been six at the beginning but by the time the meeting ended . . . many people had come in and out and others had returned and there must have been about fifteen people . . . it was then we concluded that the room was too small."

12. R. Williams, "A History of the Association of Black Psychologists: Early Formation and Development," *Journal of Black Psychologists* 1 (1974): 9–23.

13. J. White, "Toward a Black Psychology," *Ebony Magazine* (September, 1970).

14. A. Hilliard, *Return to the Source*. Slide show produced by South Carolina Educational Television (Public Broadcasting System). (Columbia, South Carolina, 1987).

15. N. Akbar, *Chains and Images of Psychological Slavery* (Jersey City, N.J.: New Mind Productions, 1984).

16. W. Nobles, *African Psychology* (Oakland, Calif.: A Black Family Institute Publication, 1986). J. Baldwin, *The African Personality in America* (Tallahassee, Fla.: Nubian Nation Publications, 1992).

17. D. Azibo, "African Psychology in Historical Perspective and Related Commentary," in *African Psychology in Historical Perspective and Related Commentary* (Trenton, N.J.: Africa World Press, 1996).

18. A. Mama, *Beyond the Masks: Race, Gender and Subjectivity.* (London: Routledge, 1995), 162–165.

19. A. Smith, "The Psychometric Development of a Scale to Measure Afrocentric and Eurocentric Worldviews." Unpublished doctoral dissertation, Southern Illinois University, 1996 provides an excellent example of research concerning this concept.

▶ 7

Production of Black Psychologists in America

Howard University, the largest Black university during the early era of Black schools, became the leading Black university providing graduate and undergraduate training in psychology. Howard quickly became the leading conduit for Black students to matriculate into graduate school. Between 1919 and 1938, twenty students had enrolled in Howard's graduate program in psychology. See Table 7.1.

The importance of the Howard psychology program can be understood when its numbers are compared to a total of only thirty-six Black students enrolled in all graduate studies in psychology in institutions outside the South between 1930 and 1938. See Table 7.2.

Under the leadership of Francis Sumner, chair of Howard's psychology department, an immediate priority was placed on building a strong program in psychology. Two years after Sumner's 1928 appointment, he hired Max Meenes, a white associate professor trained as a "brass instrument psychologist" at Clark University. Meenes, formerly at Lehigh University, joined Sumner and graduate student Frederick Watts to form a three-person department. Meenes, commenting on Sumner's program for Howard psychology majors, outlined the introductory course sequencing during the 1930s. See Table 7.3.

The first course in psychology ran through three quarters. It was unique in a sense that the first quarter was psychology according

TABLE 7.1 Major Fields of Graduate Students in Black Colleges (1919–1938)

Field	Atlanta	Fisk	Hampton	Howard	Virginia State	Xavier	Total
Anthropology	—	1	—	—	—	—	1
Biology	14	6	—	—	—	—	20
Botany	—	—	—	7	—	—	7
Chemistry	10	12	—	18	—	—	40
Economics	20	—	—	4	—	—	24
Education	46	43	23	60	5	3	180
English	18	26	—	49	—	1	94
Foreign Language	11	—	—	25	—	—	36
History	26	1	—	55	—	4	86
Mathematics	19	4	—	21	—	—	44
Music	—	7	—	—	—	—	7
Philosophy	—	—	—	1	—	1	2
Physics	—	—	—	7	—	—	7
Psychology	—	—	—	**20**	—	—	**20**
Religion	—	—	—	5	—	—	5
Social Work	—	—	—	1	—	—	1
Sociology	22	16	—	3	—	—	41
Political Science	—	—	—	1	—	—	1
Zoology	—	—	—	18	—	—	18
Not Given	—	—	—	1	—	—	1
Total	186	116	23	296	5	9	635

Source: Fred McCuistion, *Graduate Instruction for Negroes in the United States* (Nashville: George Peabody College for Teachers, 1939), 43–44. Reprinted by permission.

to Titchener and we used Titchener's book. The second quarter, we were teaching psychology from the point of view of behaviorism. We used Watson's book. The third quarter, we were interested in dynamic psychology, and we used McDougall and Freud. The major [in psychology] had to have all three of these basic courses.[1]

Describing other courses in the Howard psychology program, Meenes continued:

In addition to the usual run of courses in those days, we had courses in learning, personality, mental hygiene, and so on. Dr.

TABLE 7.2 Black Graduate Students in Institutions Outside the South: Major Fields of Study and Enrollment (1930–1938)

Major Field	Enrollment		
	1930–1936	**1938–1939**	**Total**
Health	33	20	53
Home Economics	32	19	51
Zoology	29	16	45
Science—General	29	14	43
Music	23	20	43
Economics	31	11	42
French	37	5	42
Psychology	**31**	**5**	**36**
Business	17	9	26
Physics	14	9	23
Fine Arts	10	12	22
Biology	7	11	18
Political Science	10	6	16
Agriculture	7	5	12
Foreign Language	10	2	12
Latin	7	1	8
Law	8	—	8
Unclassified	3	5	8
Bacteriology	4	3	7
Classics	5	1	6
Library Science	5	1	6
Engineering	4	2	6
German	3	2	5
Anthropology	4	—	4
Industrial Arts	2	2	4
Philosophy	2	2	4
Botany	2	—	2
Dramatics	—	2	2
Journalism	1	—	1
Physiology	—	1	1
Total	1,084	663	1,747

Source: Fred McCuistion, *Graduate Instruction for Negroes in the United States* (Nashville: George Peabody College for Teachers, 1939), 57–58. Reprinted by permission.

Sumner was very much interested in the psychology of religion, so we provided such a unique course. We emphasized the laboratory-experimental aspect of psychology. In that way we were different from all the other Black schools.[2]

TABLE 7.3   Courses of Instruction for the Beginning Psychology Sequence at Howard University (1932-1933)

Psychology 1, 2, and 4 form the natural approach to all advanced courses in
  Psychology and are a definite requirement of all students who major in Psychology.
Psychology 1. *General Psychology* 1. An introduction to Psychology from the
  behavioristic, introspective, and dynamic standpoints. Lectures, collateral readings,
  and demonstrations. Credit for Psychology 1 will not be given until Psychology 2 is
  completed. (Mr. Sumner, Mr. Meenes)
Psychology 2. *General Psychology* 2. A continuation of Psychology 1. (Mr. Sumner,
  Mr. Meenes)
Psychology 4. *Experimental Psychology.* An elementary laboratory course in
  Psychology. (Mr. Meenes)

Source: Howard University Catalog—Undergraduate, 1932–1933 (Washington, D.C.: Howard
University, 1932).

TABLE 7.4   Advanced Courses in Psychology at Howard University (1932–1933)

Psychology 212. *Psychological Journals.* A systematic study of current psychological
  journals.
Psychology 213. *Reading of French Psychology.* A reading of several psychological
  works in French. Prerequisites: eight courses in Psychology and a reading
  knowledge of French.
Psychology 214. *Reading of German Psychology.* A reading of several psychological
  works in German. Prerequisites: eight courses in psychology and a reading
  knowledge of German.

Source: Howard University Catalog—Undergraduate and Graduate, 1932–1933 (Washington,
D.C.: Howard University, 1932).

Howard's graduate courses in psychology were equally outstanding for
that time and were specifically designed to enable graduates to succeed
in pursuing their doctorates at the large white universities. See Table 7.4.

> Now at the graduate level we went only into the master's de-
> gree; we didn't want to issue any doctorates here because we
> thought our students should go elsewhere . . . We didn't want
> them to be ingrown. Our graduate work was perhaps a little bit
> unusual, too; we had two courses designed to enable our stu-
> dents to pass the language exams for the doctorate. One was
> readings in German psychology, and the other was readings in
> French psychology.[3]

Discussing the successes of the Howard program and the subsequent pursuit of the doctorate by Howard graduates, Meenes described the apprehensions of students who were competing in a society that was more often than not unreceptive to Black graduate students:

Our students were a little bit reluctant to face the outside competition. They worried that they might not have an adequate background. But we saw to it that they did get it. And then they came back to us, frequently quite surprised, to say, "You know, I am getting along fine. As fine as anybody." These were students who went on to Columbia, Minnesota, Wisconsin, California, and so on. Yes, they did have a good background. It really made us feel proud.[4]

On April 30, 1935, a new classroom building on the Howard campus was formally opened, providing a "spacious and modernly appointed unit" for the psychology department.[5] The new facility was the only unit in any Black institution at that time designed specifically for psychology; it compared favorably with facilities at many of the leading institutions in the United States. See Figure 7.1.

In 1938, Sumner outlined three objectives for the psychology department:

A. Servicing of students preparing for various professional lines such as business, education, law, medicine, religion, music, art, clinic work, and nursing. A certain amount of scientific psychological knowledge is requisite in all these professional lines which involve the interplay of human beings. In many instances certain course requirements in psychology are definitely stated as preparatory prerequisites. In other instances, courses in psychology are recommended although not definitely prescribed.

B. Cultural significance of psychology is stressed by the Psychology Department and this appeals to a large number of students. Here a knowledge of psychology is of importance for the deeper understanding of literature, religion, philosophy, art, crime, genius, mental derangement, history, biography, and all other creations of the human mind.

C. The preparation of a few select students for scientific pursuit of psychology in graduate study leading to the Master's and Doctor's degree.[6]

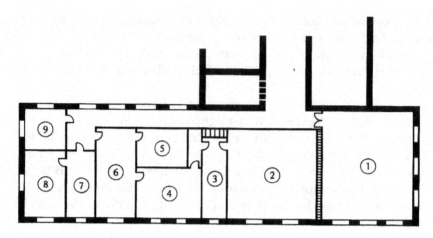

FIGURE 7.1 Psychology Unit, Douglass Memorial Hall, Howard University, Washington, D.C.: (1) a large undergraduate laboratory which seats 30 students and which has concealed cabinets for storage of apparatus, (2) a lecture room seating 48 students, (3) office of the department head, (4) a small lecture room and laboratory for graduate students, (5) a dark room furnished with a number of daylight lamps, work-benches, etc., (6) a machine shop containing a metal lathe, a wood lathe, a jig-saw, electric drill, work benches and tools, (7), (8), and (9) small laboratories for professors and graduate students.

Source: F. C. Sumner, "The New Psychology Unit at Howard University," *Psychological Bulletin,* 1935, p. 860. Copyright 1935 by the American Psychological Association. Reprinted by permission.

In 1943, the annual award of a Gold Key was established for the Howard University senior completing a major in psychology with exceptional distinction. This award, later called the Dodson Award after its benefactor, Mrs. Willie A. Dodson, was designed to provide an incentive for achievement among students in the department. The first recipient of the award was Mrs. Mauvice Winslow Brett of the Class of 1944.

Not only was Howard University producing outstanding scholars in psychology, but also the popularity of the department led Sumner, in 1947, to announce:

> During the year 1946–47 the enrollment at the graduate and undergraduate levels was the highest in the history of the Psychology Department. The scholastic ability of the undergraduate students in psychology was on the whole higher than usual.[7]

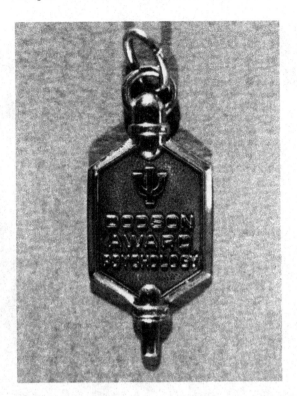

Dodson Award in Psychology. In 1943, this gold key was established as an annual award for exemplary academic achievement for Howard University psychology seniors. The award was established by former psychology graduate, Mrs. Willie A. Dodson. Howard's psychology program was the premier program among Black Colleges and Universities.

Finally, on June 2, 1947, the Howard University chapter of Psi Chi, the national honorary society for psychology, was installed:

> Dr. Max Meenes served as Installation Officer and Dr. F. C. Sumner as Sponsor. Fourteen students were initiated as chartered members. Edward Brock, a Junior, was installed as Chapter President. This Chapter is the first one of Psi Chi to be established in a Negro school.[8]

There were a few cases of Black psychologists who were unable to find jobs in psychology and went into other professional fields. One of these was J. Henry Alston, the first Black American to publish an original

Max Meenes (left) with his former students Mamie and Kenneth Clark in 1957. A native of Poland, Professor Meenes came to the United States as a child. He earned B.A. and Ph.D. Degrees at Clark University and a M.A. at Princeton. He was head of the Howard University psychology department from 1956 to 1966 and published several books and studies. Professor Meenes died in 1973. The Clarks, holders of Ph.D.'s from Columbia University, had received B.A.'s and M.A.'s at Howard.

research effort in an APA journal. Alston studied under G. Stanley Hall at Clark and became fascinated with neurology and experimental psychology. His 1920 research publication, "Psychophysics of the Spatial Conditions for the Fusion of Warmth and Cold into Heat," was received with much praise by E. G. Boring and other leading researchers. However, after receiving his M.A. in experimental psychology, he switched his academic interest to education and administration because of the lack of job opportunities in experimental psychology. Alston later recalled: "Af-

J. Henry Alston

ter writing several schools, I found that they did not need or feel the need of persons in pure psychology so I was forced by circumstances to change to education as most of our colleges were then teacher training institutes."[9] Alston eventually became a minister and presiding elder in the Christian Methodist Episcopal Church.

In several instances, Black Americans traveled to Europe to obtain graduate training. One of these was the savant Gilbert Haven Jones, who earned his doctoral degree in philosophy in 1901 at the University of Jena in Germany and later studied at the University of Gottingen in Germany. A philosopher, Jones was the first Black person with an earned doctorate to teach psychology in the United States. (At the time of Jones's graduate work, psychology was not yet a separate field of study in most universities, and the subject was covered under the broad category of philosophy.) Jones, born in Fort Mott, South Carolina, in 1883, was a professor of philosophy and education at St. Augustine College in North Carolina, A&M University in Oklahoma, and Wilberforce University in Ohio (where he was later appointed Dean, then Vice President).

Another individual, adjunct to psychology, was biologist Charles Henry Turner who received his Ph.D. degree, summa cum laude, from the University of Chicago in 1907. Turner's study of plants and animals led to important understanding of animal behavior called "behavioristic psychology." He taught at Clark University (Atlanta, Georgia); however, he spent much of his career as a public school biology teacher in St. Louis. Up to the end of his career in 1923, Turner was constantly reporting his findings to scientific circles, and numerous publications carrying his contributions gave the public the advantage of the results of his research.[10]

The training of Black scholars in psychology continued to be minuscule. The Committee on Equality of Opportunity in Psychology (APA) reported that the ten most prestigious departments of psychology in the United States granted only eight Ph.D.'s in psychology to Black candidates between 1920 and 1966 while granting a total of 3,767 Ph.D.'s during this same period; six of these leading departments had not had a single Black Ph.D.[11] The source and numbers of Black Ph.D.'s in the fields of psychology and educational psychology at all American universities for the period 1920–1950 are shown in Table 7.5.

The balance of this chapter recounts the personal histories and careers of the Black women and men who earned doctorates in psychology and educational psychology at American universities during the years 1920 to 1950. Table 7.6 gives a complete listing of these individuals and their academic degrees.

TABLE 7.5 Source and Output of Black Doctorate Holders in Psychology and Educational Psychology (1920–1950)

University	Year of Award
Clark University	1920
University of Chicago	1925, 1939
New York University	1930, 1948, 1949, 1950
Columbia University	1932, 1937, 1940, 1944
University of Cincinnati	1933
Harvard University	1933, 1939
University of Minnesota	1934, 1944, 1947
Indiana University	1935
Northwestern University	1935, 1941, 1942
Ohio State University	1937, 1946
Temple University	1937, 1939
University of California (Berkeley)	1938, 1948
University of Pennsylvania	1941, 1943
Pennsylvania State University	1946
University of Michigan	1949

TABLE 7.6 Individuals Granted Doctorates in Psychology and Educational Psychology (1920–1950)

Name	Institutions; Bachelor's and Master's Degrees	Doctorate Degree Institution	Major Subject	Year	Degree	Dissertation Title
1. Francis Cecil Sumner	Lincoln University (Pa.) Clark University (Mass.) Clark University (Mass.)	Clark University (Mass.)	Psychology	1920	PhD	Psychoanalysis of Freud and Adler
	B.A. B.A. A.M.					
2. Charles Henry Thompson	Virginia Union University University of Chicago	University of Chicago	Educational Psychology	1925	PhD	An Objective Determination of a Curriculum for Kindergarten Teachers
	B.A. M.A.					
3. Albert Sidney Beckham	Lincoln University (Pa.) Ohio State University Ohio State University	New York University	Educational Psychology	1930	PdD	The Provisions for High School Opportunity for Negro Pupils in Kentucky
	B.A. B.A. M.A.					
4. Robert Prentiss Daniel	Virginia Union University Teachers College-Columbia	Columbia University	Educational Psychology	1932	PhD	A Psychological Study of Delinquent and Non-Delinquent Negro Boys
	A.B. A.M.					
5. Inez Beverly Prosser	Prairie View College Samuel Houston College University of Colorado	University of Cincinnati	Educational Psychology	1933	PhD	Non-Academic Development of Negro Children in Mixed and Segregated Schools
	B.A. M.A.					
6. Howard Hale Long	Howard University Clark University	Harvard University	Educational Psychology	1933	EdD	Analysis of Test Results from Third Grade Children Selected on the Basis of Socio-Economic Status
	B.S. M.A.					
7. Ruth Howard Beckham	Simmons College (Mass.) Columbia University	University of Minnesota	Psychology	1934	PhD	A Study of the Development of Triplets
	B.S. M.S.					
8. Oran Wendle Eagleson	Indiana University Indiana University	Indiana University	Psychology	1935	PhD	Comparative Studies of White and Negro Subjects in Learning to Discriminate Visual Magnitude
	B.A. A.M.					
9. Martin David Jenkins	Howard University Indiana State	Northwestern University	Educational Psychology	1935	PhD	A Socio-Psychological Study of Negro Children of Superior Intelligence
	B.S. M.S.					
10. Frank Theodore Wilson	Lincoln University Columbia University	Columbia University	Educational Psychology and Religious Education	1937	EdD	A Program of Religious Education in the Liberal Arts College at Lincoln University
	B.A. A.M.					
11. Alberta Banner Turner	Ohio State University Ohio State University	Ohio State University	Psychology	1937	PhD	The Effects of Practice on the Perception and Memorization of Digits Presented in Single Exposure
	B.S. M.S.					

Continued

TABLE 7.6 *Continued*

Name	Institutions; Bachelor's and Master's Degrees		Doctorate Degree Institution	Major Subject	Year	Degree	Dissertation Title
12. John Henry Brodhead	Temple University Temple University	B.S. M.S.	Temple University	Psychology	1937	EdD	Educational Achievement and Its Relationship to the Socio-Economic Status of the Negro in the High School of Philadelphia
13. Carlton B. Goodlett	Howard University	B.A.	University of California Meharry Medical College (M.D.)	Psychology	1938	PhD	A Comparative Study of Adolescent Interests in Two Socio-Economic Groups
14. Carol Blanche Cotton	Oberlin College	—	University of Chicago	Psychology	1939	PhD	A Study of the Reactions of Spastic Children to Certain Test Situations
15. James Duckery	University of Pennsylvania	—	Temple University	Psychology	1939	PhD	An Intensive Survey of a Negro Special Class School
16. Rose Butler Browne	Rhode Island State College	—	Harvard University	Educational Psychology	1939	EdD	A Critical Evaluation of Experimental Studies of Remedial Reading
17. Kenneth Bancroft Clark	Howard University Columbia University	B.A. M.S.	Columbia University	Psychology	1940	PhD	Some Factors Influencing the Remembering of Prose Materials
18. Herman George Canady	Northwestern University Northwestern University	B.A. A.M.	Northwestern University	Psychology	1941	PhD	Test Standing and Social Setting
19. Frederick Payne Watts	Howard University Howard University	B.A. A.M.	University of Pennsylvania	Psychology	1941	PhD	A Comparative and Clinical Study of Delinquent and Non-Delinquent Negro Boys
20. James Thomas Morton, Jr.	University of Illinois Northwestern University	B.A. M.A.	Northwestern University	Psychology	1942	PhD	The Distortion of Syllogistic Reasoning Produced by Personal Convictions
21. James Arthur Bayton	Howard University Howard University Columbia University	B.A. M.S.	University of Pennsylvania	Psychology	1943	PhD	Interrelations Between Levels of Aspiration, Performance, and Estimates of Past Performance
22. Mamie Phipps Clark	Howard University Howard University	B.A. M.A.	Columbia University	Psychology	1944	PhD	Changes in Primary Mental Abilities with Age
23. Shearley Oliver Roberts	Brown University Brown University	B.A. A.M.	University of Minnesota	Psychology	1944	PhD	The Measurement of Adjustment of Negro College Youth

#	Name	Degrees	Institutions	Field	Year	Degree	Title
24.	Roger Kenton Williams	B.A. M.S.	Claflin College Claflin College	Psychology	1946	PhD	A Comparison of College Students Classified by a Psychological Clinic as Personality Maladjustment Cases and as Vocational Guidance Cases
25.	Howard Emery Wright	B.A. M.A.	Lincoln University Ohio State University	Psychology	1946	PhD	Racial Humor; A Value Analysis
26.	Alonzo Davis	B.S. M.S.	Howard University Howard University	Psychology	1947	PhD	Status Factors in Personality Characteristics of Negro College Students
27.	Mae Pullins Claytor	B.A. M.A.	Howard University New York University	Educational Psychology	1948	EdD	The Construction of a Home Adjustment Questionnaire Which May Be Used as an Aid in the Detection of Symptoms of Juvenile Delinquency
28.	Mildred McK. Satterwhite		University of California	Educational Psychology	1948	PhD	The Vocational Interests of Negro Teachers and College Students
29.	George Thomas Kyle	B.A. M.A.	University of Illinois University of Illinois	Psychology	1949	PhD	A Comparison of Normal and Schizophrenic Subjects in Level of Aspiration, Frustration, and Aggression
30.	Roderick Wellington Pugh	B.A. M.A.	Fisk University Ohio State University	Psychology	1949	PhD	An Investigation of Some Psychological Processes Accompanying Concurrent Electric Convulsive Therapy and Nondirective Psychotherapy with Paranoid Schizophrenia
31.	Herman Hodge Long	B.A. M.A.	Talledega College Hartford School of Religion	Educational Psychology	1949	PhD	Sensitivity Response Patterns of Negro and White Groups to Anger-Producing Social Stimuli
32.	Montraville Isadore Claiborne	B.A. M.A.	Fisk University University of Michigan	Psychology	1950	PhD	Classroom Mental Hygiene Practices of Teachers in Negro Public Schools and the Relation between These Practices and Certain Factors Which Influence the Quality of Teaching

Charles Henry Thompson (1896–1980)

Charles H. Thompson, the son of Patrick Henry and Sara Estelle (Byers) Thompson, was born in Jackson, Mississippi, where both of his parents were teachers at Jackson College. His father, a graduate of Wayland Theological Seminary (later Virginia Union University), sent his son to Wayland Academy in Virginia to complete his high school education. After graduation in 1914, Thompson enrolled at Virginia Union University and, by doubling his course enrollments, was graduated in 1917 with a B.A. degree.

Following a brief period as an army cadet at the army training camp in Des Moines, Iowa, he enrolled at the University of Chicago, completing a second undergraduate degree in 1918. He was then drafted into the army and stationed at Camp Grant (Illinois) and later in France. He remained in the army for nineteen months as an Infantry Personnel Regimental Sergeant Major. Upon discharge, Thompson returned to the University of Chicago. Carrying a double major in education and psychology, he was awarded the master's degree in 1920 and his Ph.D. in 1925. At Chicago Thompson studied under William Scott Gray, Harvey Carr, and C. H. Judd.

Thompson, the first Back American to receive a doctor's degree in educational psychology, had a strong desire to become a psychiatrist, but he decided on the study of educational psychology because he did not know of any Black person who was a psychiatrist at that time.

From 1920 to 1921, Thompson was an instructor in psychology at Virginia Union University. From 1922 to 1924, he was Director of Instruction at Alabama State Normal School. From 1925 to 1926, he was an instructor in psychology and social science at Sumner High School and Junior College in Kansas City, Kansas. In 1926, he began a lifelong association with Howard University, where he held positions as professor of education, Dean of the College of Liberal Arts, and Dean of the Graduate School. For more than thirty years, Dr. Thompson was editor-in-chief of the *Journal of Negro Education*. With his leadership, the journal grew to become a highly prestigious periodical; as editor, Dr. Thompson wrote more than one hundred articles and editorials.

Dr. Thompson served on a number of national and international committees on education. He was a fellow of the American Association for the Advancement of Science and held membership in a number of professional organizations.

Charles Henry Thompson

Albert Sidney Beckham (1897–1964)

A native of Camden, South Carolina, Albert Beckham was born to Calvin Albert and Elizabeth (James) Beckham on September 21, 1897. His father was a merchant and businessman in Camden. Beckham received his early education in the Presbyterian schools of Camden and was privately tutored. He attended Pennsylvania's Lincoln University and graduated with a B.A. degree in 1915. He then enrolled at Ohio State University and earned a second bachelor's degree in 1916. The following year, the twenty-year-old Beckham was awarded the M.A. degree in psychology.

As the United States was then embroiled in World War 1, Beckham applied for duty in the Air Corps. But he was refused training and told that he could contribute to the war effort by teaching psychology at a college. As a result, Beckham was assigned to the Sergeant's Army Training Corps (SATC) from 1917 to 1918 as a war professor in psychology at Wilberforce University in Ohio. He remained at Wilberforce as assistant professor of psychology until 1920.

When Beckham's parents moved from South Carolina to New York City, he joined them in New York, and in 1921 and 1922 he was editor of the New York City Dispatch until he became a Jay Gould Fellow in Psychology at New York University. In 1924, he accepted an instructorship at Howard University; from 1925 to 1928, he was an assistant professor of psychology. During this period, he founded the psychological laboratory at Howard, the first of its kind in a Black institution of higher learning. In 1928, he returned to New York and continued psychological study at NYU, where in 1930 he received a Ph.D. in psychology.

A Fellow of the National Committee for Mental Hygiene at the Illinois Institute for Juvenile Research from 1929 to 1930, Dr. Beckham also served as senior assistant psychologist at the institute from 1931 to 1935. There he conducted research and developed such reports as "Minimum Levels of Intelligence for Certain Occupations," which became a guide for state institutions for training the mentally handicapped.

Dr. Beckham was affiliated with Chicago's Board of Education, Bureau of Child Study, from 1935 to 1964. He served several school districts, but his longest term of service was spent as psychologist at DuSable High School. There he counseled thousands of Black youths, many of whom today credit his guidance as a key factor in their later (and for some, distinguished) careers. At DuSable he innovated the services of a school psychology clinic and developed parent counseling groups in which the study of adolescence helped mothers and fathers to deal understandingly with their children. The clinic reached into the community and brought together ministers whose parishes included

Albert Sidney Beckham

families of DuSable students; for the first time in that community, a church-neighborhood-school relationship became viable.

Dr. Beckham continued to publish research throughout his career. Studies from the Institute for Juvenile Research in Chicago included "A Study of Race Attitudes in Negro Children of Adolescent Age" and "A Study of the Intelligence of Colored Adolescents of Different Social Economic Status in Typical Metropolitan Areas." The latter surveyed the largest number of Black children to be included in one study.

While at DuSable High School, Dr. Beckham published several psychological studies: "Incidence of Frustration in a Counseled and Non-Counseled High School Group," "Narcolepsy Among Negroes," and "Incidence of Albinism in Negro Families."

From 1960 to 1963, he was psychological consultant at Ada S. McKinley Community House, Chicago, where he evaluated retarded children, adults, and women in vocational training classes. Here, as at other sites, he combined research with psychological service. The unpublished "A Study of Retarded Children and Their Mothers" details physical handicaps of retarded children and the relation between child's and mother's tested intelligence.

With his wife, Dr. Ruth W. Howard, Dr. Beckham conducted a practice in clinical psychology known as The Center for Psychological Service; in this capacity, he serviced private and public agencies. At one time, he was consultant to the Civil Aeronautics Administration.

His professional affiliations included the Chicago Psychology Club, Illinois Psychological Association, American Psychological Association, American Association for the Advancement of Science, and Beta Kappa Xi scientific society. He was a board member of the Chicago Friends of the Mentally Ill and the People's Rehabilitation Foundation.

His civic affiliations included service as a board member of the Boy Scouts of Chicago, the Planned Parenthood Society, and the Grace Church Community Center. He was a member of Alpha Phi Alpha fraternity, the American Heritage Society, and the American Forestry Association.

In 1945, he received an Honorary Doctor of Laws degree from Lincoln University.

Robert Prentiss Daniel (1902–1968)

Robert Daniel, the son of Charles James and Carrie (Green) Daniel, was born in Ettricks, Virginia. He graduated magna cum laude from Virginia Union University with a B.A. degree in 1924. Dr. Daniel received his master's degree in education in 1928 and his Ph.D. in educational psychology from Columbia University in 1932.

He was an instructor of mathematics at Virginia Union University from 1923 to 1925 and an instructor of English and education the following year. From 1926 to 1928, he was an assistant professor of education; from 1928 to 1936, he was professor of education and psychology and Director of the Extension Division at Virginia Union. In addition, from 1932 to 1936, Dr. Daniel was Director of the Division of Educational Psychology and Philosophy at Virginia Union, and in the summers of 1935 and 1936 he was a visiting professor of education at Hampton Institute in Virginia.

In 1936, Dr. Daniel was inaugurated as president of Shaw University in North Carolina. He remained in this capacity until 1950, when he assumed the presidency of Virginia State College, a position he held until his death in 1968.

Dr. Daniel was an ordained Baptist minister who served on numerous church governing boards and was active in many educational and psychological organizations. His professional affiliations included membership in the American Psychological Association, National Association for the Study of Negro Life, American Association of School Administrators, American Teachers Association, and the National Education Association. In 1953, he was nominated president of the Conference of Presidents of Negro Land Grant Colleges. His awards included the Distinguished Service Award in Education from the National Urban League in 1948.

Dr. Daniel was the author of "A Psychological Study of Delinquent Negro Boys" and of numerous other journal articles in the fields of psychology and education.

Inez Beverly Prosser (1897–1934)

Inez Beverly Prosser, born in Yoakum, Texas, in 1897, was the oldest daughter in a family of eleven brothers and sisters. Her father, Samuel Andrew Beverly, was a waiter, and her mother, Veola Hamilton Beverly, was a housewife. She attended public schools in Yoakum, graduating from high school in 1912. She was a very studious youngster who read constantly, and as a result her parents sent her to nearby Prairie View Normal College for teacher training. After graduation from Prairie View, she taught for a brief period in the Yoakum Colored Schools before accepting a teaching position in Austin, Texas. While teaching in Austin she attended Samuel Houston College and soon received her B.A. degree "with distinction" in education.

Following her marriage to Rufus A. Prosser, she attended the University of Colorado and earned a master's degree in educational psychology. Returning to Austin, she taught education courses at Tillotson College and became the dean and registrar of the college. During the 1929–1930 college year, Inez Prosser played a dominant role in a number of events at Tillotson, including the arrangement of the visit of Dr. George Washington Carver and the remodeling of several buildings. She received recognition as "an excellent teacher and leader."

In 1930, Inez Prosser accepted a teaching position and administrative duties at Tougaloo College in Mississippi. The award of a General Education Board Fellowship in 1931 provided her with the financial assistance to pursue further graduate studies in educational psychology at the University of Cincinnati. In 1933, Inez Prosser earned her Ph.D. in educational psychology, the first Black American woman to receive this degree. Her dissertation, the "Non-Academic Development of Negro Children in Mixed and Segregated Schools," was one of the earliest investigations into the social domain of elementary school children. At her graduation, Dr. Prosser was remembered as a "small petite woman whose doctoral gown had simply engulfed her."

Dr. Prosser was devoted to helping her brothers and sisters to secure college educations. To this end, she provided encouragement and a "college fund" to assist whatever brother or sister wanted to attend college. All her brothers and sisters completed high school and six of them completed college.

She was a tireless scholar at a time of overwhelming odds against Black people achieving such recognition as a doctor of philosophy de-

Inez Beverly Prosser

gree. One year after receiving her doctorate, she was killed in an automobile collision near Shreveport, Louisiana.

In 1968, at the HemisFair exposition in San Antonio, Texas, Dr. Prosser was cited for her contribution to Texas culture.

She was a member of Alpha Kappa Alpha sorority.

Howard Hale Long (1888–1948)

Howard Long, the son of Thomas and Annie (Vassar) Long, was born in News Ferry, Virginia, and obtained his preparatory education at the Wayland Academy in Richmond, Virginia. He received his B.S. degree and the Bachelor's Diploma in Education from Howard University in 1915. As a graduate, Long studied experimental psychology under G. Stanley Hall at Clark University, where he was awarded a master's degree in 1916. From 1916 to 1917, he was a psychology instructor at Howard University. He then served during World War I as an infantry first lieutenant in Europe.

After the war, Long became Dean at Paine College in Georgia; in 1923, he was appointed Dean of the School of Education at Knoxville College. The following year, he accepted a position as supervising principal in the public school system of Washington, D.C. From 1925 until his retirement in 1948, he was an associate superintendent in charge of educational research for the District of Columbia schools.

During this period, he published several research monographs in educational psychology and provided leadership for many research projects. His early publications, "An Analysis of Some Factors Influencing Alpha Scores by States" and "On Mental Tests and Racial Psychology" were documents frequently quoted in the field of psychometry. Howard Long received his Doctor of Education degree in educational psychology from Harvard University in 1933, the first graduate of Howard University to earn this degree.

After retiring from the District of Columbia school system, he became Dean of Administration at Wilberforce State College in Ohio. He was married to the former Ollie Mae Guerrant and was a member of Alpha Phi Alpha fraternity.

Howard Hale Long

Ruth Winifred Howard (1900–)

Ruth W. Howard became the first Black woman in the United States to receive the highest academic degree in psychology when she was awarded a Ph.D. by the University of Minnesota in 1934.

Ruth Howard was the eighth child in the family of the Reverend and Mrs. William James Howard of Washington, D.C. Throughout her childhood, she was exposed to the social work attitude of her father's ministry at the Zion Baptist Church in Washington. This, coupled with an affinity for books and reading, soon led her to recognize a desire to work with people and to study human behavior. After graduation from Dunbar High School in 1916, she attended Simmons College in Boston under a National Urban League grant. Majoring in social work, she received her B.S. degree in 1921 and her M.S. degree in 1927. From 1923 to 1929, she practiced social work, first in community organization with the Cleveland Urban League and later in child welfare with the State Welfare Agency.

A strong desire for more knowledge of human dynamics led Ruth Howard to the study of psychology. Under a Laura Spelman Rockefeller Fellowship for Parent Education, she studied at Columbia University's Teachers College and School of Social Work in 1929–1930. Continuing under a second Rockefeller fellowship, she studied at the University of Minnesota from 1930 to 1934. There she collaborated in research in areas of child development at the university's Institute for Child Development. In 1934, she received her Ph.D. in psychology and child development at Minnesota. Her doctoral research, "A Study of the Development of Triplets," was the first published study of a sizeable group of triplets of varying ages from several ethnic groups.

Shortly after completing her doctoral work, she married psychologist Albert S. Beckham and settled in Chicago. Following a clinical internship at the Illinois Institute for Juvenile Research, she entered into private practice in clinical psychology.

From 1940 to 1964, Dr. Howard served with her husband as co-director for the Center for Psychological Services. Concurrent professional duties involved her with several schools of nursing; from 1940 to 1964 she was psychologist for Chicago's Provident Hospital School of Nursing, and she consulted at schools of nursing in Kansas City, Missouri, and Jacksonville, Florida. She conducted clinics at Kentucky State College and Edward Waters College in Jacksonville. She was lecturer and consultant to adolescents for the Evanston (Illinois) public schools (1953–1955). In 1955, she was reading therapist at the University of

Ruth Winifred Howard

Chicago's Reading Clinic. From 1966 to 1968, she was a staff member for Worthington and Hurst Psychological Consultants. In 1964–1966, she was a psychologist for the McKinley Center for Retarded Children and, in 1968–1972, a psychologist for the Chicago Board of Health, Mental Health Division.

Dr. Howard continued in private practice and worked as psychological consultant for children's programs at Abraham Lincoln Centre and as consultant for Daniel D. Howard Associates in Chicago.

Dr. Howard's publications include "Fantasy and the Play Interview," "Intellectual and Personality Traits of a Group of Triplets," and "Developmental History of a Group of Triplets."

Her professional affiliations were the Chicago Psychology Club, Illinois Psychological Association, American Psychological Association, American Association for the Advancement of Science, and the International Reading Association.

Her civic affiliations included being a board member of the YWCA of Chicago, Women's International League for Peace and Freedom, American Association of University Women, and the National Association of College Women. She was a member of International House Association, Art Institute of Chicago, Hyde Park-Kenwood Community Conference, and Delta Sigma Theta sorority.

Oran Wendle Eagleson (1910–1997)

Oran Eagleson was born in Unionville, Indiana, but before he was one year old, his parents took him to Bloomington, Indiana, where he lived until a few months after completing work for the Ph.D. degree at Indiana University in 1935. It was at Indiana that he had also earned his B.A. (1931) and M.A. (1932) degrees.

The summer before entering the ninth grade, with both parents deceased, Eagleson went to work in a shoe repair shop to help out with the expenses being borne by his sister, Katie M. Eagleson, and brother, Halson V. Eagleson. (His brother later became a professor of physics at Howard University after several years on the faculty at Morehouse College.) Young Eagleson held the job as shoe shiner and shoe repair finisher through high school, college, graduate school, and even for about five months after receiving his doctorate.

At the beginning of his undergraduate training, Eagleson thought he would major in philosophy. But he found the course in introductory psychology, taught by S. L. Crawley, to be so interesting and challenging that he decided psychology would be his major subject and philosophy his minor. Both as undergraduate and graduate student, he was greatly impressed and influenced by psychologists J. R. Kantor, W. N. Kellogg, W. F. Book, and R. C. Davis (who served as chairman of his doctoral committee).

After receiving his Ph.D. in August 1935, Dr. Eagleson could not find employment in his new profession until February 1936, when he had a job offer from North Carolina College for Negroes in Durham. There he taught courses in psychology, sociology, economics, and philosophy until financial readjustments at the college and a pending salary reduction made Dr. Eagleson look elsewhere for employment. S. O. Roberts, later at Fisk University, had recently left Spelman, a woman's college in Atlanta, where he had initiated the first psychological laboratory in any of the institutions of the Atlanta University Center. His leaving vacated a teaching position in psychology that was then offered to Dr. Eagleson.

In September 1936, Dr. Eagleson accepted the Spelman College position. The new position not only paid a higher salary, but also offered the opportunity to teach just psychology courses. At this period, psychology courses were for elective or supplementary purposes—not a field in which the administration encouraged students to major; it was not until a few years later that psychology was listed as a major field of study. Dr. Eagleson encouraged many students to consider psychology as a major field, and gradually the number of psychology majors increased. In the early years of the major program, all but a few students were interested

Oran Wendle Eagleson

in teaching, social work, or homemaking, and their interest in psychology was in the application of the discipline to these areas or to the improvement of their everyday living patterns.

While teaching at Spelman, Dr. Eagleson also served as an exchange professor at Atlanta University, where he offered courses and directed theses for graduate students. His association with the supervision of theses was continued up to the time he assumed the duties of Dean of Instruction at Spelman in September 1954, a position he held until September 1970, when he was appointed Callaway Professor of Psychology.

Dr. Eagleson was associated with the research program of the Cooperative Experimental Summer School of the Atlanta University Center and was co-director of the Morehouse-Spelman Intensified Pre-College

Program. He also served as special lecturer and consultant in orientation and training projects conducted by the Peace Corps, Head Start, and several school systems in Georgia.

Dr. Eagleson's early research interests lay in racial comparisons, puzzle solving, handwriting, and musical topics. His research articles include "Comparative Studies of White and Negro Subjects in Learning to Discriminate Visual Magnitude," "The Success of Sixty Subjects in Attempting to Recognize Their Handwriting," and "Identification of Musical Instruments When Heard Directly and Over a Public-Address System."

Martin David Jenkins (1904–1978)

Martin Jenkins, the son of David and Josephine Jenkins, was born in Terre Haute, Indiana. He attended the public schools of Terre Haute, graduating from Wiley High School in 1921. He attended Howard University in Washington, D.C., receiving his B.S. degree in mathematics in 1925. From 1925 to 1930, he was a highway bridge contractor, in partnership with his father, in the firm of David Jenkins and Son. During this time, Martin Jenkins attended Indiana State College (now University) and earned a second undergraduate degree in teacher education.

In 1930, John Grandy, president of Virginia State College, visited Terre Haute on a speaking engagement and offered him a teaching post. Dr. Jenkins accepted the appointment, becoming an instructor of education at VSC from 1930 to 1932, when he was awarded a fellowship to pursue graduate studies at Northwestern University. (This was the first award of its kind to be granted to a Black American at Northwestern.) He was awarded a master's degree in 1933.

Dr. Jenkins remained at Northwestern, studied under Prof. Paul A. Witty, and received his doctorate in 1935. His dissertation, "A Socio-Psychological Study of Negro Children of Superior Intelligence," and subsequent studies, became classics in educational psychology. While many psychologists were debating the question of equality of Black-white intelligence test scores during this period, Dr. Jenkin's investigation discovered that intelligence levels for Blacks were as high as those recognized for the white population Furthermore, he identified a representative sample of "superior" Black students, one of whom had the highest IQ then on record.

From 1935 to 1937, Dr. Jenkins was registrar and professor of education at North Carolina Agriculture and Technical College. In 1937, he accepted the position of Dean of Instruction at Cheyney State Teachers College in Pennsylvania. From 1938 to 1948, Dr. Jenkins was a professor of education at Howard University with a one-year duty assignment as a Senior Specialist in Higher Education, Office of Education (HEW). In 1948, he assumed the presidency of Morgan State College in Maryland, a position he held until 1970. He was then Director, Office of Urban Affairs, American Council on Education (Washington, D.C.) from 1970 to 1974. He continued as a consultant in higher education.

Dr. Jenkins published more than eighty books, monographs, and articles. He lectured widely in the United States and abroad; under the auspices of the U.S. Department of State, he delivered lectures on educational psychology at colleges and universities in France, Norway, Sweden, Greece, Italy, and Lebanon.

Martin David Jenkins

Dr. Jenkins was a Diplomate in Clinical Psychology (ABEPP). He was decorated by the Liberian Government as Knight of the Liberian Humane Order of African Redemption. His numerous other awards include the Andrew White Medal from Loyola College, the Department of the Army Outstanding Civilian Service Medal, and a Commendation for Model Cities activities by the Departments of Health, Education, and Welfare and Housing and Urban Development.

He was awarded honorary doctor's degrees by the University of Liberia, Delaware State College, Howard University, Indiana State University, Johns Hopkins University, Lincoln University, and Morgan State College. He was a member of the Phi Beta Kappa honor society and the Kappa Alpha Psi and Sigma Pi Phi fraternities.

In 1974, the Martin David Jenkins Behavioral Science Center at Morgan State College was dedicated in his honor.

Alberta Banner Turner (1909–)

Alberta Turner, daughter of James L. and Mable Banner, was born in Chicago, Illinois, and moved to Columbus, Ohio, at a very early age. Her father was a cement contractor and her mother was a beautician who devoted her life to hard work in order to finance her daughter's college education. Alberta Turner attended the public schools of Columbus, graduating from East High School in 1925. At the age of sixteen, she enrolled at Ohio State University; she received her B.S. degree in Home Economics in 1929.

She had planned to continue as a graduate student at OSU but instead was persuaded to accept a position in the home economics department at Wilberforce University (now Central State College) in Xenia, Ohio. As head of the Department of Home Economics at Wilberforce, she attended Ohio State in the summer months and earned an M.S. degree in education in 1931. Her major field was child development and her graduate advisor was experimental psychologist S. Renshaw, who later became her doctoral dissertation advisor. In 1935, Alberta Turner received a Ph.D. in psychology from OSU.

From 1935 to 1936, she was head of the home economics department at Winston-Salem College in North Carolina. From 1936 to 1937, she was professor of psychology and head of the department of Home Economics at Lincoln University in Missouri. The years 1938 to 1939 found Dr. Turner head of the Department of Home Economics at Southern University in Louisiana. In 1939, she returned to North Carolina to head the home economics department at Bennett College for Women. She remained at Bennett until she returned to Columbus, Ohio in 1942 on maternity leave.

Unexpectedly in 1944, Dr. Turner was offered her first full-time employment in psychology as a clinician at the Ohio Bureau of Juvenile Research. For the next twenty-seven years, Dr. Turner worked at the bureau in a variety of positions, promoted from clinical psychologist to supervising psychologist and then to the position of chief psychologist. In 1963, she was promoted to the Central Administrative Office of the Ohio Youth Commission and became the Director of Research for the Ohio Youth Commission. She served in this capacity until her retirement in 1971.

During the period of her employment with the Commission, Dr. Turner found time to teach a variety of graduate courses at Ohio State University. She was also a psychologist at the Ohio Reformatory for Women. She served for four years as a member of the National Advisory Council for Vocational Rehabilitation and the Rehabilitation Institute of

Alberta Banner Turner

Chicago. She was a member of the Regional Advisory Council for the Research and Training Center at Northwestern University's McGraw Medical Center. She also served as president of the National Jack and Jill of America and national program director for Links, Inc.

In 1971, a citation from the State of Ohio and the Ohio Youth Commission read, "Alberta Banner Turner, Ph.D., has been synonymous with mention of the field of juvenile rehabilitation and treatment in Ohio for 27 years. She has played a very active role in its history." After her retirement, she became administrative assistant to Weight Watchers of Central Ohio, a position in keeping with her research interest in the psychological aspects of obesity, and was a Mary Kay cosmetics director.

Dr. Turner's publications include "The Effects of Practice on the Perception and Memorization of Digits Presented in Single Exposure" and "The Psychologist at the Juvenile Diagnostic Center: Past, Present, and Future."

Her honors and awards include Gamma Psi Kappa, Ten Women of the Year by the Columbus Citizen Journal, Alpha Kappa Alpha Award for Community and Scholastic Endeavors, and Pi Lamda Theta Citation. She served as a member of the Criminal Justice Supervisory Commission and the Ohio Society for Crippled Children and Adults.

Dr. Turner holds Diplomate status in Clinical Psychology (ABEPP) and is certified by the Ohio Psychological Association. She is married to John G. Turner, retired from the U.S. Department of Labor, and is the mother of two children. She resides in Columbus, Ohio, and Freeport, Grand Bahamas, and maintains an interest in incest cases of female adolescents.

John Henry Brodhead (1898–1951)

John Brodhead was born in Washington, New Jersey, the son of Robert and Elizabeth Brodhead. He graduated from the West Chester State Normal School in Pennsylvania in 1919. In 1937, he received his Doctor of Education degree in educational psychology from Temple University.

Dr. Brodhead was a teacher and principal in the Philadelphia school system beginning in 1919. During the 1940s, he was principal of Reynolds School, one of the largest schools in Philadelphia.

Dr. Brodhead was active in a number of educational movements and organizations. He was elected president of the American Teachers Association (ATA) in 1949. He served as president of the Association of Pennsylvania Teachers, the New Era Educational Association, and the Pennsylvania Educational Association. He was a charter member of the Philadelphia Commission on Participation of Negroes in National Defense and was a later organizer and chairman of the Citizens Committee for Integration of Negro Nurses. This committee ultimately led to the admittance of Black nursing trainees into the Philadelphia General Hospital.

He was the author of "The Educational and Socio-Economic Status of the Negro in the Secondary Schools of Pennsylvania."

Kenneth Bancroft Clark (1914–)

Kenneth Clark, born in the Panama Canal Zone, is the son of Arthur and Miriam (Hanson) Clark. At the age of seven, he came to the United States and received his public school education in New York City. He enrolled at Howard University in 1929 and several years later became a naturalized citizen. He received his B.S. degree in psychology from Howard University in 1935 and the following year was awarded the M.S. degree. He enrolled at Columbia University and, while a graduate student, was a research assistant for the comprehensive study of Gunnar Myrdal, *An American Dilemma*. He was awarded the Ph.D. degree in psychology in 1940.

Dr. Clark taught at Queens College (New York) and, beginning in 1942, was a professor of psychology at City College in the City University at New York. Dr. Clark was president of the Metropolitan Applied Research Center, which he founded in 1967 "as a catalyst for change and as an advocate for the poor and powerless in American cities." He was a visiting professor at Columbia University, the University of California at Berkeley, and Harvard University. Dr. Clark was a member of the New York State Board of Regents and a member of the Board of Trustees of the University of Chicago. He was also a member of the New York Urban Development Corporation.

Dr. Clark was awarded the Spingard Medal by the NAACP in 1961 and the Kurt Lewin Memorial Award by the Society for Psychological Study of Social Issues in 1966. Among the colleges and universities which granted him honorary degrees are Haverford College, Yeshiva University, Oberlin College, Johns Hopkins University, Amherst College, New York University, Columbia University, and the University of Massachusetts.

The U.S. Supreme Court cited Dr. Clark's work on the harmful effects of segregation in its 1954 decision, *Brown v. Board of Education*. He was the author of several books and articles, including *Prejudice and Your Child* (1955) and the prize-winning *Dark Ghetto: Dilemmas of Social Power* (1965). He was co-author, with Jeannette Hopkins, of *Relevant War Against Poverty* (1968) and co-editor, with Talcott Parsons, of *Negro American* (1968). His most recent work was *Pathos of Power* (1974).

Dr. Clark was president (1970–1971) of the American Psychological Association (the first Black to hold that office) and president of the Society for the Psychological Study of Social Issues. His fraternal member-

Kenneth Bancroft Clark

ships included Sigma Xi and Phi Beta Kappa. He recently announced plans to join Gunnar Myrdal for a new study of racial problems in the United States.

Dr. Clark was married to Dr. Mamie Phipps Clark and is the father of two children.

Carlton Benjamin Goodlett (1914–1997)

Carlton B. Goodlett, the son of Mr. and Mrs. A. R. Goodlett, was born in the Black community of Orange Hill at the outskirts of Chipley, Florida. His mother received a teaching credential from Florida A & M College, and his father completed night high school in Omaha, Nebraska, where the family had then moved. Young Goodlett attended the public schools of Omaha, graduating from Central High School in 1931. While a high school student, he "discovered what it meant to be a Black person in the white man's world." As a result, he identified strongly with his blackness and decided to attend a Black university in spite of the opportunities he had to enroll in several white universities.

Armed with a national Alpha Phi Alpha fraternity scholarship, he began studies at Howard University in Washington, D.C., then an extremely segregated city. The proud seventeen-year-old from the midwest ran head-on into the realities of racism; the accumulation of his experiences led Goodlett to devote his life's work to fighting racism and its by-products.

Receiving his B.S. degree in psychology under the tutelage of Francis C. Sumner, he proceeded to the University of California at Berkeley to earn a master's degree in abnormal psychology and made plans to attend medical school. However, several events altered his plans as well as his goals. The first Black person to study psychology in the graduate division at the University of California, Goodlett met and became the protege of Harold and Mary Jones. The Joneses, who had established several institutes of child welfare in the United States, persuaded Goodlett to work at the Berkeley Institute as a graduate student. His efforts at the Berkeley Institute eventually became the basis of his Ph.D. dissertation, "A Comparative Study of Adolescent Interests in Two Socio-Economic Groups." In 1938, he was awarded a Ph.D. in psychology at the University of California.

In 1938, Dr. Goodlett joined the faculty of West Virginia State College and taught educational psychology, learning, and statistics. While at WVSC, Dr. Goodlett attempted to organize an Institute for the Study of the Negro Child, but he could not obtain funding from the General Education Fund Foundation, which had previously funded and established child study institutes in several major white universities. He also worked with Herman Canady in an attempt to organize professional Blacks in psychology during the late 1930s (see Chapter 6).

Dr. Goodlett went on to author several articles and monographs, including "The Mental Abilities of Twenty-Nine Deaf and Partially Deaf

Carlton Benjamin Goodlett

Negro Children" and "The Reading Abilities of the Negro Elementary Child in Kanawha County, West Virginia." After two years of teaching at West Virginia State College, Dr. Goodlett enrolled in Meharry Medical College in Tennessee in 1940 to study medicine. While a student at Meharry, he taught courses in psychology at Meharry Medical College, Fisk University, and Tennessee Agricultural and Industrial College. The energetic Dr. Goodlett also found time to teach courses at Fort Valley State College in Georgia during two summer vacations.

After receiving his M.D. degree, he interned at Homer G. Phillips Hospital in St. Louis and then did a brief stint as a house physician at Maury County Colored Hospital in Columbus, Tennessee, before returning to northern California in 1945. Since that time, Dr. Goodlett became involved in community action programs and served as a catalyst in many civil rights efforts. In 1947, he became co-publisher of the San Francisco

Sun Reporter and in 1951 publisher; he became president of the National Newspaper Publishers Association—The Black Press of America.

Dr. Goodlett was president of the San Francisco NAACP, president of the San Francisco Foundation to Study Our Schools, a director of the San Francisco Council of Boy Scouts of America, and a member of the Society of Sigma Xi and the National Committee on Africa. He also served as chairman of the California Black Leadership Conference, trustee of the Third Baptist Church, and former vice president of the San Francisco Council of Churches.

In 1966, Dr. Goodlett ran in the gubernatorial primary election in California and came in third in a field of six Democrats. In 1967–1968, he taught a course at San Francisco State College entitled "Group Conflict in Urban America."

Dr. Goodlett maintained that there are two deadly menaces to the survival of Black people in the United States: racism and the effects of alcohol and drug addiction. Under his sponsorship, a three- to five-year study was projected that examined "The Role of Alcohol, Hard Drugs and Narcotics on the Black Experience," by four national Black organizations: National Newspaper Publishers Association, National Bar Association, National Business League, and National Medical Association.

Dr. Goodlett believed that Blacks in the behavioral sciences, particularly in psychology, sociology, and psychiatry, have a special responsibility to study in depth the role of racism on the quality of the Black experience in the nation and a further responsibility to lead in the development of techniques for the eradiction of racism in the United States.

Herman George Canady (1901–1970)

Herman G. Canady, the son of Rev. Howard T. and Mrs. Anna (Carter) Canady, was born in Okmulgee, Oklahoma. He attended Douglass Elementary School and Favor High School in Guthrie, Oklahoma. In 1922, he graduated from the high school department of George R. Smith College in Sedalia, Missouri.

In the fall of 1923, with the assistance of a Charles F. Grey scholarship, Canady enrolled at Northwestern University's Theological School with the intention of becoming a minister. There he discovered an intense interest in the behavioral sciences, and he decided to major in sociology. Throughout his undergraduate years, he worked at odd jobs around Evanston, Illinois, to pay his living expenses.

In June 1927, he graduated from Northwestern with a B.A. in sociology and a minor in psychology. He remained at Northwestern and the following year was awarded the M.A. degree in clinical psychology. Canady's master's thesis, "The Effects of Rapport on the IQ: A Study in Racial Psychology," criticized the neglect of the importance of the race of the examiner in establishing testing rapport and offered suggestions for establishing an adequate environment. This document became a historical treatise and a classic in its field.

In September 1928, after the departure of Francis Sumner from West Virginia Collegiate Institute (now West Virginia State College), Canady accepted an offer to join that faculty and assume the vacant chairmanship of the psychology department. Under Canady's vigorous leadership, WVSC became the nation's leading Black college in psychological research. During a three-year period, 1936–1939, Canady conducted a host of social-psychological research projects and published many journal articles. Of these studies, "Adapting Education to the Abilities, Needs and Interests of Negro College Students" and "Individual Differences and Their Educational Significance in the Guidance of the Gifted and Talented Child" became significant resources for many Black educational institutions. His "Psychology in Negro Institutions" was the only published research effort that evaluated the status, training, and research efforts of early psychologists in Black colleges and universities.

In 1939, Canady was awarded a General Education Board fellowship, which allowed him to take a leave of absence from West Virginia in 1939 and 1940 to return to Northwestern and complete his Ph.D. studies. In June 1941, he was awarded a doctorate in psychology. His dissertation, "Test Standing and Social Setting: A Comparative Study of the Intelligence-Test Scores of Negroes Living Under Varied Environ-

Herman George Canady

mental Conditions," became a widely quoted study in sociology as well as in psychology.

Upon his return to West Virginia, Dr. Canady again assumed a research leadership posture and conducted a series of significant studies in social psychology. His record as a psychologist and researcher was eminent.

Dr. Canady was a visiting lecturer to schools and colleges under the auspices of the American Friends Service Committee (1946) and consultant to the Pacific Coast Council on Intercultural Education and Intercultural Projects of the San Diego City Schools (1947). He was a part-time clinical psychologist for the Mental Health Unit, Veterans Administration, Huntington, West Virginia (1948–1953) and for the West Virginia Bureau of Mental Hygiene (1947–1968).

In 1950, Dr. Canady was designated Diplomate, American Board of Examiners in Professional Psychology. His awards included Man of the Year, 1949, from Alpha Chapter of Omega Psi Phi fraternity, and Middle-

Eastern Provincial Achievement Award, 1951, from Kappa Alpha Psi fraternity. He held fraternal memberships in Sigma Xi, Alpha Kappa Delta, and Kappa Alpha Psi. His professional memberships included Fellow of the American Association for the Advancement of Science, Fellow of the American Psychological Association, American Teachers Association (Chairman of the Department of Psychology, 1938–1945), American Association of University Professors, West Virginia State Psychological Association (President, 1954–1955), West Virginia Academy of Science (Chairman of the Department of Psychology, 1952–1953 and 1955–1956), and the West Virginia State Teachers Association.

Dr. Canady, who retired in 1968, was a faculty member and chairman of the psychology department at West Virginia State College for forty years. He was an active participant in the struggle for equal rights. He received Northwestern University's Alumni Merit Award and an honorary doctor's degree from West Virginia State College.

In 1934, Herman Canady married the former Julia Witten of Tip Top, Virginia. He was the father of Joyce A. and Herman G. Canady.

Frederick Payne Watts (1904–   )

Frederick Watts was born in Staunton, Virginia. His father, Charles H., an avid reader, was at one time a farmer and later performed house maintenance services; his mother, Harriett, was intensely interested in rearing her five children. His parents instilled high ideals in all their children and encouraged them to become college educated—with the result that one became a physician, one a dentist, and one a psychologist.

Frederick Watts completed elementary and high school in Washington, D.C. His early professional goal was to become an ophthalmologist, and to this end he enrolled at Howard University with the intention of becoming a physician. To help finance his education, he worked at many odd jobs. The Army ROTC program at Howard was financially helpful. Watts's intense interest in "why people misbehave" led him to enroll in several psychology courses, and his psychology professor, the dynamic Albert S. Beckham, inspired him to major in psychology.

After graduating from college in 1926, with a double major in French and psychology, he received a teaching fellowship in psychology which provided him with the financial assistance needed to complete his master's degree at Howard. After a brief year of teaching at Kittrell College in North Carolina, he returned to Howard University to teach in the summer of 1928. By this time Beckham had left Howard, and Francis Sumner joined Watts forming a two-person department of psychology. Watts remained at Howard until 1942, teaching psychology with Sumner and another colleague, Max Meenes, who joined the department in 1930. During this period Watts published with Sumner a scholarly investigation of the "Rivalry Between Uniocular Negative After Images and the Vision of the Other Eye" and his own research on "A Comparative and Clinical Study of Delinquent and Non-Delinquent Negro Boys."

In 1941, Watts received his Ph.D. in clinical psychology from the University of Pennsylvania, the first black person to receive this degree from that institution. While at Pennsylvania, he studied under L. Witmer, M. Viteles, and S. Fernberger.

In October 1942, Dr. Watts was called to serve in the army as a preinduction classification officer and personnel consultant during World War II. In this capacity, he assisted in setting up psychological testing facilities for the Baltimore induction station and supervised in the assignment and counseling of enlisted personnel in various military installations. Upon his discharge, as a captain in the adjutant general's department, he was appointed assistant chief clinical psychologist for the Veterans Administration regional office in Philadelphia.

Frederick Payne Watts

In 1948, Dr. Watts returned to Howard to establish the Liberal Arts Counseling Service, which was later expanded to encompass the total student body (and renamed the University Counseling Service). Watts conducted a number of institutional studies at Howard, including "Initial Group Counseling of Freshmen" and "A Study of the College Environment." Other studies accomplished at this time included "The Development of a Behavior Judgment Scale" and "Developmental Counseling."

Dr. Watts was affiliated with a number of professional organizations and was a Diplomate in Clinical Psychology (ABEPP). He was director of the University Counseling Service and taught psychology part-time until his retirement from Howard University in 1970.

He was married to the late Louise Armstead Watts and is the father of four daughters. Today he resides in Washington, D.C., and his current interests continue to be in counseling and clinical psychology

James Arthur Bayton (1912–1990)

James Bayton, born in Whitestone, Virginia, was the son of George and Helen Bayton; his father was a physician and a graduate of Howard University's medical school. Bayton graduated from Temple University's high school in 1931, and he then enrolled at Howard University as a chemistry major with the intent of eventually entering medical school. But Bayton enjoyed his psychology courses, taught by Francis Sumner, Max Meenes, and Frederick Watts, and it was not long before he had taken enough of them to declare psychology a major subject. After graduation with a B.A. in 1935, and with the assistance of a graduate scholarship, Bayton began studies for the M.S. degree in psychology.

When he was awarded the graduate degree at Howard, it was clear that the medical profession had lost out to his desire to become a professional psychologist. Bayton entered Columbia University in 1936, studying under R. S. Woodworth and A. T. Poffenberger; however, at the death of his father, Bayton transferred his graduate studies to the University of Pennsylvania in order to be nearer his home. At Pennsylvania, he studied under L. Witmer, S. W. Fernberger, M. G. Preston, and M. Viteles. (It is interesting to note that Fernberger had also taught Francis Sumner and Max Meenes at Clark University and Frederick Watts at Pennsylvania.)

With his dissertation research under way, Bayton was offered a teaching position at Virginia State College. The prestige of VSC and the financial depression of the late 1930s together led Bayton to interrupt his studies to become an associate professor of psychology. He remained in this position from 1939 to 1943, during which time he performed research and published journal articles. Among his students at Virginia State was an enthusiastic young man who later became chairman of the psychology department at Florida A & M University, Dr. Joseph Cyrus Awkard. In 1943, with the aid of the prestigious Harrison fellowship at the University of Pennsylvania, Bayton was awarded his Ph.D. in psychology.

During the war years 1943–1945, Dr. Bayton was a social science analyst with the U.S. Department of Agriculture, working with R. Likert, D. Cartwright, and A. Campbell. In 1945, he was appointed professor of psychology at Southern University in Louisiana. In 1946, Bayton moved to Morgan State College in Maryland as professor of psychology. In 1947, he returned to his alma mater, Howard University, as a professor of psychology. In 1948, Bayton answered a request to rejoin the Department of Agriculture, on a part-time basis, to provide assistance in their consumer behavior studies. His work with the Department of Agriculture

James Arthur Bayton

was recognized by a Superior Service Award for "superior accomplish-ments in the development and application of psychological concepts and techniques in the field of commodity market research and for out-standing ability and leadership."

Dr. Bayton held a number of positions concurrent with his teaching duties. He was vice president of National Analysts, 1953–1962 and again 1966–1967; vice president of Universal Marketing Research, 1962–1966; senior fellow at the Brookings Institution, 1967–1968; and senior staff psychologist at Chilton Research Services, 1968 to 1976.

He served on several advisory committees, including the Research Advisory Committee, Social Security Administration, HEW (1962–1964), and the Advisory Committee on Agricultural Science, Department of

Agriculture (1965–1968). He was chairman of the committee appointed to study equal employment opportunity policies in the National Aeronautics and Space Administration. He also conducted lectures and seminars in many of America's leading universities.

Dr. Bayton's skill in directing marketing research was of national record; his projects included research for DuPont, IBM, Armstrong Cork, Chrysler, Eli Lilly, Curtis Publishing, Johnson and Johnson, Schick, Pet Milk, American Dairy Association, Federal Reserve Board, Smith Kline, French, Proctor and Gamble, and the Office of Naval Research. He was responsible for another series of research projects over a period of thirty years dealing with the self-concept of Black people. He also served as an expert witness for the NAACP Legal Defense Fund in cases dealing with legal aspects of school desegregation and discrimination in employment.

His later interests were in government and corporate policy research, motivation, and consumer behavior. Dr. Bayton was the author of *Tension in the Cities—Three Programs for Survival* and a host of professional journal articles, including "Single Stimulus Versus Comparative Methods in Determining Taste Preferences," "Method of Single Stimulus Determinations of Taste Preferences," "Interrelations Between Levels of Aspiration, Performance, and Estimates of Past Performance," and "Intervening Variables in the Perception of Racial Personality Traits." A major project of his studied the identification of factors related to racial tension in military settings.

Dr. Bayton was chairman of the psychology department at Howard from 1966 to 1969. He was a member of Phi Beta Kappa, Sigma Xi, and Omega Psi Phi fraternities.

James Thomas Morton, Jr. (1911–1974)

Born in Greenwood, South Carolina, James Morton was taken to Evanston, Illinois, by his parents when he was eighteen months old. As an active, civic-minded youngster growing up in Evanston, Morton found mathematics and French easy subjects and reading an enjoyable but insatiable habit. He was athletically inclined and won numerous awards from the city recreational department for his athletic ability. Much of his time was spent with youth groups in attempts to open in them an awareness of the possibilities for a better intellectual and economic life for the youth of that day. On a voluntary basis, he taught classes in Negro history to members of the Evanston community and various church groups. His involvement in the Ebenezar Methodist Church of Evanston led to still more community activities.

James Thomas Morton, Jr.

After graduation from Evanston Township High School in 1931, Morton matriculated at the University of Illinois at Champaign. His desire to major in psychology was discouraged by one university counselor who informed him that "psychology was no career for the Negro and it was best for him to go into law or medicine." Nevertheless, he graduated with a B.A. in psychology in 1934.

With an accumulation of courses in both psychology and sociology, Morton enrolled at Northwestern University and received his M.A. in 1935. He began his teaching career at Bennett College in North Carolina, but he returned to Northwestern to earn his Ph.D. in psychology in 1942. Returning to Bennett, he was appointed Dean of Instruction.

Then Dr. Morton was drafted into the army as a private. His military career was uneventful; however, near the end, he was given a direct commission as a psychologist, the only Black American to receive such an appointment during World War II.

Upon his discharge, he accepted a position at Dillard University in Louisiana as a professor and counselor. In 1946, he accepted an appointment at Tuskegee Veterans' Hospital in Alabama, becoming the first Black chief psychologist for the VA. While in Alabama, he produced a study (unpublished) of Black psychologists, hoping to use the data to assist in the recruitment of young Black scholars in psychology. He also compiled an immense data bank relating to the intelligence of Black Americans as measured by the Wechsler-Bellevue Intelligence Test. In 1948, Dr. Morton was designated Diplomate in Clinical Psychology in the APA's first listing of Diplomate status awards. Morton was later elected to Fellow status in the APA.

In 1953, Dr. Morton returned to Evanston, Illinois, entered private practice, and subsequently became employed at the VA Hospital at Downey, Illinois. He also affiliated with other hospitals and educational institutions in the Chicago area. At the time of his death, in 1974, he was coordinator of training for psychology Ph.D. candidates at the VA Hospital at Downey.

For many years, Dr. Morton was a pioneer for Blacks in clinical psychology and a strong advocate for equal education and employment opportunities for minority youth. His chief professional interests were in clinical and social psychology. He was married to the former Lorraine Hairston and the father of one child, Elizabeth.

Mamie Phipps Clark (1917–1983)

Mamie Phipps Clark was born in Hot Springs, Arkansas, the daughter of Harold H. and Katie F. Phipps. Her father was a physician in Hot Springs, where she attended public schools from elementary to high school. Upon graduation from Langston High School in 1934, she enrolled at Howard University with the intent of majoring in mathematics; while at Howard she met her future husband, Kenneth B. Clark, and through his influence decided to major in psychology. In 1938, she was awarded the B.A. degree, magna cum laude, in psychology. With University Fellow status, she remained at Howard and subsequently earned her M.A. in psychology in 1939. In 1944, as a Rosenwald fellow at Columbia University, Mamie Clark received her Ph.D. in psychology.

Mamie Phipps Clark

Dr. Clark's professional experiences included duties as a research psychologist for the American Public Health Association from 1944 to 1945; from 1945 to 1946, she assumed duties as a research psychologist for the United States Armed Forces Institute, New York Examination Center at Teachers College, Columbia University. In 1946, Dr. Clark became executive director of the Northside Center for Child Development in New York City, a position she held until her death.

Dr. Clark at the same time held many other positions; she was a psychologist for the Riverdale Children's Association (1945–1946) and a visiting professor of experimental methods and research design at Yeshiva University (1958–1960). She was a member of the board of directors for the New York Mission Society, Teachers College at Columbia University, New York City Public Library, American Broadcasting Company, Museum of Modern Art, and the Phelps Stokes Fund. Dr. Clark served with several advisory groups including the Harlem Youth Opportunities Unlimited (HARYOU) and the National Headstart Planning Committee. In 1957, she received the Alumni Achievement Award of Howard University for outstanding post-graduate service in psychological research. In 1972, Dr. Clark received the honorary Doctor of Humane Letters degree from Williams College.

She held membership in the American Psychological Association and Phi Beta Kappa, and she was a fellow of the American Association of Orthopsychiatry. She authored numerous monographs and research studies. Her publications, "Segregation as a Factor in the Racial Identification of Negro Pre-school Children," "The Development of Consciousness of Self and the Emergence of Racial Identification in Negro Pre-school Children," and "Skin Color as a Factor in Racial Identification of Negro Pre-school Children" (all with K. B. Clark), became classics in the field of psychology.

Shearley Oliver Roberts (1910–1984)

S. O. Roberts, born in Alexandria, Virginia, was the son of George and Esther (Ragland) Roberts. He graduated from Howard High School in Wilmington, Delaware, in 1928. His B.A. and M.A. degrees (with honors) were granted at Brown University in June 1932 and June 1933, respectively. His major was psychology and his minor work was in education and economics; his principal teachers at Brown were L. Carmichael and H. Schlosberg.

The University of Minnesota in 1944 conferred on Roberts a Ph.D. in child welfare (child development) and psychology. He had studied there with J. E. Anderson, F. Goodenough, B. F. Skinner, and D. G. Paterson, under a George Davis Bivin grant in mental hygiene. Special work in human development on a General Education Board fellowship was done at the University of Chicago with R. J. Havighurst and E. W. Burgess.

Dr. Roberts's experiences included teaching, serving as dean of students, individual and group psychological testing and interviewing, and research in child development. He held positions at Atlanta University (instructor, 1933–1936), Dunbar Junior College (acting dean, 1942–1943), and at Arkansas AM&N College (teacher and Dean of

Shearley Oliver Roberts

Students, 1939–1942 and 1944–1945). The psychology department at Fisk was established under his chairmanship in 1951–1952.

Dr. Roberts was the recipient of numerous federal and private foundation grants. His areas of special interest were child development, mental health principles, testing, cultural differences, and personality adjustment.

He was a delegate to the White House Conference on Youth in 1950; he participated in a number of other organizations and special meetings (the Thayer Conference on Psychology and Schools was one of these). He was editor of the Fisk-Meharry Local Preparatory Commission's Report on "Negro American Youth, Mental Health and World Citizenship." He was a Fellow of the Society for Research in Child Development and of the Division of Developmental Psychology of the American Psychological Association. He was a member of the American Educational Research Association and of Sigma Xi and Psi Chi societies. He served on the Council of Psychological Resources in the South, the Governor's Committee on Training and Research in Tennessee, the board of the Mental Health Center of Middle Tennessee, the Nashville Metropolitan Action Commission (as member and vice chairman), and other scientific and professional groups. Dr. Roberts was a professor of psychology and of education and the chairman of Fisk University's psychology department. He was lecturer in psychology at Meharry Medical College. At Fisk, he inaugurated the Program in Child Life and Development in 1950.

He married Marion Pearl Taylor of Little Rock, Arkansas, and had three daughters, Esther Pearl Ashley, Barbara Taylor Stone, and Kay George.

Roger Kenton Williams (1914–1989)

Roger Williams was born in Harrisburg, Pennsylvania, where his father, James H. Williams, was a public school teacher and his mother, Carrie Williams, was busy rearing him, his two brothers, and a sister. After his graduation from Harris Senior High School in 1932, he attended Claflin College in South Carolina, where he earned his B.A. degree, magna cum laude, in sociology. While an undergraduate, Williams was president of the Student Government Association and class president, as well as other campus leadership positions.

Following his graduation in 1936, he remained at Claflin College as an assistant to the Dean in charge of student personnel. During that time, Williams realized the need to learn more about human behavior and the behavioral sciences. A decision to attend graduate school resulted in his enrollment at Pennsylvania State University in College Park in 1940.

Roger Kenton Williams

In 1941, Williams accepted an appointment as associate professor of education and psychology at North Carolina Agricultural and Technical College, where he remained until his career was interrupted by military duty during World War II. For more than three years, Williams served in the U.S. Coast Guard as a Chief Yeoman in Recruitment and Morale. After his discharge in 1945, and with the financial assistance of the G.I. Bill of Rights, he returned to PSU and completed his Ph.D. studies in psychology in 1946. His dissertation focused on "A Comparison of College Students Classified by a Psychological Clinic as Personality Maladjustment Cases and as Vocational Guidance Cases." At Pennsylvania State University, he studied under C. C. Peters, E. B. Ormer, and R. G. Bernreuter.

In 1946, Dr. Williams returned to North Carolina A&T College as a professor of psychology and Director of the Veterans Administration Guidance Center. He remained in these positions until 1948, when he accepted appointments as professor of education and Director of Student Personnel at Morgan State College. From 1949 to 1972, he was professor of psychology and chairman of the psychology department. From July 1968 to January 1969, he was in addition acting dean of the graduate school at Morgan. From February 1972 to June 1973, he held the position of Vice President for Academic Affairs. Later, Dr. Williams was named Vice President for Planning and Operations Analysis at Morgan State University.

He also held a number of concurrent positions. From 1957 to 1968, Dr. Williams was director of Morgan's Independent Study Project, and for several years he was a consultant to the Ford Foundation. In 1972, he was named chairman of the Maryland State Board of Examiners of Psychologists. His research publications include "Creating Institutional Opportunities for Producing More Black Ph.D.'s in Psychology" (with Bayton and Roberts), "Appearance, Features and the Concept of Black Militancy" (with Gregory Shannon), and a number of academic placement tests. Other research interests included student research supervision, independent study designs, and statistical application of qualitative data.

Dr. Williams married the former Beryl E. Warner and had one son.

Howard Emery Wright (1908–1988)

Howard Wright, the son of William H. and Evelyn (Ferguson) Wright, was born in Philadelphia. He attended elementary school in Washington, D.C., and Atlantic City High School in New Jersey. He entered Lincoln University in Pennsylvania in 1928 and received his B.A. degree in 1932. He then enrolled in the graduate school at Ohio State University and, in 1933, Wright was awarded the M.A. degree in psychology. His thesis research, "An Analysis of Results with Certain Tests of Interests and Attitudes," indicated his early interest in social psychology.

At twenty-five years of age, Wright became principal of the Campus Laboratory School at Albany State College in Georgia, a position he held until 1934. From 1936 to 1939, he was principal of Aracoma High School in Logan, West Virginia, and from 1940 to 1945, he was principal of the Campus Laboratory School at Prairie View College in Texas.

Howard Emery Wright

At Prairie View he was also associate professor of education and director of teacher training. Wright then returned to Ohio State in 1945 as a graduate teaching assistant; he completed his Ph.D. in psychology in 1946.

From 1945 to 1948, Dr. Wright was chairman of the psychology department at North Carolina College in Durham. In the fall of 1948, he became chairman of the division of education and psychology at Texas Southern University, remaining in this position until 1953, when he returned to North Carolina to reassume the chairmanship of the psychology department.

In 1961, Dr. Wright was appointed president of Allen University in South Carolina. In 1965, he was regional director of Community Action Programs for the Office of Economic Opportunity in Washington, D.C. From 1966 to 1967, he was branch chief of the Division of College Support for the U.S. Office of Education. Wright accepted the academic deanship at Maryland State College in Princess Anne in 1967; three years later he became acting chancellor at the University of Maryland.

In 1972, Dr. Wright became Director, Division of Social Sciences at Hampton Institute in Virginia, and in September 1974, he became professor of psychology at Salisbury State College in Maryland.

Dr. Wright served as a board member of the Home for Dependent Children (Houston, Texas), Child Guidance Clinic (Durham, North Carolina), and Advisory Committee to the Civil Rights Commission and Vice President of Victory Savings Bank (Columbia, South Carolina). His fraternal memberships included the Elks, the Masons, and Omega Psi Phi. His professional affiliations included the American Association of University Professors and the American Psychological Association. His research interests remained in the areas of social psychology and attitudinal testing.

In 1936, he married the former Anne M. Nelson of Walkertown, North Carolina, and had two children, Beverly and Howard Wright.

NOTES

1. From taped interview conducted by the author with Max Meenes at Howard University on November 28, 1972.

2. Ibid.

3. Ibid.

4. Ibid.

5. F. C. Sumner, "The New Psychology Unit at Howard University," *Psychological Bulletin* (1935): 859–860.

6. F. C. Sumner, Howard University Annual Reports, 1938–1940, Department of Psychology, pp. 1xxiii–1xxiv.

7. Ibid., 1946–1947, pp. 212–213.

8. Ibid., p. 213.

9. Personal correspondence with Reverend Alston, September 4, 1974.

10. "Negroes Distinguished in Science," *Negro History Bulletin.* Washington, D.C.: Association for the Study of Negro Life and History, II no. 8 (May 1939), 68.

11. L. Wispe, el at., "The Negro Psychologist in America," *American Psychologist,* 24 no. 2 (1969), 142–150.

▶ 8

Francis Cecil Sumner
Father of Black American Psychologists

It was 1920, eleven years after the Department of Psychology at the small, prestigious Clark University in Worcester, Massachusetts, had propelled the seclusive psychoanalytic movement to consequence by inviting Sigmund Freud to the United States. Freedom from slavery was scarcely fifty years old and nearly one-quarter of the country's Black people were designated as illiterate. History at this time had recorded a total of 2,239 lynchings of Black people in the United States. Overt racial discrimination was the order of the day; racist views were not only accepted among the masses but also were significantly present in scholarly journals, textbooks, and medical reports.

Between 1876 and 1920, only eleven Blacks out of a total of ten thousand recipients had earned Ph.D. degrees in the United States. Edward S. Bouchet, who received the doctor of philosophy degree in physics at Yale in 1876, is thought to be the first Black to receive a doctorate degree in the United States.

The first American to receive a doctorate in psychology was Joseph Jastrow at Johns Hopkins in 1886, but not until thirty-four years later did a Black American accomplish the same goal.[1] In 1920, a twenty-five-year-old Black World War I veteran successfully defended his doctoral dissertation before a group of prominent scholars and psychologists at Clark University. Francis Cecil Sumner thus became the first Black man to receive the doctor of philosophy degree in psychology, a feat accom-

Francis C. Sumner

plished in spite of innumerable social and physical factors mitigating against such achievements by Black people in this country. Francis C. Sumner was born in Pine Bluff, Arkansas, on December 7, 1895. He had one brother, Eugene. His parents, David Alexander and Ellen Lillian Sumner, adopted their last name "in token of respect for the one time Massachusetts Senator Charles Sumner."[2] Francis Sumner received his early education in the elementary schools of Norfolk, Virginia, and Plainfield, New Jersey; since secondary education for Blacks during the early 1900s was rare, he did not have a formal high school education. Instead, as his father had done, young Sumner advanced his own education through intense reading and discussion on a wide variety of subjects. His parents provided guidance in his quest for knowledge by securing for him old textbooks and other reading materials. Reading was not only an

Clark University

Worcester, Massachusetts, U. S. A.

To all to whom these presents may come, Greeting:

Be it known that

Francis Cecil Sumner

having submitted a dissertation entitled **Psychoanalysis of Freud and Adler**

and having creditably sustained the examinations required, is admitted to the degree of

Doctor of Philosophy

and is entitled to all the Honors, Rights, and Privileges to that degree appertaining.

Given at the City of Worcester, in the Commonwealth of Massachusetts this **fourteenth** day of **June** in the year of our Lord One Thousand nine hundred **twenty**

Witness the Seal of the University, by the hands of the authorized representatives of the Trustees and of the Faculty:

for the Trustees

G. Stanley Hall
Karl J. Karlson
Edwin G. Boring.
Samuel W. Fernberger
for the Faculty

Francis Sumner's degree from Clark University.

early habit with Sumner but also a major contributor to his academic success and a lifelong pattern of behavior.

Lincoln University: 1911–1915

In the fall of 1911, at the age of fifteen, Sumner was permitted to enroll as a freshman at Lincoln University in Pennsylvania after passing a written examination since he had no high school diploma. (He had received private instruction from his father in secondary subjects since no academic high school was available.) His parents worked to pay their son's fees and tuition at Lincoln, and Sumner himself worked, part-time and during the summer breaks, at many odd jobs to contribute to his college expenses. In 1915, at the age of twenty, Sumner graduated from Lincoln, magna cum laude with special honors in English, modern languages, Greek, Latin, and philosophy. During this time, he began a series of correspondences with James P. Porter, a professor of psychology and Dean of the College at Clark University, concerning his possible enrollment at Clark College. In an interesting juxtaposition, the president of Clark, G. Stanley Hall, who had applied for a chemistry professorship at Howard University in 1896 (see appendix) and taught pedagogy at Howard in 1904–1905, previously expressed views that would be considered as racist in a more contemporary time, and yet, Hall's actions toward Blacks would have to be considered liberal even by today's standards.[3] Hall openly solicited Black students to enroll at Clark and in order to facilitate this, he openly encouraged a connection with Howard University and allowed Clark's entrance examination to be taken at several Black colleges. As noted in Chapter 6, a number of leading Black scholars were trained at Clark.

In the spring of 1915, Dr. Porter notified Sumner of his acceptance to Clark's undergraduate college for the fall semester of 1915 and later arranged for Sumner to live with a "fine colored family in Worcester."[4]

Clearly, it was Sumner's fondness for reading that led him to want to become a great writer. There was little doubt of his ability to succeed in this arena, for his talent had been recognized at Lincoln University by most of his teachers. Dr. Hall noted Sumner's literary skills and interest and that he was an "extraordinarily voracious reader."[5] In 1914, Sumner continued to express his desire to be a writer: "My sole ambition is to write. Yet I shall have to fall back on something—teaching—or Government employ as an immediate means of livelihood."[6] He went on: "Many have endeavored to discourage me in my projected career and yet a few old heads have advised me to follow my own bent rather than in the least to be dissuaded by anyone."[7]

Clark College: 1915–1916

When Sumner enrolled at Clark College in 1915, he pursued his literary interests by enrolling in English courses (The Novel; Advanced Composition; Versification) and taking electives in foreign languages and psychology. This combination of studies led him to be described a year later by his fellow students as "more or less of a psychologist, and you can usually find him at the last table at the further end of the library reading something in the line of 'psychological' novels."[8] In June 1916, Sumner was awarded a second B.A. degree in English.

Sumner and Hall

The relationship between Francis Sumner and G. Stanley Hall steadily grew into one of mutual respect. There is little doubt that Sumner's admiration for Hall led him seriously to consider psychology as a graduate major. In many ways, Hall provided support and encouragement to Sumner as well as to other Black students without publicity and often through anonymity. Furthermore, Hall always found time to maintain correspondence during Sumner's World War I military service. An act of Sumner's admiration for Hall is evidenced by his "To the Memory of G. Stanley Hall 1844–1924" dedication in his manuscript, "The Structure of Religion."[9] In this manuscript, Sumner recalled the support and guidance of Hall during his days at Clark. Hall's enthusiasm toward his writings during a seminar in the autumn of 1917 was recalled with pride: "Dr. Hall proposed at the time that I enlarge upon the matter under the title, 'Modern Surrogates for Old Religious Ideas' as my doctoral thesis. However, it appeared that my interest in the subject had terminated, for try as I might, I could not kindle a passion for the proposed study." In further discussing Hall's strong suggestion that he pursue the religious treatise as a possible dissertation: "it was then as it was always to be against my nature to write to order. Then again, I was at Clark University among people who believe for the most part as I did, hence there was no inspiration from opposition."[10] It is interesting to note that Hall's racial liberalism extended as far back as 1872 as witnessed by his teaching application to Howard University. His statement, "I have strong preferences for your university" suggest evidence of his tolerance. (See Appendix D.)

Lincoln University: 1916–1917

In the fall of 1916, he returned to Lincoln University as graduate student and instructor of psychology and German. During the year at Lincoln he studied religious psychology, philosophy, and German. Teaching, which was part of his graduate course assignment, constituted the bulk of his program; he taught psychology of religion, mysticism, and rationalism; experimental psychology; social psychology; and intermediate and advanced German.

Near the end of his first semester of work at Lincoln, Sumner recognized a desire to continue in the field of psychology and a need for further advanced training. He began to investigate graduate schools, including the American University and the University of Illinois, for possible admission and financial assistance. Early in 1917, he again sought the advice and assistance of Dean Porter at Clark:

> The old problem of getting situated or of finding one's level is again before me. I am convinced that I can't do the work I want to do without further study. The chief hindrance to carrying out the latter is financial backing.[11]

While Sumner was strongly interested in psychology, he vacillated between psychology and German as his possible major, for he felt that graduate programs in German offered the best chances for financial assistance. Nevertheless, his leaning toward psychology was evident:

> Psychology appears the most vital subject in which I would specialize. Many have tried to discourage me from that subject, saying that it was not much in demand among colored people. However, I seem to see a great latent demand for it.[12]

Dean Porter's reply reinforced Sumner's bias toward psychology:

> I would not say one word to dissuade you from the study of German if you feel that is your strongest interest. I thoroly (sic) believe that if you make of your study of psychology a practical matter you can be of the greatest service to your own people.[13]

Porter continued to spell out occupational possibilities in psychology:

> This need not to be confined to teaching, for the reason that many opportunities are more and more in evidence in which the knowledge of psychology may be turned to practical account for those in whom you may be interested.[14]

Finally, on March 28, 1917, after discouraging responses from American University and the University of Illinois, Sumner wrote G. Stanley Hall to ask his consideration for a junior fellowship in psychology award "to study race psychology."[15] Since Sumner's teaching and graduate study arrangement at Lincoln University was without pay, he further impressed upon Hall his need for financial assistance and his inability to find a teaching position: "I would drop out of school and teach for awhile if I could get an appointment but so far none has appeared."[16] Shortly after Sumner received his M.A. degree from Lincoln in June 1917, he received word that he had been accepted at Clark and awarded a fellowship as a senior scholar in psychology.

Clark University: 1917–1918

As Sumner prepared to return to Massachusetts to enter the Ph.D. program at Clark, the American Expeditionary Forces began landings in France; the United States had entered World War I. Sumner was immediately classified *1-A* for military service, and he was well aware that he might be drafted in spite of the government's intention "to limit the number of colored troops in the Army."[17] Nevertheless, Sumner began his graduate studies, and on October 15, 1917, G. Stanley Hall, Sumner's major professor, approved his application for candidacy for the Ph.D. degree in psychology. The following week, Sumner passed his French and German language qualifying examinations and was well into his course studies.

Sumner's acute awareness of social injustice toward Black people in the United States led him to recognize the inconsistencies of popular accusations against World War I German kultur as being "symbolic of barbarity, immorality, and irreligiousness."[18] The ensuing conflict in his mind resulted in his writing several letters to the local newspaper expressing what was to become an unpopular view to several of Worcester's leading white citizens. Sumner's first letter to the editor said, in part:

> Within the soul of each member of my race the conscious self is saying, Serve your country, while the unconscious from the depths is thundering, You have a poor cause to serve. On the one side the martial music and the tramp of soldiers exhort to arms and patriotism; on the other side in movements of sweet, silent thought the words "God punish America" ring of salvation.[19]

Several months later, as the fighting in Europe increased, Sumner wrote another lengthy letter criticizing the claim that the United States was "a self-appointed paragon of virtue."[20] In this letter, Sumner made an interesting psychoanalytic analysis of racism in the United States—which inflamed the local citizenry.

Sumner's statements, with their detailed arguments, resulted in several verbal attacks against the "Fellow in Psychology who has raised a traitor's voice in defamation of American ideals and of the spirit of American people."[21] The reaction to Sumner's letters reached such proportions that he was summoned to the U.S. Post Office in Worcester to give reason why he should not be listed as an enemy alien and his mail held up. The case was referred to the Boston regional post office; Sumner convinced the postal authorities of his good intentions and his loyalty to the United States, and no further action was initiated by the post office.

On May 28, 1918, Sumner formally apologized in a letter to the newspaper for the circumstances of his "disloyalty to my native country."[22] A later, unsigned memorandum, undoubtedly written by Hall, cleared the air by suggesting further explanations for Sumner's actions:

> Having lived in the South, he has taken a great interest, under the influence of the colored leader Du Bois, who was Booker Washington's chief rival, in lynchings, of which he has a ghastly collection of newspaper accounts, and some of which have come pretty near to him . . . He was also smarting under the fact that by a rearrangement of the tables at the dining-hall, there happened to be at least some one at each table who preferred not to eat with a negro, so that a special table had been arranged for him and others who had befriended him.[23]

As the spring semester drew to a close, so did much of the discussion of Sumner's letters to the newspaper.

During this time, Sumner had finished a study, "Psychoanalysis of Freud and Adler," and was attempting to have it published by Badger Publishing Company. In the summer of 1918, he wrote Hall to ask him to consider the merits of this work as a potential doctoral dissertation.[24] Before he was able to elicit a response from Hall, Sumner was drafted into the army.

Military Service: 1918–1919

As soon as he had completed his basic training with the 48th Company, 154 Depot Brigade at Camp Meade, Maryland, Sumner wrote to Hall to bring him "up-to-date." He expressed disappointment over the interruption of his graduate studies and commented that he was "trying hard to take my medicine with the courage befitting a regular soldier." Sumner found time to humor his mentor in the same letter by drawing a parallel between army food and one of Hall's theoretical postulates:

> I noticed here at camp that they feed one so much of raw onion to give one long wind. I find that it does have something of that effect upon me and that the fact has caused me to associate it with the "second breath" phenomena.[25]

Sumner felt he had a good chance of attending the army officer training camp and in another letter asked Hall to write his commanding officer to recommend him for such training.[26] Hall promptly responded with a recommendation for officer training, but it was too late: Sumner had been transferred to Company M, 808th Pioneer Infantry, and he was on his way to the battlefields of France as a twenty-two-year-old company sergeant.

Recalling his overseas experiences several years later, Sumner described the horrifying effects of the war:

> The greatest fear I have ever experienced was that which I experienced when first introduced to the cannonade of German artillery. I did not fear submarines in crossing the Atlantic against which so many precautions were being taken; I did not fear exposure to the elements, to sleeping on the frozen ground, or in rain-drenched fields; I did not fear the ravages of influenza, but my resistances broke when quartered in a little shell-ranked town upon which enemy artillery was trained. The man-size projectiles would burst with the fury of gigantic explosion, causing to shudder within me every fibre.[27]

Though the Armistice was signed on November 11, 1918, Sumner's unit remained in France until mid-1919. During this time, he took leaves to southern France (Chambery, Lyons, Dijon) and to Paris. He also began to prepare for his return to the United States and to Clark University. A letter to Hall early in 1919 asked for consideration for reappointment as a senior fellow in psychology and readmission for the 1919–1920 school year.[28] On May 2, 1919, Hall approved Sumner's appointment as a senior fellow for the academic year 1919–1920. Writing from the Pontanezen Barracks at Brest, Sumner expressed his appreciation to Hall and spoke of his travels in France telling how much he enjoyed that country and expressing a desire to live there.[29]

Clark University: 1919–1920

After his discharge, Sumner returned to Clark in the fall of 1919. With the assistance of a YMCA scholarship for veterans and the money he had saved during the war, he enrolled in psychology courses taught by Hall, E. G. Boring, S. W. Fernberger, and K. J. Karlson. On June 11, 1920 beginning at 3:00 PM, Francis Sumner, G. Stanley Hall's last graduate student, defended his doctoral dissertation, "Psychoanalysis of Freud and Adler"; Sumner's defense was approved and his thesis was "accepted" on

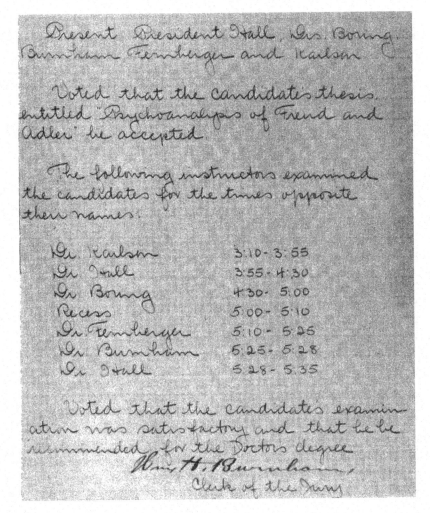

FIGURE 8.1   Examination Notice of Francis Cecil Sumner

Source: University Archives, Goddard Library, Clark University, Worchester, Mass. Reprinted with permission.

the same day (Figure 8.1). The following day, the Action of the Faculty labeled his doctoral candidacy as "passed." On June 14, 1920, Francis Cecil Sumner became the first Black American to receive the Ph.D. degree in psychology.

Sumner's dissertation, published in the *Pedagogical Seminary* (later renamed *The Journal of Genetic Psychology*), was called an outstanding interpretation of psychoanalytic theories. Hall commented on Sumner's work:

> [He] has made what I think a remarkable compilation of opinions, with a genuinely new contribution, for his Doctor's thesis on the Freudian psychanalysis (sic) . . . Sumner had a strong penchant for it [psychoanalysis] and really has shown unusual facility in mastering and even pointing out the limitations and defects of the great authorities in that field.[30]

The one journalistic account of Sumner's graduation was in *Crisis Magazine* in its annual article, "The Year in Negro Education." The article noted that two Doctor of Philosophy degrees and twelve Master of Arts degrees had been awarded to Black graduate students during 1920:

> Since the cessation of the war many Negroes who ordinarily would have continued their education, instead have entered into industry. This is inevitable; however, we are especially proud of those of our race who keep the ranks in education . . . Ph.D., Francis C. Sumner in psychology.[31]

West Virginia Collegiate Institute: 1921–1928

Dr. Sumner's first teaching position was as a professor of psychology and philosophy at Wilberforce University (Ohio) during the 1920–1921 school year. In the summer of 1921, he taught at Southern University (Louisiana). In February, 1921, Carter G. Woodson, Dean at West Virginia, wrote Dr. Porter of Clark:

> I am looking for an instructor in Experiment Psychology to head this department in this college. Dr. Francis C. Sumner has applied for this position. What can you say of his qualifications in this field? I understand that he has worked under you. Have you another Negro graduate better qualified?[32]

Professor Porter's reply spoke of his "good work as a member of my class in Social Psychology" and his graduate work under his instruction in comparative psychology. Porter continued:

> He not only did good work in my courses but I know of his work in other courses . . . He is an able and serious student. He has

personal qualities which should make him a very useful man on your faculty . . . I strongly suggest that you give him favorable consideration.[33]

In the fall of 1921, Sumner accepted an appointment as instructor of psychology and philosophy in the college department at West Virginia Collegiate Institute (now West Virginia State College). In a letter to Dean Porter at Clark, Sumner proudly told of the beauty of the campus, his salary, and plans by the state of West Virginia to make the Collegiate Institute a first class college.[34]

Shortly after his arrival at West Virginia, his lifelong emotional reaction to lightning and fire inspired him to make a contribution to the *American Journal of Psychology* upon being awakened one morning by a spring thunderstorm. Sumner's description of the "Core and Context in the Drowsy State"[35] was the first of a number of significant journal articles during his seven-year tenure at West Virginia (1924a, 1924b, 1925, 1926a, 1926b, 1927).

In one of his most timely articles, he attacked the classic heredity and environment dispute of the 1920s:

> In the current struggle between the respective protagonists of heredity and environment, the bone of contention has not been whether heredity or environment contributes all but rather whether heredity or environment contributes more in the determination of an individual's achievement. The proponents of the above mentioned explanations in their eagerness to defend the myth of Nordic superiority have intentionally or unintentionally assumed that which is to be proved, namely, that heredity counts all.[36]

All of Sumner's research studies at West Virginia were done without outside financial assistance. He complained bitterly of the refusals he received when applying to white agencies for funds for research projects. His own field of psychology had to be neglected because of what he referred to as the factor of race prejudice, which barred him from positions in northern universities, isolated him from his white colleagues, and, worst of all, exerted a peculiar effect upon his scholarship. He referred to this effect as the obsession of race persecution and observed its attendant pathological symptoms, which forced him to engage most of his mental energies in contending with race prejudice. Moreover, he called attention to the many Black intellectuals who were forced to teach in rural environments because so many Black institutions of higher learning were located in out-of-the-way sections of the country that were generally difficult to get to. In Sumner's words:

> The intellectual Negro is often deprived by reason of the fact that Negro universities and colleges are more frequently located in almost inaccessible rural districts . . . In order to increase one's income that was at best half of that of a white professor, he is forced to seek ways and means of increasing the family income. These side occupations run from preaching to common labor."[37]

In a series of controversial articles in 1926 and 1927, Sumner strongly endorsed some of the fundamentalist reforms of Booker T. Washington. Sumner declared "Negro education is cryingly in need of a new dispensation. It needs awakening to the serious responsibility of morally redeeming the soul of black folk."[38] To accomplish this "new dispensation," he suggested that certain virtues be instilled in Black students:

> "Physical Well-Being; Simplicity in Living; Belief in God; Fondness for Literature, Art, and Music; Industry; A Contempt for Loud and Indiscreet Laughing and Talking; Thrift; Honesty; Courteousness; Respect; Race Pride; and Punctuality."[39]

Sumner believed that their acceptance as a part of western culture would clear the path for Black people to enter the mainstream of U.S. society. He also believed that there were far too many substandard Black colleges and universities; he proposed "a drastic reduction in the number of Negro colleges from 40 to about five."[40] He wrote:

> With only four or live large colleges advantageously located, with the resources of [the existing] forty institutions merged into the support of the smaller number and with salaries placed on a standardized basis, the teaching personnel [would] be rigorously selected on the basis of academic and professional qualifications.[41]

And, thus would he create first-class institutions of higher learning. He further suggested a

> division of labor among the five colleges of the new order. Two, at least should be technical, that is, devoted to applied sciences

such as home economics, business administration, electrical, chemical, civil, and mechanical engineering, social service education, library science and agriculture. One college should specialize in the fine arts and literature, giving thorough training in music, painting, architecture, commercial art, sculpture, the histrionic art, and the writing of poetry and fiction. Two colleges should specialize in the liberal arts and sciences and should also have added to them professional schools of medicine, dentistry, law, and religion.[42]

Finally, Sumner criticized the practice of the semester system of instruction. He believed that the semester division of the school year did not allow adequate time for content mastery: "It is far more important for a student to learn thoroughly and in all their ramifications three subjects a year (rather) than in isolated fragments ten or twelve subjects."[43]

In writing for the *Institute Monthly* in 1927, Sumner tackled the issues surrounding the earmarks of high intelligence when he assigned self-education and creativeness as "two infallible signs of high intelligence."[44] And in one of his final articles at West Virginia, Sumner's treatise on "The Nature of Emotions" systematically evaluated several concepts of emotion from a behavioristic stance. In this evaluation, Sumner called for the importance of understanding and training the emotions of children. He criticized the "great evil of undisciplined emotions in the home" and illustrated how his resulted in an "unfortunate augmentation of the conflict of the Individual with the social milieu."[45]

Clearly, Sumner was becoming restless at West Virginia by its rural setting, removal from other psychologists, and need to fulfill his mission in a larger institution. The administration at West Virginia, sensing that Sumner might leave for a better offer and aware of the frequent faculty "raids" by nearby Howard University, urged the State Board of Education to change Sumner's annual salary from $2400 to $2700 with the comment: "We shall be able to hold Dr. Sumner for this amount." President John Davis further commented to the Board, "I do not need to call your attention to the result which would come to this institution if Dr. Sumner accepted one of the positions to which he is now being called. You will note that we have just lost, to Howard University, Professor Julian, Head of our Department of Chemistry."[46]

The effort was futile. Sumner resigned from West Virginia effective August 31, 1928 and headed eastward to Howard. (Herman Canady was hired to succeed Sumner.)

Howard University: 1928–1954

When Sumner left West Virginia, he assumed the acting chairman-ship of the department of psychology at Howard University.[47] He was convinced that in order to develop a strong program to train Black psychologists adequately, psychology departments needed to be autonomous units divorced from departments of philosophy and schools of education. (This scheme then current in most Black schools left psychology to be taught as an ancillary subject to education and/or linked to philosophy as the case in West Virginia.) With the aid of Howard's relatively new president, Mordecai W. Johnson, a separate department of psychology was permanently established at Howard, and Sumner was appointed full professor and head of the department in 1930. A young graduate assistant, Frederick P. Watts, was at Howard when Sumner arrived in 1928, and he assisted Sumner during the early days; but it was clear that more help was needed to carry out Sumner's plans for an expanded department. With the recommendation of E. G. Boring, one of his former professors at Clark University, Sumner sought thirty-year-old Max Meenes at Lehigh University in Pennsylvania as a new colleague. Meenes, a white man holding a Ph.D. degree from Clark, had been trained as a "brass instrument psychologist" and had the desired specializations and credentials. Meenes elected to join Sum-ner at Howard in 1930:

> I was teaching at Lehigh from 1926–1930 and I had received a promotion from instructor to assistant professor and it seemed clear that the next step to associate professor might take quite many years, and in the meantime I had received a letter in early 1929 from Dr. Sumner at Howard University. He wanted another psychologist . . . he made me an offer that was attractive, so I said goodby to Lehigh and came down here. I knew that Dr. Sumner was Black and that Howard was a Black school, but I was a teacher of psychology and I wanted to teach students in psychol-ogy wherever they were. Dr. Sumner had an excellent reputation and was a brilliant scholar, so I joined him.[48]

A lifelong association was formed between Sumner, Meenes, and Watts in the creation of a three-person psychology department for training Black students.

During World War II, Sumner stressed the need for Howard to train more psychologists:

The demand for Negroes trained in psychology has been larger during the present emergency than heretofore, in fact larger than the supply. It is believed that the greatest immediate need . . . is the . . . training of specialized personnel particularly in the case of the better grade student.[49]

By 1946, as the program produced more psychologists, Sumner declared that "the enrollment at the graduate and undergraduate level was the highest in the history of the Psychology Department. The scholastic ability . . . (was) higher than usual."[50] It was clear, as the 1940s came to an end, that Sumner's plan for a "first-class department of psychology" had reached fruition. (See Appendix E.)

Sumner, who professed religion publicly at the age of sixteen, read exhaustively American literature on religious psychology; subsequently, he drafted a paper entitled, "The Idea of Holiness."[51] In May 1931, Sumner had the opportunity to attend the First International Congress for Religious Psychology held at the University of Vienna. At this conference he presented a paper entitled, "Mental Hygiene and Religion" and met many leaders among European psychologists of religion. After being inspired at this conference by the "vast religion-psychological movement in Europe,"[52] Sumner began importing an extensive library of works from Europe. He began offering courses in the subject during the 1940s. His massive manuscript, "The Structure of Religion: A History of European Psychology of Religion," serves as a testament of his growing interest.[53] Sumner was also responsible for instigating studies and research into the relationship between psychology and the law. Along these lines, his research expanded into several additional areas during his life.

Several important early studies were conducted in the late 1930s and 1940s assessing the attitudes of Blacks and whites toward the administration of justice.[54] Sumner, with his graduate students, surveyed more than two thousand college students culminating in several procedures that promised to administer justice on a more democratic basis.

Sumner was described by former students as a "low keyed and very dedicated psychologist"; as a "very quiet and very unassuming individual who was brilliant with a tremendous capacity to make an analysis of an individual's gestalt"; and as "Howard's most stimulating scholar."

His colleagues spoke of his deep interest in his students (See Appendix F) and recalled "the mimeographed newsletter he prepared and issued periodically, giving items of interest about graduates from his department."[55] His enjoyment of reading and his constant quest for knowledge led Sumner to write many reviews of a wide variety of books.

He became an official abstractor for the *Psychological Bulletin* and for the *Journal of Social Psychology*. In this capacity, he translated more than three thousand articles from German, French, and Spanish.

He was a fellow of the American Psychological Association and held memberships in the American Association for the Advancement of Science, American Educational Research Association, Eastern Psychological Association, Southern Society for Philosophy and Psychology, and the District of Columbia Psychological Association. His fraternal memberships included Psi Chi, Pi Gamma Mu, and Kappa Alpha Psi. His lifelong membership in Kappa Alpha Psi was active and dedicated; he wrote frequent publications in their national journal. His first marriage was to Francees H. Hughston in 1922, and his second marriage was to Nettie M. Brooker in 1946. He had no children.

On January 12, 1954, Dr. Francis Cecil Sumner suffered a fatal heart attack while shovelling snow at his home in Washington, D.C. President Mordecai W. Johnson of Howard University delivered the eulogy at the University Chapel, and a tribute was paid by J. St. Clair Price, Dean of the College of Liberal Arts at Howard. There was a military honor guard, in memory of Sumner's service in World War I, as he was buried at Arlington Cemetery in Virginia.[56] Dr. Sumner's role in the development of Black psychologists is a monument to perseverance, scholarship, and dedication.

NOTES

1. Clark's first Black graduate, Louis C. Tyree of Indianapolis, enrolled in 1909 and received his B.A. degree in 1912.

2. Personal correspondence from G. Stanley Hall, 1918, University Archives, Goddard Library, Clark University, Worcester, Massachusetts.

3. Hall's liberalism and concern for Blacks is evident in spite of his earlier writings and commentary to the contrary. In his application to teach at Howard University, he spoke of his "preference for your University on personal and other grounds." (See Appendix.) For an excellent view into Hall's attitudes toward Black and women students, see William A. Koelsch's *Clark University: A Narrative History*, Clark University Press, 1987.

4. Personal correspondence, James P. Porter, 1915, University Archives, Goddard Library, Clark University.

5. Personal correspondence, F. C. Sumner, June 16, 1915, University Archives, Clark University.

6. Personal correspondence, F. C. Sumner, 1915, University Archives, Clark University.

7. Ibid.

8. "Who's Who, 1916," *Clark College Yearbook*, Clark University, Worcester, Massachusetts.

9. F. C. Sumner, "The Structure of Religion: A History of European Psychology of Religion." Unpublished manuscript. Howard University, 1934.

10. Ibid.

11. Personal correspondence, F. C. Sumner, June 1917, University Archives, Goddard Library, Clark University.

12. Ibid.

13. Personal correspondence, James P. Porter, 1917, University Archives, Goddard Library, Clark University.

14. Ibid.

15. Personal correspondence, F. C. Sumner, June 1917, University Archives, Goddard Library, Clark University.

16. Ibid.

17. Personal correspondence, G. Stanley Hall, 1918, University Archives, Goddard Library, Clark University.

18. F. C. Sumner in "The Forum of the People," *Worcester Gazette*, May 25, 1918, Worcester, Massachusetts.

19. Ibid., February 15, 1918.

20. Ibid., May 25, 1918.

21. H. Chamberlin in "The Forum of the People," *Worcester Gazette*, May 27, 1918.

22. F. C. Sumner in "The Forum of the People, *Worcester Gazette*, May 29, 1918.

23. Personal correspondence, G. Stanley Hall, 1918, University Archives, Goddard Library, Clark University.

24. Personal correspondence, F. C. Sumner, June 1918, Goddard Library, University Archives, Clark University.

25. Ibid.

26. Ibid.

27. Ibid.

28. Personal correspondence, F. C. Sumner, 1919, University Archives, Goddard Library, Clark University.

29. Ibid.

30. Personal correspondence, G. Stanley Hall, 1920, University Archives, Goddard Library, Clark University.

31. M. G. Allison, "The Year in Negro Education," *The Crisis*, (July 1920): 126.

32. C. G. Woodson, Personal Correspondence to James Porter, Clark University, February 25, 1921.

33. J. P. Porter, Personal Correspondence to C. G. Woodson, West Virginia Collegiate Institute, March 2, 1921.

34. Personal correspondence, F. C. Sumner, June 1919, University Archives, Goddard Library, Clark University.

35. F. C. Sumner, "Core and Context in the Drowsy State," *American Journal of Psychology* (April 1924).

36. F. C. Sumner, "Environic Factors Which Prohibit Creative Scholarship Among Negroes," *School and Society* 22 (1928).

37. Ibid.

38. F. C. Sumner, "The Philosophy of Negro Educating," *Educational Review* LXXI (January 1926): 42–45.

39. Ibid.

40. F. C. Sumner, "Morale and the Negro College," *Educational Review* LXXIII (March 1927): 168–172.

41. Ibid.

42. Ibid.

43. Ibid.

44. F. C. Sumner, "Earmarks of High Grade Intelligence," *The Institute Monthly*, Institute, West Virginia (May 1927): 6–8.

45. F. C. Sumner, "The Nature of Emotion," *Howard Review* 1 (June 1924).

46. J. Davis, Personal correspondence to the West Virginia State Board of Education and Advisory Council, July 19, 1927.

47. Many of Howard's early faculty members previously taught at West Virginia State College.

48. From a taped interview conducted by the author with Max Meenes at Howard University on November 28, 1972.

49. Ibid.

50. Ibid.

51. Sumner, "Structure of Religion."

52. Ibid.

53. Ibid.

54. Sumner's early research regarding Black and white college attitudes about administration of justice began in 1944.

55. Each year Sumner edited *The Record,* which was a compilation of the Master Graduates in Psychology. This mimeographed newsletter contained a record of Howard graduates, their accomplishments, and their statistical summaries.

56. "Funeral at Howard for Dr. F. Sumner," The *Washington Afro-American Newspaper,* January 16, 1954, p. 5.

▶ Part III

Conclusion

Chapter 9
The Past Is Prologue

▶ 9

The Past Is Prologue

In many ways we have come full circle since the birth of "scientific" psychology. Some of the dubious research of the 1920s has lingered as a phantom-like apparition of pseudointellectualism. Proclamations purporting to present evidence of limited intellectual capacities in Black Americans resemble the claims of biased 1920 educational psychologists; race betterment policies and recommendations for genetic control of the "socially unacceptable" continue to reemerge with the same bigotry. These theories recur with an appearance of enough "newness" to obscure the cobwebs of the past and actually encourage a repeat of the same defenses utilized decades ago. Current arguments concerning the utilization of IQ tests and the allegations of inherited deficits in Black and brown children still exist. Even among the "elite" white psychologists who discouraged Black students since the early 1940s to avoid aspects of psychology as a major, these openly brazen barriers no longer exist.[1] But it was these and other negativisms that created the atmosphere for the formation of minority professional caucuses to counterargue and to provide specialized agendas and unified forces.

Part One of this book focused on research activities that impacted on scientific perspectives of Black people. These views resulted from the connections between psychology and physical anthropology and attempts to detect, measure, and report minute variations in humans. While activities of the two disciplines appear to be discrete, it is important to note that they shared similar philosophical biases, strongly influenced one another, and contributed heavily to the belief that one race was inherently superior to another. One could dismiss the early anthropometric findings as quaint examples of misguided scientists during a period of widespread racism were it not for the fact that these views molded the psyches of many Americans in various mixtures of arrogance and fear. Furthermore, these findings either created or reinforced unfortunate views concerning what is considered idealized skin coloring or concepts of "good hair" or "bad hair," all which became precursors for human problems of self-concept and self-esteem. Quantification of physical attributes also encouraged beliefs that psychological traits, too, could be measured. While the quantification of physical differences has now lost much of its credibility and acceptance, the idea that mental attributes could be measured has grown.

THE MYTH OF MENTAL MEASUREMENT

During the twentieth century, attempts to measure and report individual and group intellectual capabilities in the form of a single score took center stage. The logic of a single score to represent an individual's potentiality to learn or to declare the intellectual capacity to learn is a holy grail in the profession. Entwined in this tragedy has been the basic assumption that a generalized, broad-based definition of intelligence could be created and, consequently, the propriety of assigning blanket terms to all problem-solving behaviors has resulted in a highly debatable issue. This has become especially obvious with wide variations in the cognitive life-styles of American society. With factorial studies showing that a number of elements, normally ignored by conventional IQ tests, underlie the problem-solving behaviors of individuals regardless of cultural difference, the often quoted statement that "intelligence is whatever it is that intelligence tests test" sums the existing state of past efforts and becomes a poor recommendation for the continual use of such concepts.

Many Americans, Black and white, understand that IQ tests are not valid but are helpless in the system that has constructed and perpetuated a myth of mental measurement. Billions of dollars have been poured into the psychometric profession, making it difficult for those directly or indirectly involved in the industry to agree that the IQ concept is null and void. Just as the Binet test was legally contested in 1916 during the height of the "race betterment movement" when institutionalization and sterilization were the issues, legal aspects concerning the propriety of assigning IQ scores based on psychological tests were revisited in the California public school system where children had been placed in classes for the mentally retarded. These scenarios will repeat, undoubtedly, in order to necessitate challenges to misuse of test scores. As these issues occur, similarly, the old heredity-environment debate will continue to resurface.

PSYCHOLOGY AND POLITICS

The 1954 Supreme Court decision that required public schools to racially integrate their classrooms "with all deliberate speed" rekindled the issue of inherited intellectual differences between racial groups. Former APA president Henry Garrett became the states' rights and segregationalist's "in-house psychologist" to provide a host of "reasons" why Black children could not compete intellectually with white children. (It should be recalled that Garrett was involved in the early mental measurements of World War I and strongly supported the hereditarian point of view of that time.) Garrett's most vociferous attack against school integration was a widely distributed twenty-four-page booklet, "How Classroom Desegregation Will Work," which drew heavily on selected IQ test results and anthropological data. The booklet was blatantly racist in content and remindful of the early studies of Ferguson and Mayo (see Chapter 2). Garrett, a distinguished professor at Columbia University, also preached that Black Americans should not pursue studies in social psychology because they were not suited for the study. During the 1960s, individuals who supported the importance of heredity over environment voiced strong objections to President Lyndon Johnson's Great Society programs. Important elements of Johnson's War on Poverty proposals deemphasized hereditarian views and designed programs that would reduce the environmental differences between Black and white Americans. A notable example, Project Head Start, the comprehensive preschool program for the children of the poor, was based on a recognition of the importance of environmental factors in learning; Head Start supported the notion that intelligence was malleable and not strongly deterministic. J. McV. Hunt's influential attack on the prevailing notion of genetically determined and fixed intelligence, *Intelligence and Experience*, and Benjamin Bloom's *Stability and Change in Human Characteristics*, argued that intelligence was plastic in the preschool and early elementary years and did not reach stability until about age twelve.[1] During the decade between 1964 and 1975, several studies directly or indirectly criticized the efforts of the federal government's compensatory programs. These criticisms shifted the blame for declared scholastic failures of the programs to the problems of the students or their parents. Under President Nixon's regime the dismantling of the War on Poverty's Office of Economic

Opportunity (OEO) took place. Leaders in these analyses were Daniel Moynihan, James Coleman, William Schockley, and Arthur Jensen.

OLD WINE, NEW BOTTLES

In 1965, *The Negro Family: The Case for National Action* (The Moynihan Report) concentrated almost solely on what was termed "negative" in the Black experience. The report's findings proclaimed that "deep-seated structural distortions in the life of the Negro American" existed and concluded that "the present tangle of pathology" would continue unless white intervention occurred. Moynihan reached his conclusions by comparing the absenteeism of the Black male in the household with crime and delinquency data; as in earlier cases, the Black family was viewed from a white middle-class perspective and the assumptions drawn from this bias resulted in gross oversimplifications of the data compiled. (The use of the white middle-class family as a "norm" insinuated that the white father-headed family was the idea model for stability.) Interestingly, during the 1990s views held by many white feminists support the "power" and the desirability of the female-headed household. The Moynihan perspective failed to comprehend the practical adaptation to racially different treatment while the white feminist perspective comes from other adaptations.

The Coleman Report (1966), *Equality of Educational Opportunity*, reinforced Moynihan's findings by declaring that the principal sources of scholastic failure of Black children stemmed not from the schools but rather from the student's home environment and family background. This report concluded that "schools bring little influence to bear on the child's achievement that is independent of his background and general social context." This finding was suspect on two counts: first, a number of the schools sampled in the survey failed to return the lengthy questionnaires (this raised doubts of the representativeness of the sample); second, the questionnaire items themselves reflected a strong middle-class bias.[2]

THE BELL CURVE: 'ROUND AND 'ROUND WE GO

Physicist William Schockley's entry into the hereditarian arena of human affairs created a resurgence of eugenic views when his paper, "Population Control or Eugenics," was made public.[3] His eugenic philosophy became more explicit when he spoke at a symposium sponsored by Gustavus

Adolphus College in Minnesota on "Genetics and the Future of Man" in 1965. Even though Schockley possessed no credentials in the fields of genetics or psychology, his status as a former Nobel Prize winner (co-inventor of the transistor, 1956) increased his acceptance and attracted audiences that would otherwise have been indifferent to him. Schockley advocated a national genetics control program to counteract what he termed as "dysgenics, a retroactive evolution through the disproportionate reproduction of the genetically disadvantaged." According to this view, the reported lower IQ scores of Black Americans are due to inheritance rather than to environmental factors.

Schockley extended his dysgenic notion to explain that many of the "large improvident families with social problems have constitutional deficiencies in those parts of the brain which enable a person to plan and carry out plans."[4] (He localized this deficiency in the brain's frontal lobe.) In order to halt the dysgenic trend, he called for a bonus plan in which cash payments would be paid to Black people with IQs below 100 who would voluntarily submit to sterilization operations. Schockley's suggestions differ very little from the Laughlin Report of 1914, which discussed the "best practical means of cutting off the defective germ-plasm in Americans."

To support his genetic attribution theory of intelligence and social problems, Schockley drew upon studies comparing the IQs of identical white twins separated at birth and subsequently reared in different environments. These studies reported that the measured IQs were similar in identical twins regardless of environmental differences. Schockley interpreted these data to be conclusive evidence of the importance of heredity. His database was from the studies of the infamous Sir Cyril Burt to whom Arthur Jensen lent support regarding this conjecture.

Jensen, then a University of California educational psychologist, attracted national attention in 1969 with his article, "How Much Can We Boost IQ and Scholastic Achievement?" This lengthy study drew on the author's analysis of the IQ heritability among 122 pairs of white twins—which he extrapolated to account for differences in IQ scores among Black and white children. Both Schockley and Jensen concluded inheritance accounts for a whopping 80 percent of the variability in intelligence, with environment accounting for the remaining 20 percent. These percentages are identical to Edward Thorndike's calculations in 1920 (see Chapter 3). During the mid-1990s, Richard Herrnstein and Charles Murray attracted the media's attention with similar views of the non-malleability of the IQ. And in doing so, they chronicled "failed" attempts to raise IQs of school children with the all too common argument that heredity is the major determinant of intelligence. In spite of the immense criticism of their methodologies and conclusions, it can be safely predicted that future social research will continue to pursue validation of the inferiority-superiority rankings of races. At the same time, it is likely that these researchers will declare that it is unscholarly to claim that no single measure of intelligence exists.

Part Two of this book made an effort to recount events leading to the establishment of Black higher education in hope that the reader would develop an appreciation for the problems faced by Black colleges and the enormous difficulties that Black graduates had to overcome to secure postgraduate training. Biographical articles were included to provide brief personal and career histories of Black psychologists, a close analysis of which should reveal that most of the work of these early psychologists was in the mainstream, more or less, of traditional psychological work in the area of racial differences. For this reason, the work of these psychologists in countering the biases of white psychologists utilized the same paradigms of the profession. At present there exists a scientific community of Black scholars who focus their research primarily on the Black experience. This has brought about a number of concerns on a number of issues within the discipline of psychology. Whereas during the 1970s concerns over inappropriate research stances (deficit modeling) and applied programs (urban and community psychology) were among the major priorities, the waning years of the twentieth century witnessed a heavy emphasis toward Egyptology and allied concerns in hope that establishing a philosophical base in the history of Black people would affect the concerns of Black psychology. In the first edition of this book, I stated that "while at present it is difficult to justify the existence of a Black psychology, there is a theoretical basis for it." Hopefully these editions of *Even the Rat Was White* will contribute to its history.

NOTES

1. Distinguished psychologist and then APA president, Henry Garrett, wrote in a letter of recommendation for his student Mamie Clark that "I am somewhat doubtful whether it is wise for Negro students to work on topics in Social Psychology; but in Mrs. Clark's case I feel that she will do an honest and conscientious job." (Fortunately, the Rosenwald Foundation committee did not heed the warning and Mamie P. Clark was awarded the grant.) It is important to note that this prohibiting view of Black students' inappropriateness to be considered as social psychology majors was held by many white academic psychologists for decades. It certainly points to the lack of

encouragement received by Black students who desired to pursue social psychology as a profession.

2. D. P. Moynihan and F. Mosteller (Eds.). *On Equality of Educational Opportunity.* New York: Vintage, 1972.

3. William Schockley, "Is Quality of U.S. Population Declining?" *U.S. News and World Report,* November 22, 1965.

4. Ibid.

APPENDIX A

Statement on Racial Psychology by the Society for the Psychological Study of Social Issues (SPSSI), 1938

Text of the Protest

The current emphasis upon "racial differences" in Germany and Italy, and the indications that such an emphasis may be on the increase in the United States and elsewhere, make it important to know what psychologists and other social scientists have to say in this connection.

The fascists and many others have grossly misused the term *race*. According to anthropologists, the term *race* may legitimately be used only for such groups as possess in common certain physical or bodily characteristics which distinguish them from other groups. It is impossible to speak correctly of a "German race" or of an "Italian race," since both of these groups have highly diversified physical characteristics.

A South German may resemble a Frenchman from Auvergne or an Italian from Piedmont more closely than he does a German from Hanover. North Italians are markedly dissimilar from those living in Sicily or Naples.

More important still, the emphasis on the existence of an "Aryan race" has no scientific basis, since the word *Aryan* refers to a family of language and not at all to race or to physical appearance.

As far as the Jews are concerned, scientific investigations have shown them to be tall or short, blond or dark, round-headed or long-headed, according to the particular community studied. In the light of this wide variation in physical characteristics, almost all anthropologists outside of Germany and Italy would agree that it is scientifically impossible to speak of a "Jewish race," much less of an "Aryan race."

In the experiments which psychologists have made upon different peoples, no characteristic, inherent psychological differences which fundamentally distinguish so-called "races" have been disclosed. This statement is supported by the careful surveys of these experiments in such books as "Race Psychology" by Professor T. R. Garth, of the University of Denver; "Individual Differences" by Professor Frank S. Freeman, of Cornell University; "Race Differences" by Professor Otto Klineberg, of Columbia University; and "Differential Psychology" by Dr. Anne Anastasi, of Barnard College.

There is no evidence for the existence of an inborn Jewish or German or Italian mentality. Furthermore, there is no indication that the members of any group are rendered incapable by their biological heredity of completely acquiring the culture of the community in which they live. This is true not only of the Jews in Germany, but also of groups that actually are physically different from one another. The Nazi theory that people must be related by blood in order to participate in the same cultural or intellectual heritage has absolutely no support from scientific findings.

Members of the SPSSI Council for the Statement on Racial Psychology

Members of the council were Dr. F. H. Allport, Syracuse University; Dr. Gordon Allport, Harvard University; Dr. J. F. Brown, University of Kansas; Dr. Hadley Cantril, Princeton University; Dr. L. W. Doob, Yale University; Dr. H. B. English, Ohio State University; Dr. Franklin Fearing, University of California at Los Angeles; Dr. George W. Hartmann, Columbia University; Dr. I. Krechevsky, University of Colorado; Dr. Gardner Murphy, Columbia University; Dr. T. C. Schneirla, New York University; and Dr. E. C. Tolman, University of California.

APPENDIX B

List of Respondents to the 1930 Questionnaire Concerning the Validity of the Mulatto Hypotheses (Chapter 3)

Psychologists

1. Floyd H. Allport (Syracuse)
2. Gordon W. Allport (Dartmouth)
3. J. E. Anderson (Minnesota)
4. Ada H. Arlitt (Cincinnati)
5. F. A. Aveling (Univ. of London)
6. C. H. Bean (La. State)
7. C. E. Benson (New York)
8. Madison Bentley (Cornell)
9. Edwin G. Boring (Harvard)
10. J. W. Bridges (McGill)
11. Carl C. Brigham (Princeton)
12. Mary W. Calkins (Wellesley)
13. E. H. Cameron (Illinois)
14. Harvey A. Carr (Chicago)
15. J. E. Coover (Stanford)
16. S. A. Courtis (Michigan)
17. Elmer Culler (Illinois)
18. K. M. Dallenback (Cornell)
19. J. F. Dashiell (North Carolina)
20. C. B. Davenport (Carnegie Institute)
21. Walter F. Dearborn (Harvard)
22. Raymond Dodge (Yale)
23. Knight Dunlap (Johns Hopkins)
24. U. Ebbecke (Bonn)
25. Beatrice Edsell (Univ. of London)
26. H. B. English (Antioch)
27. S. W. Fernberger (Pennsylvania)
28. F. S. Freeman (Cornell)
29. T. R. Garth (Denver)
30. A. I. Gates (Columbia)
31. A. R. Gilliland (Northwestern)
32. Kate Gordon (Univ. of Calif., Los Angeles)
33. C. T. Gray (Texas)
34. W. T. Heron (Minnesota)
35. N. D. M. Hirsch (Duke)
36. H. G. Hotz (Arkansas)
37. W. S. Hunter (Clark)
38. A. M. Jordan (North Carolina)
39. D. Katz (Rostock)
40. T. L. Kelley (Stanford)
41. F. A. Kingsbury (Chicago)

42. H. L. Koch (Texas)
43. D. A. Laird (Colgate)
44. H. S. Langfeld (Princeton)
45. L. N. Lanier (Vanderbilt)
46. Mark A. May (Yale)
47. William McDougall (Duke)
48. H. Meltzer (Psychiatric Clinic, St. Louis)
49. F. A. Moss (Geo. Washington)
50. R. M. Ogden (Cornell)
51. Jean Piaget (Geneva)
52. D. S. Patterson (Minnesota)
53. F. A. C. Perrin (Texas)
54. Joseph Peterson (Geo. Peabody)
55. Henri Pieron (Sorbonne)
56. Rudolph Pintner (Columbia)
57. S. L. Pressey (Ohio State)
58. C. M. Reinhoel (Arkansas)
59. M. L. Reymert (Wittenberg)
60. Peter Sandiford (Toronto)
61. C. E. Seashore (Iowa)
62. Mandel Sherman (Child Research Center, Washington, D. C.)
63. L. M. Terman (Stanford)
64. R. H. Thouless (Glasgow)
65. L. L. Thurstone (Chicago)
66. H. A. Toops (Ohio State)
67. M. R. Trabue (North Carolina)
68. M. S. Viteles (Pennsylvania)
69. H. C. Warren (Princeton)
70. Margaret Washburn (Vassar)
71. Paul V. West (New York)
72. H. H. Woodrow (Illinois)
73. R. S. Woodworth (Columbia)
74. Helen T. Woolley (Columbia)
75. R. M. Yerkes (Yale)
76. C. S. Yoakum (Michigan)
77. P. C. Young (La. State)

Sociologists and Anthropologists

1. Franz Boas (Columbia)
2. E. S. Bogardus (Southern California)
3. E. W. Burgess (Chicago)
4. Fay Cooper-Cole (Chicago)
5. Jerome Dowd (Oklahoma)
6. Ellsworth Faris (Chicago)
7. Ross L. Finney (Minnesota)
8. Loomis Havemeyer (Yale)
9. E. A. Hooton (Harvard)
10. Carl Kelsey (Pennsylvania)
11. J. M. Mechlin (Dartmouth)
12. R. D. McKenzie (Univ. of Washington)
13. Howard W. Odum (North Carolina)
14. H. A. Miller (Ohio State)
15. Wm. F. Ogburn (Chicago)
16. Robert Redfield (Chicago)
17. E. B. Reuter (Iowa)
18. J. H. Sellin (Pennsylvania)
19. F. G. Speck (Pennsylvania)
20. A. M. Tozzer
21. Donald Young (Pennsylvania)
22. Kimball Young (Wisconsin)

Educationists

1. W. C. Bagley (Columbia)
2. J. F. Bobbitt (Chicago)
3. F. G. Bonser (Columbia)
4. W. H. Burnham (Clark)
5. W. H. Burton (Chicago)
6. H. E. Burtt (Ohio State)

7. C. E. Chadsey (Illinois)
8. W. W. Charters (Ohio State)
9. G. S. Counts (Columbia)
10. J. O. Creager (New York)
11. E. P. Cubberley (Stanford)
12. John Dewey (Columbia)
13. J. J. Doster (Alabama)
14. I. N. Edwards (Chicago)
15. F. C. Ensign (Iowa)
16. F. N. Freeman (Chicago)
17. M. E. Haggerty (Minnesota)
18. C. H. Judd (Chicago)
19. Wm. H. Kilpatrick (Columbia)
20. H. D. Kitson (Columbia)
21. F. O. Kreager (La. State)
22. E. A. Lincoln (Harvard)
23. E. L. Morphet (Alabama)
24. L. A. Pechstein (Cincinnati)
25. C. C. Peters (Penn State)
26. B. F. Pittinger (Texas)
27. F. W. Reeves (Kentucky)
28. V. M. Sims (Alabama)
29. David Snedden (Columbia)
30. P. W. Terry (Alabama)

APPENDIX C

Miscegenation Laws in the United States

State	Year Passed	Groups Prohibited from Marrying White Persons
Alabama	1923	"Negro or descendent of a Negro to the 3rd generation inclusive."
Arizona	1928	"Negroes, Mongolians, Indians, Hindus or members of the Malay race."
Arkansas	Unknown	"Negroes and Mulattoes."
California	1929	"Negroes, Mongolians, Mulattoes or Members of the Malay race."
Delaware	1915	"Negro or Mulattoes."
Florida	1920	"Any Negro (person having one-eighth or more of Negro blood)."
Georgia	1926	"Persons with African descent;" "all Negroes, Mulattoes, Mestozos and their descendants having any ascertainable trace of either Negro or African West Indian or Asiatic Indian blood in their veins," Mongolians."
Idaho	1919	"Mongolians, Negroes or Mulattoes."
Indiana	1926	"Persons having one-eighth or more Negro blood."
Kentucky	1922	"Negro or Mulatto."
Louisiana	1926	"Persons of color."
Maryland	1924	"Negro or person of Negro descent to the third generation or a member of the Malay race."
Mississippi	1930	"Negro or Mulatto or Mongolian."
Missouri	1929	"Persons having one-eighth or more Negro blood," "Mongolian."
Montana	1921	"Negro or a person of Negro blood or in part Negro," "Chinese person," "Japanese person."
Nebraska	1922	"Person having one-eighth or more Negro, Japanese or Chinese blood."
Nevada	1929	"Any person of the Ethiopian or black race, Malay or brown race, Mongolian or yellow race."
North Carolina	1919	"Negro or Indian," "or person of Negro or Indian descent to the third generation inclusive."
North Dakota	1913	"Negro."
Oklahoma	1921	"Any person of African descent."
Oregon	1930	"Any Negro, Chinese or any person having one-fourth or more Negro, Chinese or Kanaka blood, or more than one-half Indian."
South Carolina	1929	"Any Indian or Negro."
South Dakota	1929	"Any person belonging to the African, Corean, Malayan or Mongolian race."
Tennessee	1917	"African or the descendants of Africans to the third generation inclusive."
Texas	1925	"Negro or Mongolian."
Utah	1927	"Negro or Mongolian."
Virginia	1930	"Colored persons."
West Virginia	1923	"Negro."
Wyoming	1920	"Negroes, Mulattoes, Mongolians or Malays."

APPENDIX D

Application to Howard University in 1872 for a Professorship in Chemistry from G. Stanley Hall

2 East 46 :. St. N.Y.
16th May 1872

Pres. E. Whimbley.
        Dear Sir.
                Your note
was received two days ago. I regret
much to find that I had been
misinformed as to the prospective
vacancies in your professorial corps
I have strong preferences for your
University on personal & other
grounds. This in fairness I ought
to mention. During my European
curriculum (2 years) I was enrolled
in the philosophical department & attended
lectures on history, philology & some of
the natural sciences, in accordance with
their sequence in the Hegelian encyclopædia
(which I am now editing). On the basis
of the usual College course in chemistry

& mineral. (working myself in the laboratory with the professor), I attended in Berlin one semester of Hoffmann's lectures on theoretical chemistry. & one of Du Bois Raymond on organic chemistry. Now. after thinking the matter over as carefully as I could in so short a time. & after consulting with my friends, I have determined to apply for the vacancy in the Howard U. <u>provided</u> only that a decision may be definitely made <u>soon</u>. In order that, at once. after making a hasty resumé with Prof Silliman of Yale, I may go back to Berlin for special preparation until Sept, or such later time as might be granted me. From the nature of the department & from the circle of my acquaintance I am not <u>now</u> nearly with references as substantial

for this as for the other department. Still I have not arrived at the above decision without a careful survey of the ground on without competent advice neither, I may add, without consulting the tendency of my own tastes in the lines of study. I should leave nothing in my power undone to build up the department in a manner worthy of the service of the university with its fair prospects of the University.

Yours very respectfully

G. Stanley Hall.

2 East 46th St.
N.Y.

APPENDIX E

Psychology Instructors at Howard University, 1867–1940

Albert Beckham	1923–1928
J. Edmund Bryant	1930–1935
Alonzo J. Davis	1932–1933
McLeod Harvey	1913–1923
Jacob C. Kelson	1930–1931
J. S. Lemon	1901–1903
Max Meenes	1930–1973
Augustus Nasmith	1910–1911
Peter Ridley	1931–1932
Francis C. Sumner	1928–1954
Frederick P. Watts	1928–1970

Source: W. Dyson, *Howard University: The Capstone of Negro Education* (Washington: Graduate School, Howard University, 1941).

APPENDIX F

Master Degree Graduates in Psychology, Howard University, 1927–1950

1927

Henderson, Tillman H.
Watts, Frederick P.

1928

Honesty, Eva Hilton

1931

Ridley, Peter S.

1932

Cardoza, Frances
Davis, Alonzo
Sumner, Francees

1933

Gill, Dudley
Greene, John W.
Sneed, William H.

1934

Morton, Mary A.
Whitehurst, Keturah

1936

Bayton, James A.
Clark, Kenneth B.

Mitchell, Elsie V.
Smith, Clyde S.

1937

Hicks, Arthur
Scott, Huitt L.

1938

Dodson, W. A.
Jones, Clifton W.
Luck, Teresa L.

1939

Brandon, Nancy E.
Campbell, Astrea S.
Chilsolm, Helen E.
Clark, Mamie P.
Greene, Paxton
McLaurin, Phyllis C.

1942

Johnson, Walter I., Jr.
Lee, Jeane A.

1943

DeHaney, Kenneth G.

1944

Taylor, Inez L.

1945

Shaed, Dorothy L.

1946

Brett, Mauvice W.
Robinson, Mary K.
Wheatley, Louis
Withers, Yolanda J.

1947

Clark, Neville
Hall, Marcel E.
Houston, Thomas J.
Hunton, Vera D.

1948

Armstrong, Doris E.
Barnett, Evelyn E.
Jefferson, Fedricka Y.

Johns, Eugene H.
Leacock, Kent L.
McEachron, Shirley B.
Toms, Delores C.
Whyte, Ester C.

1949

Bell, Ernestine
Davage, Robert H.
Dawson, Gilbert L.
Johnson, Edward E.
Pennington, Steward G.
Polk, Ethel D.
Scott, Royston B.
Terrence, Euretta F.

1950

Early, Lavina A.
Robinson, James McK.
Somerville, Addison W.
Tooks, Kelly T.
Ward, Dorothy E.
Williams, Lexie A.

APPENDIX G

Selected Bibliography of Psychological Studies, 1920–1946

1920

J. Henry Alston, "The Spatial Condition of the Fusion of Warmth and Cold in Heat," *American Journal of Psychology*, July.

1922

Francis C. Sumner, "Psychoanalysis of Freud and Adler or Sex-Determinism and Character Formation," *Pedagogical Seminary*, June.

1924

Francis C. Sumner, "Core and Context in the Drowsy State," *American Journal of Psychology*, April.
———, "The Nature of Emotion," *Howard Review*, 1, June.
———, "Environic Factors Which Prohibit Creative Scholarship Among Negroes," *School and Society*, 22, 558.

1925

Francis C. Sumner, "The Fear of Death and the Belief in a Future Life," *Kappa Alpha Psi Journal*, 12, December.

1926

Francis C. Sumner, "The Philosophy of Negro Education," *Educational Review*, January.

1927

Howard H. Long, "Educational Research, *Washington, D.C. Board of Education Reports*.

Francis C. Sumner, "Morale and the Negro College," *Educational Review,* March.

1929

Albert S. Beckham, "Is the Negro Happy?" *Journal of Abnormal and Social Psychology,* 24.

Howard H. Long, "Individual Differences Among Children," *Washington, D.C. Board of Education Reports.*

1934

Albert S. Beckham, "A Study of Race Attitudes in Negro Children of Adolescent Age," *Journal of Abnormal and Social Psychology,* 39, 1, April–June.

Horace M. Bond, "Investigation of Racial Differences Prior to 1910," *Journal of Negro Education,* 3, July.

Herman G. Canady, "The Motive of Human Behavior and Personality Adjustment," *Kappa Alpha Psi Journal,* 21.

Paul A. Witty and Martin D. Jenkins, "The Educational Achievement of a Group of Gifted Negro Children," *The Journal of Educational Psychology,* November.

1935

Paul A. Witty and Martin D. Jenkins, "The Case of 'B'—A Gifted Negro Child," *Journal of Social Psychology,* 6.

1936

Herman G. Canady, "Individual Differences Among Freshman at West Virginia State College and Their Educational Bearings," *West Virginia State College Bulletin,* 23, 2.

———, "The Intelligence of Negro College Students and Parental Occupation," *American Journal of Sociology,* 42.

———, "The Effect of Rapport on the IQ—A New Approach to the Problem of Racial Psychology," *Journal of Negro Education,* 5.

———, *Behavior Adjustment,* West Virginia State College Press.

Martin D. Jenkins, "Socio-Psychological Study of Negro Children of Superior Intelligence," *Journal of Negro Education,* 5.

Martin D. Jenkins, "Gifted Negro Children," *The Crisis,* 48, November.

Francis C. Sumner and Frederick P. Watts, "Rivalry Between Uniocular Negative After-Images and the Vision of the Other Eye," *The American Journal of Psychology,* 48.

1937

Herman G. Canady, "Individual Differences and Their Educational Significance in Guidance of the Gifted and Talented Child," *The Quarterly Review of Higher Education Among Negroes,* 5.
——, "Adjusting Education to the Abilities, Needs and Interests of Negro College Students," *School and Society,* 46.

1938

——, "Sex Differences in Intelligence Among Negro College Freshmen," *Journal of Applied Psychology,* 4.

1939

Herman G. Canady, "Psychology in Negro Institutions," *West Virginia State College Bulletin,* 26, 3.
Kenneth B. Clark and Mamie P. Clark, "The Development of Consciousness of Self and the Emergence of Racial Identification in Negro Pre-School Children," *Journal of Experimental Education,* 8.
Carlton B. Goodlett, "Negro Youth and Educational System," *School and Society,* 50.
Martin F. Jenkins, "Intelligence of Negro Children," *Educational Method,* 19.
——, "Mental Ability of the American Negro," *Journal of Negro Education,* 8.
Francis C. Sumner, "Measurement of the Relevancy of Picture to Copy in Advertisements, *The Journal of Psychology,* 7.
——, "Attitudes Toward the Administration of Justice," *The Journal of Psychology,* 8.

1940

Kenneth B. Clark and Mamie P. Clark, "Skin Color as a Factor in Racial Identification of Negro Pre-School Children, *Journal of Social Psychology,* 11.
Kenneth B. Clark, "Some Factors Influencing the Remembering of Prose Material," *Archives of Psychology,* 253.
Carlton B. Goodlett, "The Educational Problems of Minority Youth," *School and Society,* 52.
Martin D. Jenkins, "Racial Differences and Intelligence," *American Teacher Magazine.*

1941

James A. Bayton, "Racial Stereotypes," *Journal of Abnormal and Social Psychology*, 30.

———— and M. G. Preston, "Differential Effect of a Social Variable Upon Three Levels of Aspiration," *Journal of Experimental Psychology*, 29.

Daniel P. Clarke, "Role of Psychology in Race Survival," *Journal of Negro Education*, 10.

————, "Stanford-Binet "L" Response Patterns in Matched Racial Groups," *Journal of Negro Education*, 10.

Frederick P. Watts. "A Comparative Clinical Study of Delinquent and Non-Delinquent Negro Boys," *Journal of Negro Education*, 10.

1942

James A. Bayton, "Psychology of Racial Morale," *Journal of Negro Education*, 11.

————, "Correlations Between Levels of Aspiration, *Journal of Negro Education*, 13.

Herman G. Canady, "The American Caste System and the Question of Negro Intelligence," *Journal of Educational Psychology*, 2.

Herman G. Canady et al., "A Scale for the Measurement of the Social Environment of Negro Youth," *Journal of Negro Education*, 11.

Herman G. Canady, "The Methodology and Interpretation of Negro-White Mental Testing," *School and Society*, 55.

————, "The Question of Negro Intelligence and Our Defense Program, *Opportunity*, 20.

Kenneth B. Clark and Francis C. Sumner, "Some Factors Influencing a Group of Negroes in Their Estimation of the Intelligence and Personality Wholesomeness of Negro Subjects," Howard University unpublished Manuscript.

Kenneth B. Clark, "Morale Among Negroes," A chapter in Goodwin Watson's *Civilian Morale*, 1942 Yearbook of the Society for the Psychological Study of Social Issues.

1943

Herman G. Canady, "The Problem of Equating the Environment of Negro-White Groups for Intelligence Testing in Comparative Studies," *Journal of Social Psychology*, 17.

————, "A Study of Sex Differences in Intelligence Test Scores Among 1,306 Negro College Freshmen," *Journal of Negro Education*, 12.

Herman G. Canady, "Interrelations Between Levels of Aspiration, Performance and Estimates of Past Performance," *Journal of Experimental Psychology*, 33.

Roderick W. Pugh, "Comparative Study of the Adjustment of Negro Students in Mixed and Separate High Schools," *Journal of Negro Education*, 12.

1944

Kenneth B. Clark, "Group Violence; A Preliminary Study of the Attitudinal Pattern of its Acceptance and Rejection: A Study of the 1943 Harlem Riot," *Journal of Social Psychology*, 19.

Mamie P. Clark, "Changes in Primary Mental Abilities with Age," *Archives of Psychology*.

Ruth W. Howard, "Fantasy and the Play Interview," *Character and Personality*, 13.

Martin D. Jenkins et al., *The Black and White Rejections for Military Service*, The American Teachers Association.

Francis C. Sumner, "The Newer Negro and His Education," *West Virginia State College Bulletin*, 2.

Francis C. Sumner and Nettie M. Brooker, "Prognostic and Other Values of Daily Tests," *Journal of Applied Psychology*, 28.

1945

Herman G. Canady, "Differences Among the Peoples of the World," (Chapter 23) *Psychology for the Armed Forces*, E. G. Boring (Ed.), The Infantry Journal.

Kenneth B. Clark, "Zoot Effect on Personality: A Race Riot Participant," *Journal of Abnormal and Social Psychology*, 40.

Francis C. Sumner and Dorothy L. Shaed, "Negro-White Attitudes Towards the Administration of Justice as Affecting Negroes," *Journal of Applied Psychology*, 29.

1946

Herman G. Canady, "The Psychology of the Negro," In *Encyclopedia of Psychology*, P. L. Harriman (Ed.), Philosophical Library.

Kenneth B. Clark et al., "Variations in the Angioscotoma in Response to Prolonged Mild Anoxia," *Journal of Aviation Medicine*.

Ruth W. Howard, "Intellectual and Personality Traits of a Group of Triplets." *The Journal of Psychology*, 21.

Francis C. Sumner and Luis Andres Wheatley, "Measurement of Neurotic Tendency in Negro Students of Music, *Journal of Psychology*, 22.

Bibliography

Alston, J. Henry. "Psychophysics of the Spatial Condition of the Fusion of Warm and Cold in Heat." *American Journal of Psychology* (July 1920).

American Anthropological Association. "The New York Meeting of the American Anthropological Association." *Science* (New Series) 89 (1939): 29–30.

Anonymous. "Some Suggestions Relative to a Study of the Mental Attitude of the Negro." *Pedagogical Seminary* 23 (1916): 199–203.

Arber, E., and A. G. Bradley, eds. *Travels and Works of Captain John Smith.* London: Wilson, 1910.

Armstrong, M. F., and H. W. Ludlow. *Hampton and Its Students.* New York: Putnam, 1875.

Bache, M. "Reaction Time with Reference to Race." *Psychological Review* 2 (1895) 475–586.

Barzun, J. *A Study in Superstition: Race.* New York: Harper and Row, 1935.

Bastain, P. W. A. *A Tropical Dependency.* London: Frank Cass, 1906.

Bayton, James A. "Correlations Between Levels of Aspiration." *Journal of Negro Education* 13 (1942).

Bayton, James A. "Differential Effect of a Social Variable Upon Three Levels of Aspiration." *Journal of Experimental Psychology* 29 (1941).

Bayton, James A. "Psychology of Racial Morale." *Journal of Negro Education* 11 (1942).

Bayton, James A. "Racial Stereotypes." *Journal of Abnormal and Social Psychology* 30 (1940).

Beckham, Albert S. "Is the Negro Happy?" *Journal of Abnormal and Social Psychology* 24 (1929).

Beckham, Albert S. "A Study of the Intelligence of Colored Adolescents of Different Socio-Economic Status in Typical Metropolitan Areas." *Journal of Social Psychology* 4 (1933) 70–91.

Beckham, Albert S. "A Study of Race Attitudes in Negro Children of Adolescent Age." *Journal of Abnormal and Social Psychology* 29, part 1 (April–June 1935).

Bellamy, R. "Measuring Hair Color." *American Journal of Physical Anthropology* 14, part 1 (January–March 1930): 75–77.

Berstein, M., and S. Robertson. "Racial and Sexual Differences in Hair Weight." *Journal of Physical Anthropology* 10, part 3 (July 1927): 379–385.

Bey, P. As quoted by J. C. Prichard in *Natural History of Man*, ed. E. Norris. London: Wilson and Ogilvy, 1855.

"The Binet Test in Court." *Eugenical News* 1 (August 1916).

Blackwood, B. "A Study of Mental Testing in Relation to Anthropology." *Mental Measurement Monographs* 4 (December 1927): 113.

Bloom, Benjamin. *Stability and Change in Human Characteristics*. New York: Wiley, 1964.

Bond, Horace M. "Intelligence Tests and Propaganda." *The Crisis* 28, part 2 (June 1924).

Bond, Horace, M. "Some Exceptional Negro Children." *The Crisis* 34 (October 1927): 257–280.

Borman, H. A. "The Color-Top Method of Estimating Skin Pigmentation." *American Journal of Physical Anthropology* 14 (January–March 1930): 59–70.

Broca, P. *Instructions generales pour les recherches anthropologiques a faire sur le vivant*. 2nd ed. Paris, 1879.

Brunschwig, L. "Opportunities for Negroes in the Field of Psychology." *Journal of Negro Education* (October 1941).

Buck v. Bell, Superintendent. United States Supreme Court, 1927. 274 US 200.

Buffon, G. *Historie naturelle, generale et particuliere, avec la description du Cabinet de roy*. Paris: Penaud, 1750.

Burmeister, Hermann. *The Black Man: The Comparative Anatomy and Psychology of the African Negro*. New York: W. C. Bryant, 1853.

Burlingame, M., and C. P. Stone. "Family Resemblance in Maze-Learning Ability in White Rats," in National Society for the Study of Education, *Nature and Nature, Their Influence Upon Intelligence*. Bloomington, Ill., Public School Publishing Company, 1928. Twenty-Seventh Yearbook, part 1, pp. 89–99.

Canady, Herman G. "Adjusting Education to the Abilities, Needs and Interests of Negro College Students." *School and Society* 46 (1937).

Canady, Herman G. "The American Caste System and the Question of Negro Intelligence." *Journal of Educational Psychology* 2 (1942).

Canady, Herman G. *Behavior Adjustment.* West Virginia State College Press, 1936.

Canady, Herman G. "Differences Among the Peoples of the World." *Psychology for the Armed Forces.* Chapter 23. E. G. Boring, ed. *The Infantry Journal,* 1945.

Canady, Herman G. "The Effect of 'Rapport' on the IQ: A New Approach to the Problem of Racial Psychology." *Journal of Negro Education* 5 (1936): 209–219.

Canady, Herman G. "Individual Differences Among Freshman at West Virginia State College and Their Educational Bearings." *West Virginia State College Bulletin* 23, part 2 (1936).

Canady, Herman G. "Individual Differences and Their Educational Significance in Guidance of the Gifted and Talented Child." *The Quarterly Review of Higher Education Among Negroes* 5 (1937).

Canady, Herman G. "The Intelligence of Negro College Students and Parental Occupation." *American Journal of Sociology* 42 (1936).

Canady, Herman G. "Interrelations Between Levels of Aspiration, Performance and Estimates of Past Performance." *Journal of Experimental Psychology* 33 (1943).

Canady, Herman G. "The Methodology and Interpretation of Negro-White Mental Testing." *School and Society* 55 (1942).

Canady, Herman G. "The Motive of Human Behavior and Personality Adjustment." *Kappa Alpha Psi Journal* 21 (1934).

Canady, Herman G. "The Problem of Equating the Environment of Negro-White Groups for Intelligence Testing in Comparative Studies." *Journal of Social Psychology* 17 (1943).

Canady, Herman G. "Psychology in Negro Institutions." *West Virginia State Bulletin* 3 (June 1993).

Canady, Herman G. "The Psychology of the Negro," in P. L. Harriman, ed. *Encyclopedia of Psychology.* New York: Philosophical Library, 1946.

Canady, Herman G. "The Question of Negro Intelligence and Our Defense Program." *Opportunity* 20 (1942).

Canady, Herman G. "A Scale for the Measurement of the Social Environment of Negro Youth." *Journal of Negro Education* 11 (1942).

Canady, Herman G. "Sex Differences in Intelligence Among Negro College Freshmen." *Journal of Applied Psychology* 4 (1938).

Canady, Herman G. "A Study of Sex Differences in Intelligence Test Scores Among 1,306 Negro College Freshmen." *Journal of Negro Education* 12 (1943).

Carter, A. M. "An Assessment of Quality in Graduate Education." *American Council on Education,* Washington, D.C., 1966.

Clark, Kenneth B. *Dark Ghetto: Dilemmas of Social Power*. New York: Harper and Row, 1967.

Clark, Kenneth B. "Group Violence: A Preliminary Study of the Attitudinal Pattern of its Acceptance and Rejection: A Study of the 1943 Harlem Riot." *Journal of Social Psychology* 19 (1944).

Clark, Kenneth B. "Morale Among Negroes," in Goodwin Watson, *Civilian Morale*. Yearbook of the Society for the Psychological Study of Social Issues, 1942.

Clark, Kenneth B. *Pathos of Power*. New York: Harper and Row, 1974.

Clark, Kenneth B. *Prejudice and Your Child*. Boston: Beacon Press, 1963.

Clark, Kenneth B. "Some Factors Influencing the Remembering of Prose Material," *Archives of Psychology* 253 (1950).

Clark, Kenneth B. "Zoot Effect on Personality: A Race Riot Participant." *Journal of Abnormal and Social Psychology* 40 (1945).

Clark, Kenneth B., and Mamie P. Clark. "The Development of Consciousness of Self and Emergence of Racial Identification in Negro Pre-School Children." *Journal of Social Psychology* 10 (1939).

Clark, Kenneth B., and Mamie P. Clark. "Segregation as a Factor in the Racial Identification of Negro Pre-School Children." *Journal of Experimental Education* 8 (1939).

Clark, Kenneth B., and Mamie P. Clark. "Skin Color as a Factor in Racial Identification of Negro Pre-School Children." *Journal of Social Psychology* 11 (1940).

Clark, Kenneth B., and Francis C. Summer. "Some Factors Influencing a Group of Negroes in Their Estimation of the Intelligence and Personality Wholesomeness of Negro Subjects." Howard University unpublished manuscript, 1942.

Clark, Kenneth B. et al. "Variations in the Angioscotoma in Response to Prolonged Mild Anoxia." *Journal of Aviation Medicine,* 1946.

Clark, Mamie P. "Changes in Primary Mental Abilities with Age." *Archives of Psychology,* 1944.

Clarke, Daniel. "Role of Psychology in Race Survival." *Journal of Negro Education* 10 (1941).

Clarke, Daniel. "Stanford-Binet 'L' Response Patterns in Matched Racial Groups." *Journal of Negro Education* 10 (1941).

Coleman, James, et al. *Equality of Educational Opportunity*, U.S. Dept of Health, Education, and Welfare. Washington, D.C.: U.S. Government Printing Office, 1966.

Cooper, P. "Notes on Psychological Race Differences." *Social Forces* 8 (1919): 426.

Crane, A. L. *Race Differences in Inhibition*. New York: The Science Press. Archives of Psychology, 1923. Vol. 63.

Cronbach, L. J. *Essentials of Psychological Testing*. New York: Harper and Row, 1949.

Cross, William. *Shades of Black: Diversity in African-American Identity*. Philadelphia: Temple University Press, 1991.

Cross, William. "The Thomas and Cross Models of Psychological Nigrescence: A Review." *Journal of Black Psychology* 5 (1978): 13–31.

Danielson, F. H., and C. B. Davenport. *The Hill Folk: Report on a Rural Community of Hereditary Defectives*. Cold Spring Harbor, N.Y.: New Era Press, 1912.

Davenport, C. B. *Guide to Physical Anthropology and Anthroposcopy*. Cold Spring Harbor, N.Y.: Eugenics Research Association, 1927.

Davenport, C. B. *Heredity in Relation to Eugenics*. New York: Arno Press, 1972 (1911).

Davenport, C. B. *The Trait Book*. Cold Spring Harbor, N.Y.: Eugenics Record Office, 1912. Vol. 6.

Davenport, C. B., and M. Steggerda. *Race Crossing in Jamaica*. Washington, D.C.: Carnegie Institution, 1929. Vol. 395.

Davis, Arthur P. "The Negro Professor." *The Crisis* (April 1936): 103.

Deniker, J. *The Races of Man: An Outline of Anthropology and Ethnography*. Freeport, N.Y.: Books for Library Press, 1900.

Dennett, R. E. *At the Back of the Black Man's Mind*. London: Macmillan, 1906.

Downey, J. E. *The Will-Temperament and Its Testing*. Yonkers, N.Y.: World Book Company, 1924.

Drew, Charles R. "Negro Scholars in Scientific Research." *Journal of Negro Education* 35 (1950).

Dugdale, R. L. *The Jukes: A Study in Crime, Pauperism, Disease, and Heredity*. New York: Putnam, 1910.

Eells, K. *Intelligence and Cultural Differences: A Study of Cultural Learning and Problem Solving*. Chicago: University of Chicago Press, 1933.

Ellison, R. *Invisible Man*. New York: Random House, 1992.

Embree, E., and J. Waxman. *Investment in People: The Story of the Julius Rosenwald Fund*. New York: Harper, 1949.

Estabrook, A. H. *The Ishmaelites*. Washington, D.C.: Carnegie Institution, 1917.

Estabrook, A. H. *The Jukes in 1915*. Washington, D.C.: Carnegie Institution, 1916.

Estabrook, A. H., and I. E. McDougle. *Mongrel Virginians: The Win Tribe*. Baltimore: Williams and Wilkins, 1926.

264   *Bibliography*

Ferguson, G. O., Jr. *The Psychology of the Negro: An Experimental Study.* New York: The Science Press, 1916.

Finlayson, A. *The Dack Family: A Study in Hereditary Lack of Emotional Control.* Cold Springs Harbor, N.Y.: Eugenics Record Office, 1915.

Fitzgerald, J. A., and W. W. Ludeman. "Intelligence of Indian Children." *Journal of Comparative Psychology* 6 (1926).

Flugel, J. C., and D. J. West. *A Hundred Years of Psychology.* New York: Macmillan, 1964.

Folkmar, D., and E. C. Folkmar. "Dictionary of Races or Peoples." Document No. 662. Washington, D.C.; The Immigration Commission, 1911. p. 150.

Franklin, J. H. *From Slavery to Freedom: A History of Negro Americans.* 3rd ed. New York: Knopf, 1967.

Fritsch, G. "Bermerkungen zu der Hautfarbentafel." *Mitt Anthrop Ges Wien,* Berlin, 1916. Vol. 16, pp. 183–185.

Galton, F. "Annals of Eugenics," *Galton Laboratory for National Eugenics* 1, part 1 (October 1925): 3

Garth, T. R. "The Will-Temperament of Indians." *Journal of Applied Psychology* 11 (1927): 512–518.

Garrett, Henry. *How Classroom Desegregation Will Work.* Richmond, VA.: Patrick Henry Press, 1968.

de Gobineau, A. *The Inequality of Human Races.* New York: Putnam, 1915.

Goddard, H. H. *The Kallikak Family: A Study in the Heredity of Feeble-mindedness.* New York: Macmillan, 1912.

Goodlett, Carlton B. "The Educational Problems of Minority Youth." *School and Society* 52 (1940).

Goodlett, Carlton B. "Negro Youth and Educational System." *School and Society* 50 (1939).

Gray, J. "A New Instrument for Determining the Colour of the Hair, Eyes, and Skin." *Man* no. 27 (1908): 54–58.

Grier, W., and P. Cobbs. *Black Rage.* New York: Basic Books, 1968.

Haddon, A. C. *History of Anthropology.* London: Watts, 1934.

Haeckel, E. H. *Generelle Morphologie der Organismen.* Berlin: G. Reimer, 1866.

Hall, G. S. "The Negro in Africa and America," *Pedagogical Seminary* (1912).

Hakluyt, R. "The First Voyage of Robert Baker to Guinie," in *Principall Navigations, Voiages and Discoveries of the English Nation.* London, 1589. p. 132.

Helms, Janet, ed. *Black and White Racial Identity: Theory, Research, and Practice.* New York: Greenwood, 1990.

Herrnstein, Richard, and C. Murray. *The Bell Curve: Intelligence and Class Structure in American Life.* New York: The Free Press, 1994.

Herskovits, Melville J. "Age Changes in Pigmentation of American Negroes." *American Journal of Physical Anthropology* 9, part 3, (1926): 323.

Herskovits, Melville J. *The Anthropometry of the American Negro.* New York: Columbia University Press, 1930.

Herskovits, Melville J. "A Critical Discussion of the 'Mulatto Hypotheses'." *Journal of Negro Education* (July 1934): 401.

Herskovits, Melville J. *The Negro and Intelligence Tests.* Hanover, N.H.: Hanover, 1927.

Howard, Ruth W. "Fantasy and the Play Interview." *Character and Personality* 13 (1944).

Hrdlicka, Ales. *Anthropometry.* Philadelphia: Wistar Institute of Anatomy and Biology, 1939.

Hrdlicka, Ales. "Directions for Collecting Information and Specimens for Physical Anthropology." Washington, D.C.: United States National Museum, 1904. No. 39, Part R, p. 25.

Hunt, J. *Intelligence and Experience.* New York: Ronald Press, 1961.

Hunter, W. S. "Indian Blood and Otis Intelligence Test." *Journal of Comparative Psychology* 2 (1922).

Hunter, W. S., and E. Sommermier. "The Relation of Degree of Indian Blood to Score on the Otis Intelligence Test." *Journal of Comparative Psychology* 2 (1922): 257–277.

Hurlock, E. B. "The Will-Temperament of White and Negro Children." *Pedagogical Seminary* 38 (1930): 91–99.

Jamieson, E., and P. Standiford. "The Mental Capacity of Southern Ontario Indians." *Journal of Educational Psychology* 19 (1928): 536–551.

Jenkins, Adelbert. *Psychology and African Americans,* 2nd ed. Boston: Allyn and Bacon, 1995.

Jenkins, Martin D. "Gifted Negro Children." *The Crisis* 48 (November 1936).

Jenkins, Martin D. "Intelligence of Negro Children." *Educational Method* 19 (1939).

Jenkins, Martin D. "Mental Ability of the American Negro." *Journal of Negro Education* 8 (1939).

Jenkins, Martin D. "Racial Differences and Intelligence." *American Teacher Magazine* (1940).

Jenkins, Martin D. "A Socio-Psychological Study of Negro Children of Superior Intelligence." *Journal of Negro Education* 5 (1936): 175–190.

Jenkins, Martin D. et al. *The Black and White Rejections for Military Service.* The American Teachers Association, 1944.

Jensen, Arthur. "How Much Can We Boost IQ and Scholastic Achievement?" *Harvard Educational Review* 39 (1969): 1–123.

Joncich, G. *The Sane Positivist: A Biography of Edward L. Thorndike.* Middletown, Conn.: Wesleyan University Press, 1968.

Jones, James. *Prejudice and Racism,* 2nd ed. New York: McGraw Hill, 1996.

Jordon, W. D. *White Over Black.* Chapel Hill: The University of North Carolina Press, 1968.

Karier, Clarence J. "Testing for Order and Control in the Corporate Liberal State." *Educational Theory* 22 (Spring 1972).

Klineberg, O. "An Experimental Study of Speed and Other Factors in 'Racial' Differences." *Archives of Psychology* 93 (1928): 111.

Klineberg, O. *Race Differences.* New York: Harper and Row, 1935.

Klineberg, Otto. "A Study of Psychological Differences Between 'Racial' and National Groups in Europe," *Archives of Psychology.* New York: Science Press, 1931.

Korn, James, et al. "Historians' and Chairpersons' Judgment of Eminence Among Psychologists," *American Psychologist* (July 1991): 371–374.

LaRue, D. W. "Teaching Eugenics." *Eugenical News* (August 1917): 62.

Laughlin, H. H. *Eugenics Record Office.* Cold Spring Harbor, N.Y.: June 1913. Vol. 1.

Laughlin, H. H. *Report on the Committee to Study and to Report on the Best Practical Means of Cutting Off the Defective Germ-Plasm in the American Population.* Cold Spring Harbor, N.Y.: Eugenics Record Office, February 1914.

Linnaeus, C. von. *Systema Natura.* Lugduni, Batavorum, 1735.

Long, Howard H. "Analyses of Test Results from Third Grade Children Selected on the Basis of Socio-Economic Status." Unpublished Doctoral Dissertation, Harvard University, 1933.

Long, Howard H. "Educational Research." *Washington, D.C., Board of Education Reports,* 1927.

Long, Howard H. "Individual Differences Among Children." *Washington, D.C., Board of Education Reports,* 1929.

Malthus, T. R. "An Essay on the Principle of Population." London, 1803.

Mama, Amina. *Beyond the Masks: Race, Gender and Subjectivity.* London: Routledge, 1995.

Mayo, M. J. *The Mental Capacity of the American Negro.* New York: The Science Press, 1913. Archives of Psychology, Vol. 28.

McCuistion, F. *Graduate Instruction for Negroes in the United States.* Nashville, Tenn.: George Peabody College for Teachers, 1939.

McFadden, J. H., and J. F. Dashiell. "Racial Differences as Measured by the Downey Will-Temperament Test." *Journal of Applied Psychology* 7 (1923): 30–53.

Miller, George A. *Psychology*. New York: Harper and Row, 1962.

Miller, Herbert. "Science, Pseudo-Science and the Race Question." *The Crisis* 30, part 6 (October 1935).

Miller, Herbert. "Some Psychological Considerations on the Race Problem," in W. E. B. Du Bois, ed., *The Health and Physique of the Negro American*. Atlanta University Press, 1906. pp. 54–56.

Moore, H., and I. Steele. "Personality Tests." *Journal of Abnormal and Social Psychology* 29 (1934–1935): 45–52.

Morgan, D. C., and H. A. Murray. "A Method for Investigating Fantasies: The Thematic Apperception Test." *Archives of Neurological Psychiatry*, 34 (1935): 289–306.

Morse, J. "A Comparison of White and Colored Children Measured by the Binet Scale of Intelligence." *The Popular Science Monthly* 84, part 1 (January 1914): 75–79.

Moynihan, D. *Negro Family: The Case for National Action*. Washington, D.C.: U.S. Labor Department, Office of Policy Planning and Research, 1965.

Moynihan, D. P., and F. Mosteller, (Eds.). *On Equality of Educational Opportunity*. New York: Vintage, 1972.

Myrdal, G. *An American Dilemma*. New York: Harper and Row, 1944.

Novick, Peter. *That Noble Dream: The 'Objectivity Question' and the American Historical Profession*. New York: Cambridge University Press, 1988.

Parham, Thomas. *Psychological Storms: The African American Struggle for Identity*. Chicago: African American Images, 1993.

Paschal, F. C., and L. R. Sullivan. "Racial Factors in the Mental and Psychical Development of Mexican Children." *Comparative Psychology Monographs* 3 (October 1925): 46–75.

Phillips, B. A. "The Binet Test Applied to Colored Children." *Psychological Clinic* 8 (1914): 190–196.

Plato. *Republic*, trans. Paul Shorey. Loeb Classical Library. New York: Putnam, 1935.

Popenoe, P., and R. Johnson. *Applied Eugenics*. New York: Macmillan, 1920.

Porteus, S. D. *The Psychology of a Primitive People*. New York: Longmans, Green, 1931.

Pugh, Roderick W. "Comparative Study of the Adjustment of Negro Students in Mixed and Separate High Schools." *Journal of Negro Education* 12 (1943).

Pyle, W. H. "The Mind of the Negro Child." *School and Society* 1 (1915): 358.

Reisman, J. M. *The Development of Clinical Psychology.* New York: Appleton, 1966.

Saint-Hilaire, I. *Historie Anecdotique, Politique et Militaire de la Garde Imperiale.* Paris: E. Penaud, 1847.

Sanchez, G. I. "Group Differences and Spanish-Speaking Children—A Critical Review." *Journal of Applied Psychology* 16 (1932): 549–558.

Schockley, William. "Is Quality of U.S. Population Declining?" *U.S. News and World Report* (November 22, 1965).

Schultz, Duane, and S. Schultz. *A History of Modern Psychology,* 6th ed. Fort Worth: Harcourt Brace, 1996.

Schwinfurth, J. *Heart of Africa.* Berlin: Junker and Dunnhaupt, 1938.

Searle, L. V. "The Organization of Hereditary Maze-Brightness and Maze-Dullness." *Genetic Psychology Monograph* 39 (1949): 279–325.

"Selection of Negroes," *Eugenical News* 2 (March 1917).

Shaxby, J. H., and H. E. Bonnell. "On Skin Colour," *Man* (April 1928): 41–42, 60–64.

Spearman, Z. C. "General Intelligence Objectively Determined and Measured." *American Journal of Psychology* 15 (1904): 193–201.

Spruzheim, G. *Examination of the Doctrines of Gall and Spruzheim.* London: Walker and Greig, 1817.

Stanton, W. *The Leopard's Spots, Scientific Attitudes Toward Race in America 1815–1859.* Chicago: University of Chicago Press, 1960.

Stern, W. *Uber Psychologie der Individuellen Differenzen.* Leipzig, 1900.

Stetson, G. R. "Some Memory Tests of Whites and Blacks." *Psychological Review* 4 (1985): 285–289.

Sullivan, L. R. *Essentials of Anthropometry, A Handbook for Explorers and Museum Collectors.* rev. ed. H. L. Shapiro. New York: American Museum of Natural History, 1928.

Sumner, Francis C. *Annual Reports, 1938–1947.* Howard University, Department of Psychology.

Sumner, Francis C. "Attitudes Toward the Administration of Justice." *The Journal of Psychology* 8 (1930).

Sumner, Francis C. "Core and Context in the Drowsy State." *American Journal of Psychology* (April 1924).

Sumner, Francis C. "Environic Factors Which Prohibit Creative Scholarship Among Negroes." *School and Society* 22, p. 558.

Sumner, Francis C. "The Fear of Death and the Belief in a Future Life." *Kappa Alpha Psi Journal* 12 (December 1925).

Sumner Francis C. "Measurement of the Relevancy of Picture to Copy in Advertisements." *The Journal of Psychology* 7 (1939).

Sumner, Francis C. "Morale and the Negro College." *Educational Review* (March 1927).

Sumner, Francis C. "The Nature of Emotion." *Howard Review* 2 (June 1924).

Sumner, Francis C. "Negro-White Attitudes Towards the Administration of Justice as Affecting Negroes." *Journal of Applied Psychology* 29 (1945).

Sumner, Francis C. "The New Psychology Unit at Howard University." *Psychological Bulletin* (1935): 859–860.

Sumner, Francis C. "The Newer Negro and His Education." *West Virginia State College Bulletin* 2 (1944).

Sumner, Francis C. "The Philosophy of Negro Education." *Educational Review*, January 1926.

Sumner, Francis C. "Psychoanalysis of Freud and Adler or Sex-Determinism and Character Formation." *Pedagogical Seminary*, June 1922.

Sumner, Francis C., and Nettie M. Brooker. "Prognostic and Other Values of Daily Tests," *Journal of Applied Psychology* 28 (1944).

Sumner, Francis C., and Frederick P. Watts. "Rivalry Between Uniocular Negative After-Images and the Vision of the Other Eye." *The American Journal of Psychology* 48 (1936).

Sumner, Francis C., and Luis Andres Wheatley. "Measurement of Neurotic Tendency in Negro Students of Music." *Journal of Psychology* 22 (1946).

Sunne, D. "Personality Tests—White and Negro Adolescents," *Journal of Applied Psychology* 9 (1925): 256–280.

"Survey of Negro Colleges and Universities." *Bureau of Education Bulletin.* United States Department of the Interior, 1928. Vol. 7.

Szasz, Thomas. *The Manufacture of Madness: A Comparative Study of the Inquisition and the Mental Health Movement.* New York: Harper and Row, 1970.

Taylor, Dalmas, and S. Manning. *Psychology, A New Perspective.* Cambridge, Mass.: Winthrop Press, 1975.

Terman, L. *Intelligence Tests and School Reorganization.* New York: World, 1923.

Terman, L., and M. A. Merrill. *Measuring Intelligence.* Boston: Houghton Mifflin, 1937.

Thomas, Charles, and S. Thomas. "Something Borrowed, Something Black." In C. W. Thomas, ed., *Boys No More.* Beverly Hills: Glencoe, 1971.

Thompson, Charles H. "The Conclusion of Scientists Relative to Racial Differences." *The Journal of Negro Education* 3 (July 1934): 494–512.

Thorndike, E. L. "Eugenics: With Special Reference to Intellect and Character." *The Popular Science Monthly* 83 (1913): 126.

Thorndike, E. L. *Human Nature and the Social Order.* New York: Macmillan, 1940.

Todd, T. W., B. Blackwood, and H. Beecher. "Skin Pigmentation." *American Journal of Physical Anthropology* 11, part 2 (1928): 187–205.

Todd, T. W., and L. Van Gorder. "The Quantitative Determination of Black Pigmentation in the Skin of the American Negro." *American Journal of Physical Anthropology* 4, part 3 (1921): 239–260.

Tryon, R. C. "Genetic Differences in Maze Learning in Rats," in National Society for the Study of Education, *Intelligence: Its Nature and Nurture.* Bloomington, Ill: Public School Publishing Company, 1940. Yearbook 39, part 1, pp. 111–119.

Van de Water, M. "Racial Psychology." *Science-Supplement* (September 1938).

Virchow, Rudolf. *Zeitschrift für Ethnologie.* Berlin: Heft, 1895. Vol. 11.

Waitz, Theodor. *Introduction to Anthropology.* London: Longmans, 1863.

Watts, Frederick P. "A Comparative Clinical Study of Delinquent and Non-Delinquent Negro Boys." *Journal of Negro Education* 10 (1941).

Wechsler, David. *The Measurement of Adult Intelligence.* Baltimore: Williams and Wilkins, 1939.

Welsing, F. As quoted in "Soul: The Sixth Sense," in *New Directions* by Genevieve E. Kaete. Washington, D.C., Howard University, Spring, 1974.

Wispe, L., P. Ash, J. Awkard, K. Hicks, M. Hoffman, and J. Porter. "The Negro Psychologist in America." *American Psychologist* 24, part 2 (1969): 142–150.

Witty, P., and Martin D. Jenkins. "The Case of 'B'—A Gifted Negro Girl." *Journal of Social Psychology* 6 (1935): 117–124.

Witty, P., and Martin D. Jenkins. "The Educational Achievement of a Group of Gifted Negro Children." *Journal of Educational Psychology,* November 1934.

Woodworth, R. S. *History of Psychology in Autobiography,* Carl Murchison, ed. Worcester, Mass.: Clark University Press, 1932. Vol. 2.

Woodworth, R. S. "Racial Difference in Mental Traits." *Science* (February 1910): 171.

Name Index

Subject Index